Romantic Consciousness

Romantic Consciousness

Blake to Mary Shelley

John B. Beer
Emeritus Professor of English Literature
University of Cambridge
and Fellow of Peterhouse

palgrave
macmillan

© John Beer 2003

First published 2003 by
PALGRAVE MACMILLAN
Houndmills, Basingstoke, Hampshire RG21 6XS and
175 Fifth Avenue, New York, N. Y. 10010
Companies and representatives throughout the world

PALGRAVE MACMILLAN is the global academic imprint of the Palgrave Macmillan division of St. Martin's Press, LLC and of Palgrave Macmillan Ltd. Macmillan® is a registered trademark in the United States, United Kingdom and other countries. Palgrave is a registered trademark in the European Union and other countries.

ISBN 1–4039–0324–7 hardback

This book is printed on paper suitable for recycling and made from fully managed and sustained forest sources.

A catalogue record for this book is available from the British Library.

Library of Congress Cataloging-in-Publication Data

Beer, John B.
    Romantic consciousness: Blake to Mary Shelley / John Beer.
        p. cm
    Includes bibliographical references (p.) and index.
    ISBN 1–4039–0324–7 (cloth)
        1. English literature–19th century–History and criticism.
    2. Consciousness in literature. 3. Shelley, Mary Wollstonecraft,
    1797–1851–Knowledge–Psychology. 4. Blake, William,
    1757–1827–Knowledge–Psychology. 5. Romanticism–Great Britain. I. Title.

PR468.C66B44 2003
820.9'355–dc21
                                                        2003044150

10   9   8   7   6   5   4   3   2   1
12   11   10   09   08   07   06   05   04   03

Printed and bound in Great Britain by
Antony Rowe Ltd, Chippenham and Eastbourne

For Gillian

Contents

List of Illustrations

Abbreviations

Place of publication is London unless otherwise indicated.

APrW	Matthew Arnold, *Complete Prose Works*, ed. R.H. Super (11 vols., Ann Arbor, MI, 1960–77)
APW	Matthew Arnold, *Complete Poems*, ed. Kenneth Allott; 2nd edn., ed. Miriam Allott (1979)
BE	*The Poetry and Prose of William Blake*, ed. D.V. Erdman and H. Bloom (New York, 1965)
BK	Blake, *Complete Writings, with Variant Readings*, ed. G. Keynes, 1957; reprinted with additions and corrections in the Oxford Standard Authors series (Oxford, 1966)
BLJ	Byron, *Letters and Journals* ed. L.A Marchand (12 vols., 1973–94).
BPW	Byron, *Works*, new edition: *Poetry*, ed. E. H. Coleridge (7 vols., 1898–1904).
CAR	Coleridge, *Aids to Reflection* [1825], ed. John Beer, *CC* 9 (1993).
CBL	Coleridge, *Biographia Literaria*, [1817]; ed. James Engell and Walter Jackson Bate, *CC* 7 (2 vols., 1983).
CC	*The Collected Works of Samuel Taylor Coleridge*, general ed. Kathleen Coburn, associate ed. Bart Winer (Princeton, NJ and London 1969–2002).
CCS	Coleridge, *On the Constitution of the Church and State* [1829], ed. John Colmer *CC* 10 (1976).
C Friend	Coleridge, *The Friend* [1809–18]; ed. Barbara Rooke, *CC* 4 (2 vols., 1969).
CL	Coleridge, *Collected Letters*, ed. E.L. Griggs (6 vols., Oxford 1956–71).
C Lects (1795)	Coleridge, *Lectures 1795: On Politics and Religion*, ed. Lewis Patton and Peter Mann, *CC* 1 (1971).
CLS	Coleridge, *Lay Sermons* [1816–17]; ed. R.J. White, *CC* 6 (1972).
CM	Coleridge, *Marginalia*, ed. George Whalley, *CC* 12 (6 vols., 1980–2001).
CN	Coleridge, *Notebooks*, ed. Kathleen Coburn (5 vols., Princeton, NJ and London 1959–2002).

CPL (1949)	*The Philosophical Lectures, hitherto unpublished, of Samuel Taylor Coleridge*, ed. Kathleen Coburn (1949).
CPW (Beer)	Coleridge, *Poems*, ed. J.B. Beer, new edn. Everyman (2000).
CPW (EHC)	Coleridge, *Poetical Works*, ed. E.H. Coleridge (2 vols., Oxford 1912)
CPW (CC)	Coleridge, *Poetical Works*, ed. J.C.C. Mays, *CC* 16 (6 vols., 2001)
CShC	*Coleridge's Shakespearean Criticism*, ed. T.M. Raysor (2 vols., 1936); 2nd edn. Everyman (2 vols., 1960).
CTT	Coleridge, *Table Talk*, ed. Carl Woodring, *CC* 14 (2 vols., 1990).
DQCS	De Quincey, *Confessions of an English Opium Eater* and *Suspiria De Profundis* (Boston 1852).
DQD	*A Diary of Thomas De Quincey, 1803*, ed. H.A. Eaton (1927).
DQW	*The Collected Writings of Thomas De Quincey*, ed. D. Masson (14 vols., Edinburgh 1889).
DWJ	*Journals of Dorothy Wordsworth*, ed. E. de Selincourt (2 vols., Oxford 1941).
HW	*The Complete Works of William Hazlitt*, ed. P.P. Howe (21 vols., 1930–4).
KL	*Letters of John Keats, 1814–1821*, ed. H.E. Rollins (2 vols., Cambridge, Mass. 1958).
KP	*Poems of John Keats*, ed. M. Allott (1970).
ML	*The Letters of Mary W. Shelley*, ed. F.L. Jones (2 vols., Norman, Oklahoma 1944).
MP	John Milton, *The Complete Poems*, ed. B.A. Wright and G. Campbell (1980).
RX	John Livingston Lowes, *The Road to Xanadu* (1927).
SBR	Charkes Robinson, *Shelley and Byron: The Snake and Eagle Wreathed in Fight* (Baltimore 1976)
SBT	E.J. Trelawny, *The Last Days of Shelley and Byron, Being the complete text of Trelawny's 'Recollections'* edited, with additions from contemporary sources, by J.E. Morpurgo (Westminster 1952). (References to Trelawny's 1878 edition of what becomes his *Records* are given separately.)
SL	*The Letters of Percy Bysshe Shelley*, ed. F.L. Jones (2 vols., Oxford 1964).

SP	*Shelley's Prose: or The Trumpet of a Prophecy,* ed. D.L. Clark (Albuquerque, New Mexico 1966).
SPW	Shelley, *The Complete Poetical Works* ed. T. Hutchinson (Oxford 1934).
SW	*The Complete Works of Percy Bysshe Shelley,* ed. R. Ingpen and W.E. Peck (10 vols., 1926–30)
TP	*The Poems of Tennyson,* 2nd edition, ed. Christopher Ricks (3 vols., 1987)
WL (1787–1805)	*The Letters of William and Dorothy Wordsworth, The Early Years, 1787–1805,* ed. E. de Selincourt, 2nd edn., revd C.L. Shaver (Oxford 1967).
WL (1821–53)	*The Letters of William and Dorothy Wordsworth, The Later Years, 1821–1853,* ed. E. de Selincourt; 2nd edn. revd A.G. Hill (4 vols., Oxford 1978–88)
W Prel	Wordsworth, *The Prelude,* ed. E. de Selincourt (1926); 2nd edn. revd Helen Darbishire (Oxford 1959).
W Prel (1799)	The 1799 text in *The Prelude 1799, 1805, 1850,* ed. Wordsworth, Abrams and Gill (New York 1979).
W Prel (1805)	The 1805 text in *W Prel* above.
WPrW	Wordsworth, *Prose Works,* ed. W.J.B. Owen and J.W. Smyser (3 vols., Oxford 1974).
WPrW (Grosart)	Wordsworth, *Prose Works,* ed. A.B. Grosart (3 vols., 1876).
WPW	Wordsworth, *Poetical Works,* ed. Ernest de Selincourt and Helen Darbishire (5 vols., Oxford 1940–9)

Preface

This book and its successor trace the shape of an argument implicit in certain works of Western culture following the challenges to conventional approval of rational consciousness at the time of the French Revolution. The overall argument throughout is that the writers chiefly covered were responding to a contemporary perception that the mental structures created in such activity were not always adequate to the representation of all that was involved in the human psyche.

For some English writers particularly, the possibility that rational consciousness might need to be subsumed into a total sense of Being – in which the human might even be linked to the divine – was prominent. Although an intuition of the kind can be traced in Blake, the writer most responsible for articulating and developing it was Coleridge, his notable interest in psychology, particularly the unusual phenomena associated with animal magnetism, leading him to investigations that bordered constantly on pantheism before his religious experience convinced him that although the creative human imagination might *reflect* that of the creator God the only form of Being with which human beings could properly form a relationship was that of a morally judging Divinity. His earlier speculations, closer to pantheism yet resisting it, provided a powerful stimulus to Wordsworth's own ideas concerning Nature, with the result that 'Being' became for a time a centrally important word in the vocabulary of both poets. This is true not only of some memorable poems of the time but of *The Prelude*, occurring crucially in central passages where Wordsworth attempts to interpret his experiences. Yet despite their common use of the word, there was a crucial disparity between their usages, fruitful not only in the nature of Coleridge's influence on future writers, but in foreshadowing the form that twentieth-century discussions of 'Being' would take.

In two subsequent chapters use of the word 'Being', as such, becomes less prominent, but the underlying issues persist. Two major successors, Keats and De Quincey, each of whom encountered Coleridge at a crucial stage of his development, were both strongly drawn by the stimulus of his psychological discourse into speculations of his own concerning the existential significance of experiences in the unconscious. In Chapter 5 the actual word 'Being' moves again into the foreground with the contention that some of the Cambridge Apostles – particularly Hallam and Tennyson – were drawn by way of discourses which Coleridge was still delivering to the young men who visited him in his old age to adopt the term as part of their own private 'Apostolic' vocabulary and their developing semi-mystical view of the world.

More intense exploration of the issues involved had already taken place earlier, however, in the interplay of mind between Shelley and Byron, and their ability to neglect even potential dangers in pursuing their respective concerns for the nature of Being, whether physical or spiritual. The volume ends with some account of their extreme attitudes, together with the effect of such discussions on the Mary Shelley who was to live on after them.

I wish to acknowledge my gratitude to the organizers of various conferences, including the annual Wordsworth Summer Conference in Grasmere, the biennial Coleridge conference at Cannington, the conference on English and German Romanticism at Houston and the All-India Teachers Conference in India, where some ideas in the book were given a first airing, Material in two chapters has been used for previous pieces: The discussion of De Quincey first appeared in the *Bicentenary Studies* of his work, edited by Robert Lance Snyder, and that of Tennyson and the Cambridge Apostles in *Tennyson: Seven Essays*, edited by Philip Collins. Both pieces, it is hoped, gain by being incorporated in the fuller argument of the present volume, the discussions in which are further complemented by those in a second, published simultaneously, *Post-Romantic Consciousness: Dickens to Plath*. This successor examines the interest in the relationship between consciousness and Being also shown by certain writers and thinkers from the mid-nineteenth century to the present day, their critical attitudes to such Romantic themes being matched, nevertheless, by evidences of a continuing debt.

1
Consciousness and the Mystery of Being

The word 'being' is one of the most unobtrusive in the English language. Since it is mostly used as a part of the verb 'to be', or (as in 'human being') a virtually redundant extra, it becomes almost invisible on the page – so much so that when it is used as a free-standing word in its own right it becomes advisable to capitalize its first letter and speak of it as 'Being'; otherwise, if set at the side of a word such as 'consciousness', it may virtually vanish. One of the purposes of this study is to argue, by contrast, that its significance for certain writers has been so considerable that it should not be allowed to escape notice through simple oversight.

Despite this unobtrusiveness some thinkers have found reason to focus upon the term in recent years – as is not unnatural at a time when the nature of humanity has itself been a matter of continual discussion. The issues involved have attracted the attention, for example, of some scientists, particularly those specializing in neurological matters, who have found them relevant to their preoccupations. In his book *Descartes' Error*, Antonio Damasio approaches them by way of a long discussion of the relationship between brain and body in which his chief contention is that reason and emotion, so far from being separate elements in human behaviour, are always intimately linked. Drawing on a series of observations, based largely on experimental work, he maintains that such links can be found at every level of behaviour. His approach is made particularly valuable by his ability to draw heavily on work – his own and others' – devoted to patients who have suffered brain lesions. Through being able to isolate particular areas of the brain for study in this way it is possible to discover exactly what has been lost in particular circumstances. While very striking results may be obtained within the parameters of such observations,

1

however, there is an area that remains obscure. So long as one is dealing with attributes and faculties that are capable of being lost, the possibilities can be investigated subtly by way of examining the patients in question; and this can extend to the cases where something like a loss of feeling-tone. But what if the 'sense of being' itself is lost?

Damasio is certainly aware of such an element in human behaviour. He thinks of it rather, however, as a *sense* underlying others:

> I call it background feeling because it originates in 'background' body states rather than in emotional states. It is not the Verdi of grand emotion, nor the Stravinsky of intellectualized emotion, but rather a minimalist in tone and beat, the feeling of life itself, the sense of being.[1]

'A background feeling,' he adds, 'corresponds ... to the body state prevailing between emotions.... If you try for a moment to imagine what it would be like to be without background feelings, you will have no doubt about the notion I am introducing. I submit that without them the very core of your representation of self would be broken.'

Most of his readers are likely to agree with him concerning the existence of the phenomenon he is describing: the question is rather whether his description is fully satisfactory. As far as emotion is concerned, his position is based on an assertion to be found in William James's writings:

> If we fancy some strong emotion and then try to abstract from our consciousness of it all the feelings of its bodily symptoms, we find we have nothing left behind, no 'mind-stuff' out of which the emotion can be constituted, and that a cold and neutral state of intellectual perception is all that remains.[2]

Damasio's own error, if it may be so characterized, is to insist on describing as a *feeling* something that should be thought of rather as a state, since in this case it may exist, it would seem, without any emotion at all being present. Such a state, indeed, need never rise into consciousness for its existence to be believed in. Although not necessarily negative, it is better described in terms of what it is not than of what it is.

In this respect, the 'sense' of being is not easily to be distinguished from the sense of life, which can show itself in myriad ways – normally through movements of one kind or another – but need not even be expressed for its existence to be readily affirmed. To all intents and purposes it may be better to identify the two senses, those of Being and of life, since while it is true that someone who is dead does not cease to exist, it is virtually impossible to imagine how a dead person could have a sense of being – at least without invoking the supernatural.

Damasio also joins some thinkers, ancient and modern, in attempting to demolish popular delusions. One of these is of the homunculus – the idea that inside each human being there is a smaller one who acts as a kind of director of operations and who can be more readily identified with that individual's mind. He supports Daniel Dennett, similarly, in dismissing the idea of a 'cartesian theatre', a stage in the mind on which is vividly played out every drama that the imagination can conjure up. In one sense, such demolitions must be accepted, particularly in so far as they get in the way of a just appreciation of the true state of affairs. Not only is there no little human being inside each one of us, but there is nothing even remotely resembling one; nor is there anything like a theatre in the human head. All we have are arrangements of cells and nerves, which do that particular work. It is as if we were to suppose that a little person existed inside each computer, or a miniature studio in each television set. It is not even as if there were any kind of localization of the sort: in order to visualize even in rudimentary fashion the nature of a television picture, we must think rather of the way in which various separate pieces of circuitry, widely separated, work together to produce the illusion of a scene in the little box.

In a particularly striking instance, Damasio's account of decisiveness, he seeks to show that much human decision-making is not a simple and straightforward process of rational thought, a weighing of the evidence this way and that – which might in any case become an endless process – but that it is frequently facilitated by the presence of what he calls 'somatic markers'. These can be regarded as essentially emotional stampings into the thought-process, which will already have been impressed by previous experience of such situations, Often, they have the effect of speeding up the time taken to reach individual decisions.

He concludes with his strongest and most central attack, on Descartes' 'cogito ergo sum', his celebrated '*I think, therefore I am*'. So far from being the self-evident proposition Descartes thought it, Damasio maintains, it is his central 'error', an attempt at identification between reasoning and true Being that has cast its shadow over

Western intellectual life ever since. He sums up his own position as follows:

> Long before the dawn of humanity, beings were beings. At some point in evolution, an elementary consciousness began. With that elementary consciousness came a simple mind; with greater complexity of mind came the possibility of thinking, and, even later, of using language to communicate and organize thinking better. For us, then, in the beginning it was being, and only later was it thinking. And for us now, as we come into the world and develop, we still begin with being, and only later do we think. We are, and then we think, and we think only inasmuch as we are, since thinking is indeed caused by the structures and operations of being.[3]

As will be observed, an important little shift has taken place. Instead of writing about emotions, Damasio now refers more exclusively to 'being'. What he appears to be saying is that emotions and thought, not thought alone, go to make up being, but he does not clarify the situation further. Whether or not his statement is accepted (and to many it will no doubt seem simple common sense), it can certainly be seen as a strong challenge to Descartes' assertion that his formula was self-evidently valid. Much has to do with the force of the 'therefore', the '*donc*'. Descartes, it seems, associated thinking and being so intimately that he saw no need to begin making distinctions; Damasio, by contrast, feels that a crucial distinction needs to be drawn, exposing the move from inference to identification. He could in his turn be said to risk an equal error, however, that of identifying Being with emotion. The position to be advanced here is that in both cases identification is inappropriate. Being should be thought of as distinguishable from both the levels of consciousness concerned, levels which are constantly fusing and intermingling with Being, yet which differ fundamentally in their own natures, the one being best described as primarily biochemical, the other as bioelectrical.

The importance of making such a distinction does not in fact seem to be widely recognized. Roger Penrose opens his wide-ranging and incisive study *The Emperor's New Mind* by identifying as a crucial issue the question whether machines can be said to think, particularly in view of the capacities that are now demonstrated in them – capacities which in recent years have become quite extraordinary. 'Indeed,' he remarks, 'the claim seems to be being made that they are conscious.'[4] His study is, however, explicitly devoted to computers, minds and the laws of physics, his aim being to demonstrate the extreme complexity of recent computational phenomena and of modern mathematics as it has developed through the centuries yet still to argue that in neither case is there need to suppose that consciousness is necessarily involved – a fact which can, in his view, itself be demonstrated mathematically.

Penrose goes on to discuss what the role of consciousness might be and to argue that an active use of it – or something corresponding to it – is always present in mathematical work. He also cites examples from the literature of creativity to show how scientific discoverers and musical composers have tried to describe the processes involved. His concern is invariably with mathematics and the development of physics, however; at no point does he give any sign of considering the possibility that consciousness might be associated with biochemical processes as well; and that those processes might not in that case be susceptible to quantitative computation in the manner that he notes as characteristic of certain mental workings.

One aspect of the creative process which he describes is particularly relevant to the present study. He discusses the part played by verbal and non-verbal elements in creative intellectual work, contending that when he is engaged in mathematical work, verbal facility tends not to be involved and can even be an inhibiting factor. Francis Galton, likewise, had described it as a 'serious drawback' to him in writing that he did not 'think as easily in words as otherwise'. Penrose affirms that as far as he himself is concerned, almost all his mathematical thinking is done 'visually and in terms of non-verbal concepts'.[5] In this respect his conclusion agrees with those of a 1945 inquiry among eminent mathematicians in North America to discover their working methods. The results showed that with only two exceptions, they thought neither in visual terms nor in algebraic symbols, but relied on visual imagery of a vague, hazy kind. Einstein, for instance, wrote:

> The words of the language as they are written or spoken do not seem to play any role in my mechanics [?mechanism] of thought, which relies on more or less clear images of a visual and some of a muscular type. It seems to be that what you call full consciousness is a limiting case which can never be fully accomplished because consciousness is a narrow thing.[6]

He preferred to consider 'certain signs and more or less clear images which can be "voluntarily" reproduced and combined'.

The testimony of such thinkers must be respected, yet it leaves open the question of the place of such thinking in those whose creative gifts are, specifically, verbal. Is the work of poets or novelists totally different in nature from that of mathematicians, or are there similarities to be discerned?

At this point, we may ask what can be called the 'Coleridgean question', following John Stuart Mill's well-known distinction:

> By Bentham, men have been led to ask themselves, in regard to any ancient or received opinion, Is it true? and by Coleridge, What is the meaning of it? ...With Coleridge ... the very fact that any doctrine had been believed by thoughtful men, and received by whole nations or generations of mankind, was part of the problem to be solved, was one of the phenomena to be accounted for.[7]

In these terms we may ask how it has come about that, following Descartes, whole generations of thinkers have been willing to accept the validity of his assertion, apparently without feeling any need to question its exact terms, and why the position should recently have changed. The answer is likely to be that what was being said chimed more closely with the intellectual needs of his time than with those of our own. As European society began to emerge from the constraints laid by the ages of religious belief there was a need to establish the sovereign power of reason as an alternative anchor. The Cartesian affirmation provided a means of validating the new interest in scientific inquiry. During the subsequent period the success of scientific experimentation and analysis would constantly offer justification for belief in the supremacy of rational processes in helping to solve problems that faced the human race generally. Those who felt that they needed to hold their own against established believers who might seek to limit the bounds of investigation could take comfort by establishing their position so strongly. In more recent times, however, scientists have increasingly questioned the value of making such absolute claims. As Damasio says, to assign such a dominant role to rational analysis is to risk overlooking important other factors in human nature. He is concerned, for example, with the rise of alternative medicine, not because he finds it comparably effective, but because he thinks its popularity may indicate the existence of needs that orthodox medicine does not address.

It is hard to fault the purport of Damasio's argument as far as it goes. Many, perhaps most, would agree that, in human terms, 'being' amounts to more than simple ratiocination. Yet there is a simple problem involved in his approach: by electing to use scientific methods of analysis to approach the question he is automatically assuming the hegemony of the reason he is trying to supplement. When he directs attention to the combined working of thought and emotion, he can demonstrate its existence persuasively, as, for example, by discussing the effects of lobotomy in depriving a subject of feeling tone, but it is much harder to demonstrate how it works – what manner of interaction is involved. It is far easier to analyse the workings of simple neural actions than to analyse chemical actions in the body, particularly in so far as they are acting together. The result is that any attempt to deal satisfactorily with these problems must involve a quite unusual mental poise, a willingness to think at one and the same time with the mental precision that is required for dealing with quantities and with the subtlety of intuition that makes it possible to move outside the boundaries imposed by a restricting rational activity.

The investigation of such processes suffers, however, from the fact that they are not totally accessible to analysis. Their elusiveness is an essential characteristic so that one is driven back to a few vivid images, such as that of the transforming well, to explain the enhancing effect of leaving thoughts and ideas to stand for a while before restoring them to the broad light of day. J.L. Lowes used this method to considerable effect in his study *The Road to Xanadu*, showing how images such as those of phosphorescence could lie steeped in Coleridge's subconscious for a time before re-emerging more vividly to participate in his poetry.[8] There is, of course, a paradox involved, since as soon as any kind of unconscious factor has been expressed it must in some sense become conscious; such elusiveness is to be found in a number of areas, such as our conception of time. Blake expressed it well in the irony of Enitharmon's despairing cry as she sees the forthcoming loss of feminine dominance through the loss of sexual secrecy: 'Between two moments bliss is ripe.'[9] She is too bound by the laws of the physical universe to perceive that this might be an emblem of release. Sexual experience as intimated here becomes the paradigm for many such experiences of the unseizable ('He who binds to himself a joy | Does the winged life destroy' is another of Blake's versions[10]). Saint Augustine's famous comment expresses the dilemma succinctly:

What then is time? I know what it is if no one asks me what it is; but if I want to explain it to someone who has asked me, I find that I do not know.[11]

When applied to the sense of Being this elusiveness has a further aspect. In what sense may it be true that our being relates to that of the divine? When the Apostle Paul, speaking to the Athenians, described God in the words 'in him we live and move and have our being',[12*] did he intend his emphasis on the Greek word for 'are' to be given literal emphasis? If so, is there a link with his statement to the Colossians: 'your life is hid with Christ in God', suggesting the existence of an element of the divine in human beings?[13*] Such ideas have not been acceptable to orthodox Christians, but they have attracted some less dogmatic believers, suggesting a way of sustaining their own faith and of finding common links with other religions. Orthodox and heterodox alike face the same problem: that of a God who is hidden, and therefore as elusive as some of the elements in their own unconscious.

One possible solution to the problem has been to suppose that the form in which the ultimate truth about things can be stated is equally clandestine. Various occult schemes have been built upon this supposition, surfacing particularly during the Renaissance and again, to a lesser degree, in the early years of Romanticism. If the Judaeo-Christian scheme did not provide a satisfying account of the universe as it was coming to be revealed by the sciences, then it was incumbent on thinkers to discover whether there might be a hidden tradition that made better sense, or, if that were not discoverable, whether it was possible to construct one. In the 1790s the young Coleridge thought he could find such a schema hidden in the works of the mythologists, and for a time his thought and poetry were coloured by the conviction. Blake, meanwhile, following a similar line, spent time in discovering what might be there to be uncovered, but even more in constructing a mythology of his own to supplement or replace what could be found in existing traditions.[14*]

If no place for such a controlling mythology was to be found, either in Christian orthodoxy or in a more esoteric tradition, the problem was not just that of finding a ground for religious belief but of explaining the human. If there is, after all, no ground of human personality in the divine, is such a basis to be found anywhere? Such considerations lead to a further probing of individual psychology and of the means by which the human being acquires a coherent identity.

Keats was one of the few to take on the question directly and try to find an answer. In a letter to his brother and sister-in-law he proposed to call the world 'The Vale of soul-making':

> Then you will find out the use of the world (I am speaking now in the highest terms for human nature admitting it to be immortal

which I will here take for granted for the purpose of showing a thought which has struck me concerning it) I say '*Soul making*' Soul as distinguished from an Intelligence – There may be Intelligences or sparks of the divinity in millions – but they are not Souls till they acquire identities, till each one is personally itself. Intelligences are atoms of perception – they know and they see and they are pure, in short they are God – how then are souls to be made? How then are these sparks which are God to have identity given them – so as ever to possess a bliss peculiar to each ones individual existence? How, but by the medium of a world like this? ... This is effected by three grand materials acting the one upon the other for a series of years – These three materials are the *Intelligence* – the *human heart* (as distinguished from intelligence or Mind) and the *World* or *Elemental space* suited for the proper action of *Mind and heart* on each other for the purpose of forming the *Soul* or *intelligence, destined to possess the sense of Identity* ... [15]

Keats had solved the problem for himself, in other words, by the simple process of assuming that human intelligences are 'sparks of the divinity'. They were, therefore, for him a part of the Being who is God, thought of in terms of vital energy. This would not have met with the approval of a thinker such as Coleridge, at least in his later years, since he would have seen this as no more than a refined version of pantheism. Yet he too clearly felt the attractions of a conception that spoke so directly to human intelligence and to the human heart. Shelley nurtured something of the same idea, thinking of God as 'the interfused and overruling Spirit of all the energy and wisdom included within the circle of existing things', of the 'collective energy of the moral and material world'.[16] His use of the word 'interfused' suggests an influence from Wordsworth's use in *Tintern Abbey* of the same word to suggest the elusive nature of the universal Being 'that rolls through all things'.

During the Romantic period, the assumption that to speak in ultimate terms about Being one must inevitably be talking about the divine (even if as a non-believer) remained fairly constant. One reason was that, at that time, questions of atheism were inseparably linked to the French Revolution and the violent events that had followed in its wake. Shelley (as will be discussed later) was bold enough to publish a pamphlet entitled 'The Necessity of Atheism'; his fate was not only to be expelled from Oxford, but to be reviled in the public press for the rest of his life. The strength of the reaction is enough to witness to the underlying fears, including a strong element of political fear – fears for the maintenance of order itself – that haunted English writers concerning the matter.

The existence of such fears also buttressed the urge to maintain conventional forms of thinking and to safeguard the boundaries of rational consciousness. New intellectual developments such as Swedenborgianism in religion, or interest in the paranormal, which had attracted young men of the time, were seen as tarred with the brush of revolutionary thinking in France and therefore either to be cast aside or, at the very best, regarded with suspicion. Yet once such new ideas had been voiced, they could not be simply hidden away again, and a conception which has since come back many times, as in the thinking of Damasio, the idea that consciousness in itself cannot be identified with the whole of what it is to be human, has remained insidiously present in human thinking ever since, giving rise to the distinction which will form the running theme of the present study: that between consciousness and what for the purposes of convenience we shall refer to (with a capitalized letter) as Being.

It must be emphasized at the outset that discussions of this matter cannot take the form of a tidy, ordered progression or a neatly presented logical argument – all the more so since we are not trying to relate comparable concepts. 'Consciousness' is something about whose nature we can generally agree, however difficult it may be to define it. 'Being', by contrast, is, as my chapter title is meant to suggest, mysterious, its nature subject for fruitful disagreement. In the unconscious the two can interact and there the definiteness of consciousness may therefore take on the elusiveness that is to be associated with Being. The complicating factor, which must be borne constantly in mind, is that while consciousness must always in some sense include Being – serving often, indeed, as a necessary filter for its expression – it is not clear how for Being will reciprocate. In order to convey what is involved, the attempt must often therefore involve resorting to impression and suggestion. The words of Wordsworth, that in order to paint such an effect he would 'need | Colours and words that are unknown to man ...'[17] re-echo in such a context.

It will be necessary, of course, to remember that writers may not mean exactly the same when they use some of the keywords involved. In particular (as has already been indicated) nineteenth-century usages tend to carry larger, metaphysical implications, where later ones will be more focused on the predicament of the individual. From the time of early Romanticism, however, neither connotation can be said to disappear, for it is in the interplay between the two potentialities that the full implications of existing as a conscious human being are kept alive. The very desire to speak of Being with some degree of emphasis betrays the human need to honour its existence as something thing more than a set of terms that is no more than the sum of what can be reached by successive conscious analyses, however fine the techniques involved.

In England, awareness of the mental phenomena to be associated with such levels of awareness increased with the growth of self-analysis, which was a characteristic of eighteenth-century culture. Philosophers began to note the contradictory movements of their own reasoning consciousness, and even, with Hume, to observe the way in which their experiences of doubt could bring them to a stand – at which point they might need to engage in a quite different kind of activity. Hume's need to dine or play a game of backgammon with his friends as a relief from the depression induced by his mental exertions[18] is a classic instance of such an activity, redressing the psychic balance when the limits of reasoning consciousness are reached.

As will be seen in the course of the following discussions,[19] writers from the Romantic period to the present day have grappled with the problem variously, since the associated questions rise in many forms, ranging from problems of personal identity to inquiries that may be seen as metaphysical in nature. During the rise of English Romanticism, however, it had an intensity that owed much to the political events of the time. From an early stage in his career, William Blake, for instance, believed that they showed how the world of rational consciousness that had been increasingly adopted by leading thinkers of the preceding period did not answer adequately to the needs of human beings. He did not examine the issues analytically, for that would in itself have been foreign to his underlying conviction, but a sense of the problems involved was to engage him throughout the whole of his life; among other things it was not for him a matter simply of positive intuition, but of deep-seated fear, giving an unusual colouring to the resulting art. With him, therefore, the study may fittingly begin.

2
Blake's Fear of Non Entity

When he was a young, aspiring painter, Samuel Palmer was taken on one occasion by John Linnell to meet the elderly William Blake, an encounter which he was never to forget:

> He fixed his grey eyes upon me, and said, 'Do you work with fear and trembling?' 'Yes, indeed,' was the reply. 'Then,' said he, 'You'll do.'[1]

In spite of the biblical overtones,[2] the ideas of 'fear' and 'trembling' may not be those that one associates with the apparently confident and forthright Blake, yet a glance at the concordance will show how often he used both words. The most notable instance of a personal reference is in his letter to John Flaxman of September 1800, where, after mentioning the 'dark horrors' of the American War, he continues,

> Then the French Revolution commenc'd in thick clouds And My Angels have told me that seeing such visions I could not subsist on the Earth, But by my conjunction with Flaxman, who knows to forgive Nervous Fear.[3]

The events surrounding the French Revolution had a profound effect on his attitude to the world. The man who wrote the *Poetical Sketches*, which were published in 1778 (though written earlier), had shown little or no sign of dissent from the political views regarded as orthodox in the England of his time. The dramatic piece 'King Edward the Fourth' and 'A War Song to Englishmen' proclaimed the need to fight valiantly for Albion's liberty and future prosperity, and contained no signals that they were intended to be read in any way ironically.

Towards the end of the century, however, particular events, including the death of his brother Robert in 1787 when he claimed to have
seen the released spirit ascending through the ceiling, 'clapping its
hands for joy',[4] the arrival of Swedenborgianism in England[5] and news
of the events in France caused Blake to revise his thinking and move
into the prophetic stance that was to be his hallmark for the rest of his
life. At one extreme, he was appalled by news of what was happening
in Paris, at the other he felt awakened to a sense of human possibilities
so vivid that he found it impossible to understand how his fellow
human beings could be so blind to it. To Johann Lavater's aphorism
that 'He who has frequent moments of complete existence is a hero,
though not laurelled, is crowned, and without crowns, a king', he
responded, 'O that men would seek immortal moments   O that men
would converse with God'.[6] Among the features of his prophetic utter-
ances was a strong line concerning the deficiencies of rational thought
when operating in isolation. The work of contemporary reason he saw
as an attempt to organize and categorize everything until the universe
itself would be reduced to the status of a mill with complicated
wheels.[7] The effects were, in fact, to be seen visibly around him as the
Industrial Revolution spread its tentacles everywhere. And if one tried
to discover who or what was in charge of this process the answer
seemed hidden. In a notebook he inquired,

> Why art thou silent & invisible,
> Father of Jealousy
> Why dost thou hide thyself in clouds
> From every searching Eye
>
> Why darkness & obscurity
> In all thy words & laws
> That none dare eat the fruit but from
> The wily serpents jaws
> Or is it because Secrecy
> gains females loud applause.

The lines he entitled 'To Nobodaddy',[8] using the term again more
vitriolically to describe in terms of the world as he saw about him the
work of such a Being if he did exist:

> Then old Nobodaddy aloft
> Farted & belchd & coughd,

> And said I love hanging & drawing & quartering
> Every bit as well as war & slaughtering.
> Damn praying & singing
> Unless they will bring in
> The blood of ten thousand by fighting or swinging.[9]

This was good political invective, but it left one with the problem raised by describing this Being in personal terms when it seemed that such a nonentity might be devoid of human characteristics altogether. In the sequel he adopted a different strategy, supposing that what existed in the universe was not a God in the Christian sense, but a loss, a missing humanity, the elements of which could still be traced in the work and teachings of Jesus, but not in the God also worshipped by Christians, who seemed more noted for his lack of humanity:

> Thinking as I do that the Creator of this world is a very Cruel Being & being a Worshipper of Christ I cannot help saying the Son O how unlike the Father   First God Almighty comes with a Thump on the Head Then Jesus Christ comes with a balm to heal it.[10]

He devised a mythology of his own, to fit his conceptions better. The hymns of Isaac Watts, which he may have known from being taken to a Baptist chapel as an impressionable child,[11] depict with some precision the God of the Old Testament as he came to see him:

> Adore and tremble, for our God
> Is a *Consuming Fire*;
> His jealous Eyes his Wrath inflame,
> And raise his Vengeance higher.[12]

This is a prototype of the 'jealous god', whom Blake conveys in Urizen; another of Isaac Watts's portraits comes even closer to the cold power that is stored in Blake's figure:

> ... Atheist, forbear; no more blaspheme:
> God has a thousand Terrors in his Name,
> A thousand Armies at Command,
> Waiting the Signal of his Hand,
> And Magazines of Frost, and Magazines of Flame.
> Dress thee in Steel to meet his Wrath;

His sharp Artillery from the *North*
Shall pierce thee to the Soul, and shake thy mortal Frame.[13]

Imagery such as this, along with that of a God with 'Stores of Lightning', seems to have been at the back of Blake's mind as he depicted Urizen in *The Four Zoas* as basing himself in the north, or in *America* (1793) described how

    ... his jealous wings wav'd over the deep;
Weeping in dismal howling woe he dark descended, howling
Around the smitten bands, clothed in tears & trembling, shudd'ring
    cold.
His stored snows he poured forth, and his icy magazines
He open'd on the deep, and on the Atlantic sea white shiv'ring
Leprous his limbs, all over white, and hoary was his visage.[14]

In Blake's work Urizen is a cold god, working through snow, ice and cold plagues. The fire and lightning are reserved for his opponent Orc, the uprising spirit of energy that cannot find humanized form.

There are many other places in which Watts's images can be discerned in Blake's writings, particularly during the early period, betraying his horror at the workings of such a God.

     Long e'er the lofty Skies were spread,
     Jehovah fill'd his Throne;
     Or *Adam* form'd, or Angels made,
     The Maker liv'd alone.[15]

So wrote Watts, who also painted a vivid picture of God making the human body, heart, brains, and lungs, in turn, and writing out his promise of redemption for men:

     ... His Hand has writ the sacred Word
     With an immortal Pen.

     Engrav'd as in eternal Brass
     The mighty Promise shines ...[16]

Translating this language into its visual imagery, Blake could have gained some strong hints towards his depiction of Urizen, who turned aside from the light, colour and harmony of the Eternals to brood in solitude, 'A self-contemplating shadow, I In enormous labours occupied', and wrote out his laws with an iron pen. When he eventually reports on his activities, it is in the words:

> Lo! I unfold my darkness: and on
> This rock, place with strong hand the Book
> Of eternal brass, written in my solitude.[17]

'The Book ... written in my solitude'. Title-page to *The First Book of Urizen*.
Courtesy of the Rare Books Division of the Library of Congress.

That 'Book' contains all the Christian virtues, but reduced to laws: 'Laws of peace, of love, of unity, I of pity, compassion, forgiveness.' Everything is reduced to standardization, in the hope of imposing permanence. Blake, by contrast, believes the human quest for permanence to be mistaken. In a world of life, fixity is impossible to achieve; the task of human beings is to learn how to live in a world where changes, shifts and transformations are part of the essential process. 'We are born to Cares and Woes,' writes Watts gloomily in one of his hymns; Blake's version sees the human condition as one of necessary alternations:

> Man was made for joy & Woe
> And when this we rightly know
> Thro the world we safely go.
> Joy & Woe are woven fine
> A Clothing for the Soul divine
> Under every grief & pine
> Runs a joy with silken twine.[18]

He did not wish to deny the existence of griefs and sorrows, but believed that a view of the world that made them central was at once mistaken and dangerous, fostering a defensive attitude in individuals and a desire for permanence that was Urizen's great mistake, reflected in the mental captivity of his eighteenth-century subjects.

Looking closely at Urizen's activities, we see that, as elsewhere, Blake's purpose was not simply to attack his predecessor. In one sense he was on the side of Watts, whose work possessed a grandeur and even visionary power that he could respect deeply. The questions that were agitating him, on the other hand, deeper than any faced by Watts, related to his own vision. How was it that the beauty and delight that he discovered everywhere in the world seemed not to be noticed at all by his fellows? Why did they persist in disregarding not only their own imaginative faculties, but also the psychic experiences induced by terror or the free exercise of energy?

What was required in his view was recognition of another level of existence, most centrally expressed by the existence of human desire for the infinite. Unless it could find fulfilment by finding a corresponding infinite object – which could only happen if it acknowledged the existence of its own genius, with its equivalent infinite quality – its human subject must end in despair:

If it were not for the Poetic or Prophetic character the Philosophic & Experimental would soon be at the ratio of all things, & stand still, unable to do other than repeat the same dull round over again.

Blake did not use the word 'unconscious' in his known writing, yet he displayed a constant awareness of its power – notably in his lines in Milton:

Come into my hand.
By your mild power descending down the nerves of my right arm
From out the portals of my brain ... [19]

'Being', as a noun, was not a word he used very much, either; when he did, it was in association with the nightmare state of death, where it appeared in response as an object of extreme desire. The concept is more often expressed in terms of the words 'Existence' and 'Entity', together with their negatives: at the end of his epic 'Vala' the 'Legions of Mystery' fall through the Immense into the Winepresses of Luvah and, forsaken of their Elements,

> vanish & are no more
> No more but a desire of Being a distracted ravening desire
> Desiring like the hungry worm & like the gaping grave.

They cry out in their agony,

> let us Exist for
> This dreadful Non Existence is worse than pains of Eternal Birth.[20]

Throughout the Prophetic Books the prospect of falling into 'Non-Entity', envisaged as a kind of abyss, is the ultimate nightmare. In 'Visions of the Daughters of Albion', Oothoon fears that she will become a 'solitary shadow wailing on the margin of non-entity';[21] Urizen begins 'Vala' with his feet 'upon the verge of Non Existence'.[22] One character, Ahania, comes to this margin, another, Enion, is repelled there.[23] Even Jerusalem, in the later epic of that name, sees her children 'In the visions of the dreams of Beulah on the edge of Non-Entity'.[24] The condition of not-Being threatens everywhere, whether as precipice, depths or wilderness. Only once in Blake's writings is it seen as involving something other than descent, when the flames roll as Los hurls his chains

> Rolling round & round, mounting on high
> Into vacuum, into non-entity
> Where nothing was ... [25]

At the conclusion of *Jerusalem* this state is redeemed, when

> the all tremendous unfathomable Non Ens
> Of Death was seen in regenerations terrific or complacent.[26]

Until then it has always remained a negative power; indeed, Blake's attitude may well have been linked to his dislike for abstract words in general, as when Fuzon arouses revolt against Urizen with the words, 'Shall we worship this Demon of smoke ... this abstract non-entity?'[27] Terms such as 'Non Ens' and 'Non Existence' betray his deep fear of falling, or being drawn, into negativity. When it comes to using a positive noun, accordingly, he prefers to use, instead of an abstract-seeming word such as 'Being', a term with more content, such as 'Genius' or 'the Poetic or Prophetic character'. 'The Poetic Genius is the true Man',[28] his extreme statement, records the larger vision behind his main theme – that all human beings are, at least potentially, informed by the universal principle of Humanity, the Eternal Man. The task of the artist is to awaken this underlying 'Being' from his sleep. The essence of his powers is to be found not in the rational mind, measuring the infinite distances of the universe until its habit of categorization brings him to despair, but in his own genius, which, being in itself fountainous, responds to fountainous energies wherever they reveal themselves, whether in the fires of the sun or in the activities of other living beings.

The motif runs through all his work. He did not need to theorize about the nature of Being, taking its existence so completely for granted that he could use it effortlessly. In one of his earliest prophetic books, 'Tiriel', he drew upon the fact that in occult science 'Tiriel' is 'the intelligence of mercury' to portray a sense of human genius at its lowest ebb. Tiriel, who at his finest might have been a winged Mercury, is here reduced to a figure who has the poisonous qualities of the element of that name, who can do nothing but curse, and who ends, appropriately, as a serpent outstretched at the feet of his faded associates, Har and Heva. When Blake wanted to produce an epic poem suitable for his time, he found his central heroic character to be a happier version of human genius, his Eternal Man, the basic representative of, and dweller in, all human beings. Instead of a warlike hero and his exploits, he would present the 'Man', with all his component 'Zoas' (his own term, close to the Greek word for 'living beings'). In this quixotic enterprise he would show how the various disorders and false emotions of individuals were all, when rightly seen, distortions from their true passions and desires. If the Eternal Man in each were to reawaken, they would find themselves instantly reharmonized in the unified Human Being who would take over.

Blake's belief in this unity of Being did not mean, however, that he himself had a such unified identity. The best one could say is that as an artist he had a visionary identity – expressed among other ways in a vivid figure that sometimes appears among his designs.

Such figures[29] are expressive more of light and running energy than of strong personal characteristics. (When one comes across such firm features in alternative representations, on the other hand, they are likely to be expressive of his streak of obstinacy; the chief note is likely to be sardonic, questioning, truculent,[30*] coming from the Blake of the notebook epigrams and derisive comments in the margins of other writers' books, a man whose strong identity contrasts with his fluency.) Quite early on Blake was thought of as 'a new kind of man',[31] and this may be related to a sense that his was a new kind of Being, to be

'Death was not, but eternal life sprung'. *The First Book of Urizen*. Courtesy of the Rare Books Division of the Library of Congress.

thought of as largely in motion, not easily to be pinned down since it was constantly realizing itself through the acts of its energy. There is about some of his most characteristic and memorable statements an immediacy that impresses. Consciousness, as a result, tended to take second place and to be suspect, since it was redolent of the Reason which he saw as responsible in his time for humanity's chief ills. This Reason produced the Spectre (pictured in his iconography with bat-wings) which lay behind all their doubting attitudes, which he found pernicious, responding to them with forceful statements such as

> If the Sun & Moon should doubt
> Theyd immediately go out.[32]

Blake's view, forcefully and even melodramatically put, never really questioned the priority of Being over such consciousness. In his case it also involved a sense of danger. Being, if once approached, was essentially ungraspable. To reach further into it would be like trying to touch the sun, or the ark of God:[33] 'For who dare touch the frowning form, I His arm is witherd to its root', as he puts it in his poem 'The Mental Traveller'.[34] Other Romantic writers, even if they viewed the position less melodramatically and had a stronger sense of the problems involved, given the development of consciousness in the recent annals of civilization, would still share his sense of portentousness – which was fitfully to re-emerge among their successors also.

3
Coleridge, Wordsworth and 'Unknown Modes of Being'

> I rather suspect that some where or other there is a radical dif-
> ference in our theoretical opinions respecting Poetry – / this I
> shall endeavour to go to the Bottom of ...[1]

So wrote Coleridge in 1802. His sense of a subterranean disagreement,
which haunts the account of his critical opinions many years later in
Biographia Literaria, was not necessarily confined to the sphere of literary criticism; it extended to many aspects, including, I shall maintain,
the ways in which the two poets regarded the very nature of Being – a
word which they became accustomed to use with a special charge of
significance.

Even in youth they had already been made aware that current theories of the human mind seemed inadequate to account for everything
in human behaviour. At the end of the eighteenth century when the
cult of animal magnetism, or hypnotism, particularly fashionable then
in France,[2*] had also made a strong impact in London, the young
Coleridge had been one of its chief beneficiaries. He derived from its
demonstration that more than one level of consciousness existed in
the human mind, sustenance for a growing interest in the imaginative
powers of human beings, evident, for example, in the first version of
The Rime of the Ancient Mariner.[3*] The clear reference to animal magnetism there disappeared from the poem after 1798, however, and the
reason can hardly have been poetic awkwardness alone. Just as the first
Lyrical Ballads volume was going through the press, he set off in the
company of the Wordsworths for Germany, where among other things
he attended the lectures of one of the most distinguished physiologists
of the time, J.F. Blumenbach. He may have hoped to learn more about
magnetism there, but if so he was destined to be disappointed, since, as

he must soon have discovered, Blumenbach was sceptical concerning the very existence and validity of hypnotic phenomena. This must have been a strong setback to his thinking, though it did not put a stop to related speculations. An important feature of this range of investigation was the challenge laid down to current ideas of reason. If it was truly the case that one could pass so fully between states of consciousness – to the extent that while in one state one had no awareness of what one did or thought in the other, a basic area of possible dissoci-ation in the psyche was suggested, which might throw a flood of light on related questions. Once the idea of a duality, or plurality, of consciousnesses had been planted in his mind it was likely to flourish there.

At the turn of the century, during their most intense collaboration,[4] this strand of thinking obliquely influenced Wordsworth's poetic thinking. It also led to some interesting developments of his own during the same period: it can be associated with his theories of 'double touch' and 'single touch', for example, the first referring to our normal conscious world, our existence in which can be confirmed by reinforcing one touch by another ('I pinched myself to make sure I was not dreaming') and the second, where no such confirmation is available, leading to experiences which can range from nightmare to ecstasy.[5] The duality involved could be further generalized into the theory of a 'primary' and 'secondary' consciousness, a division with an originality of its own, differing from the similar one that dominated later psychology – in one instance, at least, amounting to an inversion of it. Freud was to speak of 'primary' and 'secondary' consciousness, but for him the first meant simply what is signified by normal every-day consciousness. The 'secondary' layer, by contrast, was the one in which the unconscious elements had their setting and was therefore of particular interest to analysts. Coleridge's bold contention, on the other hand, was that the real key to human nature lay at this *uncon-scious* level, deserving to be promoted, therefore, as the true 'primary'.

Failure to grasp the nature of this distinction has led to some confu-sion in Coleridge studies, particularly since it also played a significant role in his important critical distinction between the 'primary' and the 'secondary' imagination. I.A. Richards, for example, maintained that, for Coleridge, the primary imagination was

> normal perception that produces the usual world of the senses ... the world of motor-buses, beef-steaks, and acquaintances, the framework of things and events within which we maintain our everyday existence, the world of the routine satisfaction of our minimum exigencies.[6]

Much as Coleridge might have liked to think this, it is clear from all he had to say about the Primary Imagination that it existed at a level removed from everyday perception, in a realm pertaining in some respects to the divine. From an early stage he had affirmed that one could not understand the mind by attending only to its powers of analysis. In one of his earlier letters, he urged the need for a holistic approach to human problems – one corresponding to the effect of, say, the resurgence of life in the spring, where the phenomena concerned work at one and the same time, with a miraculous totality. Discussing the relation between accepting notionally the principle that the Good of the whole is the Good of each individual and putting it into practice he wrote,

It is not enough that we have once swallowed it – the Heart should have fed upon the truth, as Insects on a Leaf – till it be tinged with the colour, and shew it's food in every the minutest fibre.[7]

In making this point, which he repeated in one of his political lectures,[8] Coleridge was evidently thinking of chemical processes, and the unific manner in which they may act, the result being an effect that takes place not sequentially – or indeed in any kind of identifiable order – but simultaneously. It was his sense of such magical effects of unification that particularly impressed Wordsworth – a point he stressed when he drew on the idea of primary and secondary powers in addressing to him an early version of his poem *The Prelude*:

Thou art no slave
Of that false secondary power by which
In weakness we create distinctions, then
Deem that our puny boundaries are things
Which we perceive, and not which we have made.
To thee, unblinded by these outward shows,
The unity of all has been revealed.[9]

Despite the notable change in their thought towards more conservative attitudes, which would arouse distrust among those who valued their early radicalism, it can be argued that the course both men were following at the time amounted to something more coherent and comprehensible than simple political tergiversation. Their successive writings in these years represent not so much diversion as the sustained pursuit of a discernible line of thought. Although, in the event, that under-running line issued in questions rather than answers, the overall enterprise had a life of its own, traces of which are still discernible even in their latest work. The clearest sign of its emergence is in a letter of Coleridge's in March 1798, written in answer to his brother's disquiet about his current political ideas. While it was true that he did not support the actions of the current administration, he replied, he felt himself bound to remember that the ministers might sometimes be acting on information not generally available. He went on:

> feeling this, my Brother! I have for some time past withdrawn myself almost totally from the consideration of *immediate* causes, which are infinitely complex & uncertain, to muse on fundamental & general causes – the 'causae causarum' – I devote myself to such works as encroach not on the antisocial passions – in poetry, to elevate the imagination & set the affections in right tune by the beauty of the inanimate impregnated, as with a living soul, by the presence of Life – in prose, to the seeking with patience & a slow, very slow mind 'Quid sumus, et quidnam victuri gignimur' – What our faculties are & what they are capable of becoming.[10]

Coleridge continued in a vein that reflected Wordsworth's nature philosophy of the time; the lines about setting the affections in right tune (a quotation, of course, from Milton[11]) offer a clue to the purposes of the more meditative poems that he was then writing. The most important phrases, however, are the Latin ones at the end, which would be more exactly translated as 'what we are and what we are born to become'. This investigation into the nature of what it was to be human, including 'Being' as such, was a crucial element in the whole enterprise that Coleridge and Wordsworth engaged upon in those and the following years.

There was a very good reason for undertaking it, since it sprang from the need to consider further the idea of liberty, which had come into new prominence as a result of the French Revolution, and search for something more satisfactory. It was of no use, they believed, for human beings to put their faith in it as an abstract ideal, since, as recent events in France had shown, such a course could easily lead to anarchy. Instead, they must try to identify and understand the nature of the true Being in each individual; only by taking full account of that could one propose an amelioration of the human condition.

During these years the main thrust of Wordsworth's and Coleridge's thought was, on these terms, investigative rather than dogmatic. 'Being', as pointed out, is – particularly for Anglo-Saxon readers – a word hard to monitor in view of its apparent lack of content. Written with a capital letter it can sound more like an emphatic way of speaking than an element in serious discourse. As a result, the attention paid to the word by Coleridge and Wordsworth, and by some of their nineteenth-century successors, can escape notice. Moreover, the fact that both poets used the word in their later writings in a manner more closely in line with traditional and pietistic usage, can veil the questioning and exploratory quality of their earlier usages. The point to be pursued here, however, is the greater significance of the word in the poems of their main creative period.

Shortly before he encountered Coleridge, Wordsworth had been passing through a time not simply of doubt, but of despondency at his failure to find clear answers to his questions. As he put it in *The Prelude*,

> demanding proof,
> And seeking it in every thing, I lost
> All feeling of conviction and, in fine,
> Sick, wearied out with contrarieties,
> Yielded up moral questions in despair.[12]

What is less often noticed is that his account can be matched by one that Coleridge gave of his life and thinking, describing the intellectual crisis that overtook him in roughly the same period of the 1790s. The most striking feature of this is that – even more than with Wordsworth – one might not otherwise have guessed at the disturbance going on beneath the surface. There is little or no hint of it in surviving evidence from his letters or notebooks of the time; and elsewhere in *Biographia Literaria* he describes his political and social activities as if they were all-consuming. Then, as if there were something insufficient in the story as told so far, he begins again (without explanation), recording how a year or so after he began his career in literature and politics he had passed into a state of disgust and despondency concerning the latter. The portrait he has just offered, of an apparently self-confident young man pursuing his way through the contemporary political and social scene, gives way to a quite different account:

I retired to a cottage in Somersetshire at the foot of Quantock, and devoted my thoughts and studies to the foundations of religion and morals. Here I found myself all afloat. Doubts rushed; broke upon me 'from the fountains of the great deep', and fell 'from the windows of heaven.' The fontal truths of natural religion and the books of Revelation alike contributed to the flood; and it was long ere my ark touched on an Ararat, and rested. The idea of the Supreme being appeared to me to be as necessarily implied in all particular modes of being as the idea of infinite space in all the geometric figures by which space is limited. I was pleased with the cartesian opinion, that the idea of God is distinguished from all other ideas by involving its reality; but I was not wholly satisfied. I began then to ask myself, what proof I had of the outward existence of any thing?[13]*

The importance of this account can hardly be overestimated, for it lays out the terms of an intellectual conflict that dogged Coleridge for most of his life. Impulses to accept the scientific view of the world that was growing up, particularly in the great industrial and manufacturing centres of England, and which invited the cultivation of an impersonal philosophy devoted to human improvement of the kind that was in fact to characterize many contributions to English culture in the nineteenth century, particularly from the Unitarians, struggled against a binding-back of himself (a *'religio'*) into the personally based religion of Christianity that had been an integral part of English civilization during previous centuries and in which he himself had been brought up. In some respects, the conflict would be exacerbated by his collaboration with the Wordsworths, which brought a new delight in appreciation of the beauties of the natural world, yet associated him closely with someone who was not at that time an orthodox Christian.

The most notable feature of the passage quoted is its metaphor of the Flood. Blake had used that biblical image to describe his version of the initiating catastrophe for mankind, a 'deluge of the senses' by which the power of human beings to open themselves out to infinity had been overwhelmed, leaving an impoverished state where the only way for them to construct their world was by use of finite perceptions and measurements. Coleridge's adoption explores it in more detail by exploiting the twofold nature of the biblical deluge: 'the fountains of the great deep [were] broken up, and the windows of heaven were opened'. He could thus suggest a double subversion of his intellectual position: the doctrines of natural religion and of the revealed Word of God were both 'fontal' truths, one of them to be sought in the great deep, the other in the heavens above; but when both were explored to their limits the result was overwhelming, the sceptical implications of natural religion clouding and obscuring the light from revelation above while, even as he tried to link knowledge of nature with historical religion, doubts concerning the authority of the scriptures were breaking up the firm ground on which the latter had been assumed to rest. This led to further contradictory states. As he put it later in his account, 'For a very long time indeed I could not reconcile personality with infinity; and my head was with Spinoza, though my whole heart remained with Paul and John'.

It was not simply an intellectual conflict. He was torn between allegiance to the two different groups mentioned above: the thinkers who were endeavouring to use their intelligence in the cause of human progress – and who, in the person of the Wedgwoods, were paying his way – and those who maintained the environment of Church and State in which he had been nurtured – including his god-fearing brothers. Whenever the demands of these two forces pressed on him too closely Coleridge was plunged into a corrosive anxiety. It was this intellectually troubled figure, then, who made contact with the depressed Wordsworth in 1797 while looking for help in discovering 'what our faculties are, and what they are capable of becoming'.

A question very close to this one was that of the nature of 'Life'. It would constantly come into focus for him when dealing with the Wordsworths, whether it was Dorothy, with her instinctive feeling for all living things – to which she brought a quite unusual degree of sensitivity – or William himself, with his semi-mystical claim to be able to 'see into the life of things'. He himself had already shown the degree of his own interest when writing to Thelwall in 1796:

> Dr Beddoes & Dr Darwin think that *Life* is utterly inexplicable, writing as Materialists ... Monro believes in a plastic immaterial Nature – all-pervading ... Hunter that the *Blood* is the Life – which is saying nothing at all – ... Plato says, it is *Harmony* ... and *I, tho last not least, I* do not know what to think about it – on the whole I have rather made up my mind that I am a mere *apparition* – a naked Spirit! – And that Life is I myself I! which is a mighty clear account of it.[14]

Although closely associated with this interest in life, his concern with the nature of 'Being' ('what we are', 'I myself I') has less often been generally studied.[15] During the years between 1795 and 1805, nevertheless, the word began to appear in the work of both poets with an unusual charge of meaning and in contexts that suggest that they were considering the idea back and forth between them. In the case of Coleridge, a first and foremost point of reference was the relationship with Wordsworth himself. Writing reproachfully to Robert Southey in

1795, he had said, 'I did not only venerate you for your own virtues, I prized you as the Sheet Anchor of mine!'[16] A few years later, he had told Robert Poole that he had spoken of him to Wordsworth as 'the man in whom *first* and in whom alone I had felt an *anchor!'*[17] With Wordsworth himself, the matter was different. Against his own feeling that he lacked personal identity his new friend seemed only too powerful a character, yet his poetry had a subtlety which gave the sense that a free-playing intelligence was also at play in it, offering hope that Coleridge's ranging and sometimes disorganized consciousness might now find a ground of Being by associating with Wordsworth's complementary strengths. 'You are incorporated into the better part of my being,' he wrote; 'whenever I spring forward into the future with noble affections, I always alight by your side.'[18] This sense of an intertwining of Being in which he somehow derived strength from Wordsworth's intelligent identity, his 'manliness', was to persist and develop, until in Malta he could write,

> To W[ordsworth] in the progression of Spirit... 'O that my Spirit, purged by Death of its Weaknesses, which are, alas! my *identity*, might flow into *thine*, & live and act in thee, & be Thou.'[19]

In the interval his conception of Being had come to relate the being of the individual to the whole Being of Nature. The result is seen most strikingly in 'France: An Ode'; a poem published in the *Morning Post* three weeks after Dorothy Wordsworth reported that he brought the *The Ancient Mariner* 'finished', and expressing Coleridge's disillusionment at the recent actions of the French. At the end he returns to the actual cliff-top scene where it is set, contending that the spirit of liberty that has been lost to the French can still be sensed in the movement of the winds and waves – even in the slight rustling of the trees above that mingles with the sound of the sea beyond. He then concludes:

> Yes, while I stood and gazed, my temples bare,
> And shot my being through earth, sea, and air,
> Possessing all things with intensest love,
> O Liberty! my spirit felt thee there.[20]

The 'shooting' of his 'Being' here has an outward, expansive movement which can, he is affirming, bind the human being to the rest of the living creation – and so become the ground of a universal love.

The moment is one of elevated rhetoric and exultation. Some of Coleridge's best effects in this vein came, on the other hand, when he used his powers of analysis to consider what nature might be like if the power of light and energy were withdrawn. In the subsequent period he proved himself ready to deconstruct his sense of Being into its component elements. 'So I suppose it is with all of us,' he wrote to Humphry Davy: ' – one while cheerful, stirring, feeling in resistance nothing but a joy & a stimulus; another while drowsy, self-distrusting, prone to rest, loathing our own Self-promises, withering our own Hopes, our Hopes, the vitality & cohesion of our Being! –'[21] Being, it seems, required both 'vitality' and 'cohesion' for its survival, a principle of life and a principle of form, without which one's state would be null. 'I have suffered such an extinction of Light in my mind,' he wrote in March 1799, 'I have been so forsaken by all the *forms* and *colourings* of Existence, as if the *organs* of Life had been dried up; as if only simple BEING remained, blind and stagnant.'[22] Inasmuch as Being is articulated in Coleridge's terms it is expressed through a combination of activity and effulgence, without which it would be no more than a strange nullity. If light alone were withdrawn, the resulting condition would begin to have a strange and ghostly quality, like that in the deep dell near Alfoxden, where sunlight hardly penetrates, leaving only

> the dark green file of long lank weeds,
> That all at once (a most fantastic sight!)
> Still nod and drip beneath the dripping edge
> Of the blue clay-stone.[23]

The precision of Coleridge's imagery of reduced Being here betrays the extent of his thinking on the subject. An alternative version of such deprivation turns up years later in his poem 'Limbo', where, progressing consciously from John Donne's poetry, he imagines the fear which even the appearance of something so light and aery as a flea might cause in a place of ghosts – simply by the fact of being positive at all in so insubstantial a place:

> Even now it shrinks them! they shrink in, as Moles
> (Nature's mute Monks, live Mandrakes of the ground)
> Creep back from Light, then listen for its Sound –
> See but to dread, and dread they know not why
> The natural Alien of their negative Eye.[24]

If the dell of 'This Lime-Tree Bower' exhibits the strange forms of beauty induced by a diminution of light, what would the converse world be like, where light remained but energy was withdrawn? This would not be *pure* Limbo, where there is no light. Like the dell, it would be a strange state of half-Being, but this would be the other half – which is precisely how he describes it later in the same poem. Since all energy is withdrawn, the light of the sun being replaced by that of the moon, that gives everyone and everything a strange phantasmal beauty; yet it cannot be actively seen by the chief figure in the scene, who is himself a figure of passive reflection:

> with fore-top bald & high
> He gazes still, his eyeless Face all Eye –
> As twere an Organ full of silent Sight
> His whole Face seemeth to rejoice in Light/
> Lip touching Lip, all moveless, Bust and Limb,
> He seems to gaze at that which seems to gaze on him![25]

Imagery such as this indicates an attempt to enlarge the concept of human personality beyond that set forth by the main eighteenth-century philosophers.

'We are fearfully and wonderfully made.' In exploring their sense of Being, Wordsworth and Coleridge move between the senses of fear and of wonder; but whereas Wordsworth finds that his wonder is all too often haunted by fear, Coleridge more easily makes the reverse transition, from fear to wonder. Allowing for these differences of standpoint, however, there can be little doubt that the growing emphasis on the idea of Being by both poets was a result of these differences and convergences, the discussions with each other which were sparked assuming a new charge of meaning at the time of their meetings in Racedown and after. If one is looking for a priority, that probably belongs to Coleridge, who had already been using the terms 'to be' and 'being' with an unusual emphasis. When he wrote his early 'Reflections on having left a place of Retirement', which included an image of the landscape from above the Bristol Channel as a divine temple, he continued:

> No wish profan'd my overwhelmed heart.
> Blest hour! It was a luxury, – to be!

He then continued, however, by reflecting that such a course might have been one of

> pampering the coward heart
> With feelings all too delicate for use. [26]

and that such a complacent state must be abandoned. He had already used the word 'Being', with a capital, a year before in his 'Lines on a Friend who died of a Frenzy Fever induced by Calumnious Reports':

> Is this pil'd Earth our Being's passless mound?[27]

The word began to come into further prominence when the two poets were working on their tragedies. In *The Borderers* Wordsworth presents his villain as one who had dwelt a good deal with the 'mighty objects' which

> do impress their forms
> To elevate our intellectual Being[28]

– an interesting echo from the cry of Milton's Satan: 'who would lose … this intellectual being?'[29] When the same character of Wordsworth's turned back from such impressions to contemplate the normal processes of the human world, he

> seemed a Being who had passed alone
> Into a region of futurity,
> Whose natural element was freedom –.[30]

In 'Osorio', meanwhile, Coleridge pictured his Moorish woman wishing for total solitude:

> Along some ocean's boundless solitude,
> To float for ever with a careless course,
> And think myself the only being alive![31]

Up to this point, the examples quoted are ambiguous in signification. In each case the use of the word 'being' could be regarded as examples of its weak form, the one used to speak of a 'human being' – or even refer, indifferently, to a creature as a 'being'. As the dialectic between the two men develops, however, an increasing charge of meaning can be sensed, giving particular significance whenever the word is used.

In bodily terms, both Coleridge and Wordsworth would no doubt have located the centre of Being close to, or in, the human heart. When

Coleridge wrote his 'Hymn to the Earth', a free rendering of a poem by Christian Stolberg, the line he translated as 'Into my being thou murmurest joy...'[32] was from one using the German 'Herz'. Somewhere within the idea of Being for both poets lurked the processes of pulse and flow as associated with the physical workings of the heart. That is not the crux of the matter, however, since it is clear from their usage that their version of Being moved beyond a simple model. In each case also the onward movement takes a different form. In Coleridge's, the idea of Being often, as we have seen, involves an interplay of illumination and vitality, light and energy. So during his best years as a poet Coleridge was drawn to images which could not quite be contained into static form and where in order to appreciate them the eye must itself learn to play. In such imagery birds, animals or insects move, and their movement becomes essential to the beauty of their form – the albatross flies round and round, or flocks of starlings form themselves into successive shapes while the travelling Coleridge watches,[33] or the snake's sinuous movements play a necessary part in perception of its form as beautiful. He was fascinated by bees, their honey-gathering being a prime example of energies in harmony with the vegetative, while their clustered swarming in heat caricatured the activities of fanatics. The activities of the 'bee-idiot', with his constant humming, was probably for him a sign of the persistency of the primary, life consciousness, while a particular love-emblem was the Hutchinsons' beehive,

> That ever-busy & most quiet Thing
> Which I have heard at Midnight murmuring.[34]

Coleridge's speculations had a particularly complex effect on Wordsworth's, working with directness when they affected the manuscript autobiographical poetry that became *The Prelude*. The fact that this work, which he was composing now and in the years immediately following, was eventually left to be published after his death[35]* subsequently obscured the nature of his preoccupations at the time of its writing, with the result that his central reputation was based in years to come on other works, reflecting positions that he subsequently worked out for himself. Since he also continued to work at his poem in the intervening period, it may be assumed that he was unsure of its status. Would it, he must have feared, be seen by following generations as an elaborate aberration, of no more than secondary interest? Or might critics come to share his own sense of its importance and regard it as his greatest achievement? The question is further obscured by the fact that during his lifetime it was normally called by him not 'The Prelude', but by such names as the 'Poem to Coleridge' or the 'Poem on the Growth of his Mind'. Was he not, perhaps, thinking especially of Coleridge's ideas when he described such things as how in childhood his eye might gain 'New pleasure, like a bee among the flowers'?[36]

When we cut the poem free from its moorings in nineteenth-century publishing history and look at it as a freely navigating poem in its own right, the impact of Coleridge's ideas becomes more evident. A good example may be found in Wordsworth's attempt in the third book to sum up what he has achieved so far:

> Of genius, power,
> Creation, and divinity itself,
> I have been speaking for my theme has been
> What passed within me. Not of outward things
> Done visibly for other minds – words, signs,
> Symbols or actions – but of my own heart
> Have I been speaking, and of my youthful mind.[37]

He continues to write of his life at university and of the way in which it failed to answer to his full existence since he experienced feelings he could not put into words – and indeed still finds difficulty in expressing.

> This is in truth heroic argument,
> And genuine Prowess – -which I wished to touch,
> With hand however weak – but in the main
> It lies far hidden from the reach of words.
> Points have we all of us within our souls
> Where all stand single; this I feel, and make
> Breathings for incommunicable powers.
> Yet each man is a memory to himself,
> And therefore, now that I must quit this theme,
> I am not heartless, for there's not a man
> That lives who hath not had his god-like hours,
> And knows not what majestic sway we have
> As natural beings in the strength of Nature.[38]

He then returns to his Cambridge days, suggesting that beneath the surface of his ordinary social relationships and enjoyments at that time there were other forces at work, not detectable on the surface:

> Caverns there were within my mind which sun
> Could never penetrate, yet did there not
> Want store of leafy arbours where the light
> Might enter in at will.[39]

The first two lines of that poetic sentence mark an important moment: they represent one of Wordsworth's first attempts to find an imagery for the unconscious, which turns out to be similar to that in Coleridge's *Kubla Khan*, in which the figure of commanding genius is seen decreeing his pleasure-dome

> Where Alph the sacred river ran
> Through caverns measureless to man
> Down to a sunless sea.

In this piece of psychoscaping the ordinary life of consciousness and rationality is counterpointed against the cavernous, unplumbable areas of the subconscious mind. Previously, the mind as a whole had been imaged more directly and optimistically in 'The Eolian Harp' when Coleridge contemplated a bean field with a breeze blowing over it:

> And what if all of animated nature
> Be but organic Harps diversly fram'd
> That tremble into thought, as o'er them sweeps,
> Plastic and vast, one intellectual Breeze
> At once the soul of each, and God of all?

That particular model of breeze and harp was one he continued to use at different times, though he was also both aware and wary of its pantheistic potentialities. Wordsworth, by contrast, though drawn to think of the imagination as a hidden power, regarded it as more mysterious and in some respects more fearful. Coleridge was not unaware of such effects, of course, as he shows in *The Ancient Mariner*, but his main concern in subsequent years was to pursue, particularly in letters and notebooks, the implications of his sensed distinction between the two kinds of consciousness: the analysing and the holistic. He tended to cultivate a benevolent view of imagination as a more ecstatic power – even if its potentialities when misused were fearful – by comparison with Wordsworth's conception of it as a kind of abyss in the mind. In both cases the poets were exploring the sense of a consciousness deeper than that of everyday perception.

Good evidence of the relation between his meditations on the nature of Being and Coleridge's psychological speculations can be found in some of the poetic fragments in Wordsworth's notebooks:

> In many a walk
> At evening or by moonlight, or reclined
> At midday upon beds of forest moss,
> Have we to Nature and her impulse
> Of our whole being made free gift, and when
> Our trance had left us, oft have we, by aid
> Of the impressions which it left behind
> Looked inward on ourselves, and learned, perhaps,
> Something of what we are.[40]

He writes also of 'impulses of life' that 'tell of our existence'. The binding theme of the resulting 1799 two-book *Prelude* is his memory of unusual states of mind and consciousness that made him aware of deeper modes in himself, suggesting the existence of unusual powers, involving the kind of experiences later to be described as 'spots of time': moments of quite extraordinary significance. In the episode of the stolen boat, for instance, the huge cliff that seemed to stride after him continued to haunt his consciousness:

> after I had seen
> That spectacle, for many days my brain
> Workd with a dim & undetermin'd sense
> Of unknown modes of being ... [41]

At this time the sense involved was sometimes half-objectified into one of spiritual presences: 'beings of the hills | And ye that walk the woods and open heaths | By moon or starlight', which interwove the human passions with elevated objects, 'With life & nature'.

Wordsworth was from time to time attracted into the Coleridgean conception of Being as compounding light and energy, but it was still more characteristic of his mind that on the occasions when he did so he was likely to be admonished immediately by a reminder of human mortality: once again his imagination, as it unfolds itself through his poetry, operates differently. Yet it shares a sense of ultimate elusiveness; if it can sometimes realize itself in a vivid image, it is more commonly revealed in mysteriousness and absence. Moreover, where Coleridge's version is primarily intensive his is more commonly extensive. Tracing the fortunes of the word 'Being' through the 1799 *Prelude* we find once again, central to his enterprise there, questionings about its nature, directed in his case to childhood experiences and the light they can throw. Hence his opening assertion:

> ... there are spirits which, when they would form
> A favored being, from his very dawn
> Of infancy do open out the clouds
> As at the touch of lightning, seeking him
> With gentle visitation ...[42]

He then goes on to speak of the 'severer interventions' employed by other spirits – including himself among those affected. Describing further the progress of his own complex education, he traces in the 'tempestuous workings' of his early emotions 'hallowed and pure motions of the sense' which

> surely must belong
> To those first-born affinities that fit
> Our new existence to existing things,
> And, in our dawn of being, constitute
> The bond of union betwixt life and joy.[43]

Paradoxically, this experience can itself turn eventually into a kind of otherness:

> so wide appears
> The vacancy between me and those days,
> Which yet have such self-presence in my heart
> That sometimes when I think of them I seem
> Two consciousnesses – conscious of myself
> And of some other being.[44]

Soon he wheels back on the earlier of these two senses to attempt a closer characterization:

> Bless'd the infant babe –
> (For with my best conjectures I would trace
> The progress of our Being) ...[45]

As soon as the main description of the infant's communication with the forces of life in the world is made, however, the main word is followed by two others of almost equal significance:

> Emphatically such a Being lives
> An inmate of this active Universe.[46]

'Inmate' is a further key word, linked to phrases such as 'nature's inmates';[47] the word 'active' vibrates, equally, with resonance from French theories of 'the active universe'.[48]

In this passage the word 'being' is capitalized on both occasions (the first time as an afterthought), but as Wordsworth turns back to the larger question of the effects in his own career it returns to lower case. Now he sees how what had been received passively in infancy and childhood returned to play an important part in his youthful appreciation of nature, which refused to be seen as dead:

> From Nature and her overflowing soul
> I had received so much that all my thoughts
> Were steep'd in feeling, I was only then
> Contented, when with bliss ineffable
> I felt the sentiment of being spread
> O'er all that moves, and all that seemeth still ...[49]

– and so he passes into a rhapsodic state as the 'sentiment of being' fuses with his sense of the 'one Life', now projected into the whole, various existence of nature.

As with Coleridge, however, the first, pleasurable, sense of the 'one Life' that dominated the poems of 1797–8 was to be replaced by a more analytic approach, involving questioning rather than affirmation. The early plan of *The Prelude*, relating the growth of a 'favoured being', changed, correspondingly, into a lengthier version, with further consideration of the processes – the 'growth and revolutions' – that seemed essential to its progress. The workings to be traced within his own consciousness became more complicated, signalled among other things by compound words beginning with 'under-'. In the first book of the 1805 version, for instance, he expresses a belief that he does not lack

> that first great gift, the vital soul,
> Nor general truths which are themselves a sort

> Of elements and agents, under-powers,
> Subordinate helpers of the living mind.

As the main narrative of *The Prelude* becomes concerned with the degree to which the sense of Being remained dormant during the formative period of youth, the 'under-' compounds prove increasingly useful. While he was in Cambridge, he reports,

> Hushed meanwhile
> Was the under-soul, locked up in such a calm
> That not a leaf of the great nature stirred.[50]

Other uses indicate times when the under-soul was not quite so inactive, as when he introduces his experience of displaced sublimity on crossing the Alps with the words:

> Yet still in me, mingling with these delights,
> Was something of stern mood, an under-thirst
> Of vigour, never utterly asleep.[51]

The significance of this underlying craving was that it lent *grandeur* to his experiences. Even in London, therefore, where the human mind might easily be overwhelmed by the weight of diverse sensations, the fate, he was sure, would not befall

> him who looks
> In steadiness, who hath among least things,
> An under-sense of greatest, sees the parts
> As parts, but with a feeling of the whole.[52]

In the context of such disturbances from deeper levels of Being it was all the more reassuring to glimpse elements of stability in nature; still more to glimpse them in another human being – as with his sense of Mary Hutchinson when he first knew her:

> By her exulting outside look of youth
> And placid under-countenance first revered.

After these hints and suggestions at various points in the text, however, the theme reaches a climax in the last book of the poem, when Wordsworth contemplates the complexly modified sublimity that followed his sight of the moon from Snowdon, appearing, on sub-sequent reflection, to be

> The perfect image of a mighty mind
> Of one that feeds upon infinity,
> That is exalted by an under-presence,
> The sense of God, or whatsoe'er is dim
> Or vast in its own being ... [53]

So, finally, what has been previously been described as an 'under-soul' or an 'under-sense' in himself is acknowledged as an 'under-presence' – and no other than 'the sense of God'.

In later revisions of *The Prelude* the word 'Being' still pervades, but rarely with the charge that marks its early appearances: there is no longer the sense of obstinate questioning. When in the 1838 version the word is sometimes introduced, it seems to have the function of toning down a speculation that might lead in the direction of panthe-ism.[54*] In the later development of Wordsworth's mind, that is, the word 'being' turns from a concept that is open, registering inquiry, into one more pietistic, acknowledging the ordained. During the earlier years, by contrast, there was an instability about the idea of Being which helped stimulate some of his best poetry; it continued to be reflected in later passages – though by then more often when the word 'Being' was implied than when it was actually used.

As already indicated, Wordsworth's conception of Being had always differed from Coleridge's. Or perhaps it would be truer to say that he found the negative elements in Coleridge's ideas the more impressive, more consonant with his own experience, than the positive. The idea that in the midst of desolation one might for the first time, like the Ancient Mariner, glimpse the nature of true Being was by no means uncongenial to him; the difference was that he would be more likely to stress the actual conditions of the desolation, showing how they express the grandeur associated with Being, even if it does not nor-mally reveal itself directly in equivalent splendour.

This is true also of the nature of imagination, which in Wordsworth's eyes, as in Coleridge's, was closely related to that of Being. In some of the most important places where he uses the term he does so without suggesting an inherent splendour. Nothing could be further from such a sense, for example, than the lines in *The Prelude* where he interrupts his account of crossing the Alps to suggest how at the moment when he is disturbed and bewildered by the discovery that he and his companion have actually crossed the Alps without realizing it, imagination comes to the rescue:

> Imagination! – lifting up itself
> Before the eye and progress of my song
> Like an unfathered vapour, here that power,
> In all the might of its endowments, came
> Athwart me.[55]

In 1850 he elaborates still further:

> Imagination – here the Power so called
> Through sad incompetence of human speech,
> That awful Power rose from the mind's abyss
> Like an unfathered vapour that enwraps,
> At once, some lonely traveller.[56]

Such a moment of enwrapment is bewildering, yet also strangely enabling. From now on Wordsworth learns that, in the words of Heraclitus, the way up and the way down are one and the same: as he descends through the valley his vision is heightened. On Snowdon, similarly, the imagination is identified not with the moon that shines out on the scene when they have penetrated the clouds and reached the summit but with the chasm that is revealed in the clouds, the 'deep and gloomy breathing-place' from which the roar of waters rises:

> in that breach
> Through which the homeless voice of waters rose,
> That dark deep thoroughfare, had Nature lodged
> The soul, the imagination of the whole.[57]

Once again, imagination is associated not with light but with the abyss. It is essentially unseizable, unknowable, yet the disturbing loss of bearings is accompanied by an equally ineluctable sense of power. And in this culminating experience it leads on (again in the 1805 version) to the figuring of the whole scene, the moon over clouds that are breached into a roaring abyss being seen as corresponding to a 'mighty mind' that is 'exalted by an underpresence':

> The sense of God, or whatsoe'er is dim
> Or vast in its own being ...[58]

Imagination and that which 'is dim and vast in its own being' are tightly linked here. There is a similar association between the two in the Immortality Ode, where, in addition, the evolution of some familiar lines leaves traces of Wordsworth's dealings with the nature of Being as Wordsworth's revisions over the years epitomize his developing idea.[59] Somewhere in his mind lives an idea also to be traced in Blake – that true freedom exists only where the experiences of vision and of energy combine: *The Prelude* is full of suggestions that these between them constitute for humans the true moments of Being. At the same time, as an adult and responsible figure, Wordsworth could not endorse all the implications: whatever truth it contained must be rendered obliquely, so as to guard him from any suggestion that all vision is necessarily authentic or that all expressions of energy are morally acceptable. Wordsworth the man was in any case forced to acknowledge that such moments of vision were now rare and likely to come, if at all, not directly but through memories of what it was like to be a child, sporting on the shore of the ocean, for example, and hearing its mighty roar. In the adult this sense of 'Being' can be no more than an experience of haunting.

In the summer when he was first working on the Immortality Ode, the conception turned up in just such a form as he walked along the seashore with his natural daughter Caroline Vallon on an evening of unusual splendour – the sea sounding nearby:

> Listen! the mighty Being is awake
> And doth with his eternal motion make
> A noise like thunder everlastingly.[60]

Caroline seemed oblivious to such reflections, or, in Wordsworth's words, 'untouched by solemn thought'. The reason, he comes to see, is that she has not yet endured that alienation from original Being that makes the sound of the sea so significant to him: she is still in such an organic relationship to it as to remain unwittingly instinct with its power. In the same way she needs to surmount no barrier of recollection to remain in touch with the first affections and perceptions which, as distantly recaptured by the adult,

> Uphold us, cherish, and have power to make
> Our noisy years seem moments in the being
> Of the eternal Silence.[61]

Gradually, the note of terror and the abyss which had always for him accompanied the conception modulated into a general resonance of fear and impressiveness, working through the subliminal consciousness to embrace the whole of human life. When in a previous study I explored these underlying qualities further, I invoked the concepts of *kairos,* the urge toward an all-embracing moment of fulfilled experience and that of *aion,* the resting back on a timeless sense of eternity, to suggest the extremes of a psyche such as Wordsworth's, arguing that in his youth the aspiration towards the first state was uppermost, the resulting experiences of calm being simply bonuses, occurring usually in the moment of cessation from such activity and not to be cultivated for their own sake. His 'spots of time', in other words, recorded occasions of unusual *kairos,* followed immediately by a more visionary state with all the marks of the *aionic.* Both, however, assisted his great effort in *The Prelude* to trace those sources of his own creative power, which might be thought of as a hidden but available resource for all human beings. The effect of having passed through them was, as he put it in one version of the poem, 'vivifying'[62*] – an enhancement of Being which also stressed its vitality.

The vital was, indeed, a key to the matter, since during the first part of the collaboration Coleridge's concern with the nature of the living principle had been reflected in the best of his meditative poems. In all probability Wordsworth had heard one of these, 'The Eolian Harp', soon after it was written; at all events, the picture of nature which was drawn in that poem, of an active universe in which all things harmonized, playing together with extraordinary intricacy, although disowned by Coleridge in the course of the poem itself, continued to inhabit his friend's poetry, giving its particular quality to the idea of the 'one Life' which they developed for a few years.

In this period, particularly the four years from 1796 to 1800 – the only years, according to Wordsworth, when he had been 'in blossom'[63] – he had readily made correspondences between the sensitive powers in humans and the finer influences of nature, so that the light and energy of human beings seemed in direct correspondence with the light and energy displayed by natural things. The idea was readily supported by the idea of animal magnetism, at least until what he learned during his sojourn in Germany undermined his faith. In poems such as *The Ancient Mariner* and *Christabel* appeals to beautiful scenes in living nature were an important feature, while the sense of enchantment harmonized with the magnetic idea.

The differences between his thinking and Wordsworth's, differences of which he slowly became aware, had partly to do with divergences in their concepts of Being. Already, in 1799, he had commented to Poole that whereas his own weaknesses at least had the advantage that they united him with the mass of his fellow-beings, 'dear Wordsworth appears to me to have hurtfully segregated & isolated his Being'.[64] His subsequent remark that doubtless his delights were 'more deep and sublime' indicates more about his flattering sense of his friend's nature: if he suffered from his lack of rapport with the masses, that was because his own nature was close to the divine – at least in the sense of the supreme Being at the heart of Nature. During the years immediately following it seems often to have been difficult for him to separate the two – the sense of Wordsworth and the sense of the divine. That sense in turn was linked to the idea of a creative essence at the centre of things. In 1803 he praised Thomas Jackson's *Treatise of the Divine Essence and Attributes*, in which the essence of the divine was compared to the equally incomprehensible essence in every creature, reflecting that the Roman Church had not, so far as he knew, decided between the Thomists and the Scotists 'in their great controversy on the nature of the Being which Creatures possess'.[65]

He was already exploring the importance of this element when thinking of his own self in a notebook of 1799:

Man but an half animal without drawing – but yet he is not meant to be able to communicate *all* the greater part of his being must [be] solitary – even of his consciousness.[66]

Four years later he elaborated the thought:

Without Drawing I feel myself but half invested with Language – Music too is wanting to me. – But yet tho' one should unite Poetry, Draftsmans's-ship & Music – the greater & perhaps nobler certainly all the subtler parts of one's nature, must be solitary – Man exists herein to himself & to God alone – Yea, in how much only to God – how much lies *below* his own Consciousness.[67]

For him this was only one side of the picture, however: in his own case, missing the organs of form-making and illumination, his Being could no longer relate itself properly to the world in a joyful way. Yet the other side of that personal coin was a sense of the crucial role of the sense of Being in face of the worst human experience. Shortly after writing these words he received news of the death of his second child, Berkeley, and now summoned up his philosophy of Being in its positive form as he wrote a letter of consolation to his wife:

Methinks, there is something awful in the thought, what an unknown Being one's own infant is to one! – a fit of sound – a flash of light – a summer gust, that is as it were *created* in the bosom of the calm Air, that rises up we know not how, and goes we know not whither![68]

To Poole he wrote a similar long letter, speculating,

What if the vital force which I sent from my arm into the stone, as I flung it in the air and skimm'd it upon the water – what if even that did not perish! – It was *life–!* it was a particle of *Being* – ! it was *Power!* and *how could* it perish – ? *Life, Power, Being!* – organization may & probably *is,* their *effect;* their *cause* it *cannot* be![69]

This letter continued with the reflection that 'Grief | Doth love to dally with fantastic thoughts ...'; it is clear that even if consolations such as this were not totally satisfying, he continued to be fascinated by the ways in which Being was distinguishable from consciousness. Writing to Richard Sharp early in 1804, for instance, he described how he had been too ill to read Sharp's letters, continuing,

not that my inner Being was disturbed – on the contrary it seemed more than usually serene and self-sufficing – but the exceeding Pain, of which I suffered every now and then, and the fearful Distresses of my sleep, had taken away from me the connecting Link of voluntary power, which continually combines that Part of us by which we know ourselves to be, with that outward Picture or Hieroglyphic, by which we hold communion with our Like – between the Vital and the Organic – or what Berkeley, I suppose, would call – Mind and it's sensuous Language.[70]

This sense of deprivation had been compounded in the meantime not only by ill-health, but by domestic difficulties and a growing drug addiction. Increasingly in refuge from his unhappy condition, he lapsed to analytic processes – which, as he recorded in the Dejection poem,[71] had a corrosive effect on his habits of mind generally.

Coleridge's growing sense of a disparity between his thinking and Wordsworth's can be located in the varying ideas of Being to be traced in their own consciousnesses. Diagrammatically this might be sketched as a contrast between Being as power and Being as strength. In more personal terms it could be expressed as the force of an outgoing selflessness, pitched against a fortified and self-confirming egoism. Coleridge might wish to 'merge his identity' with Wordsworth; Wordsworth never wanted to be anyone but himself. There is not, as is sometimes supposed, a power-struggle going on, simply the contentions of alternative versions of Being.

Coleridge's appreciation and veneration of his friend came to a climax in verse written when he returned from Malta and heard Wordsworth read his 'Poem to Coleridge', now completed, for the first time. In lines describing the experience, 'To William Wordsworth, composed on the night after his recitation of a poem on the growth of an individual mind', he moved from one kind of metaphor to another, beginning with the themes

> Of Tides obedient to external Force,
> And *currents* self-determin'd, as might seem,
> Or by interior Power: of moments aweful,
> Now in thy hidden Life; and now abroad,
> [When power streamed from thee, and thy soul received
> The light reflected as a light bestowed –][72]

The whole image here could be of an ocean, since just as the imagery of tides and currents might refer to the movements of the water, so the power streaming from it might render the sense of a sunny day when the impression of a brightness coming from a light of its own, and not from the sun above, is compelling. But that is in no way a necessary reading; what is clear is that the images are of energy and of light, each seen to be at once active and passive, and that the first image at least that comes to his mind is that of an ocean. Coleridge then moves to Wordsworth's experience of the Revolution in France as like a totally unexpected burst of thunder breaking over a boat becalmed on a sea beneath a cloudless sky, and so to his subsequent journey 'homeward' to his 'Heart', where he is enabled

> Oft from the Watch-Tower of Man's absolute Self,
> With Light unwaning on her eyes, to look
> Far on – herself a Glory to behold,
> The Angel of the Vision![73]

The two images which emerge most strongly from this are of a human personality which is an ocean, complemented by an 'absolute Self' which is a watch-tower. Infinite restless energies are matched by steady illumination. But when the word 'Being' itself emerges in this poem it is in connection with Coleridge's own response to the poem, which is not by now altogether pleasurable:

> O Friend! too well thou know'st, of what sad years
> The long suppression had benumb'd my soul,
> That even as Life returns upon the Drown'd,
> Th' unusual Joy awoke a throng of Pains – [74]

Once that first response, painful through evocation of intermediate sufferings, has abated, however, Coleridge can resume an oceanic image for his own soul in the passiveness induced by his listening. As the poem concluded, he records,

> Scarce conscious and yet conscious of it's Close
> I sate, my Being blended in one Thought ...[75]

From now on, however, his veneration of Wordsworth would be in decline: he had already noted how the strong identity of his friend could involve a hurtful isolation of 'his Being';[76] he would now suspect that this acted as a barrier against appreciation of the free play of sensibility accompanying his own, weaker, identity or indeed acknowledgement that it had a value of its own. He recalled a sudden insight when he grasped that Wordsworth was not as outgoing as he had supposed, through a momentary vivid impression of him: 'The *up*, askance pig look in the Boat...'[77] Yet the whole weight of that notebook entry was directed towards finding modes of avoiding the unworthy possible effects of such perceptions. A few years later, similarly, when the relationship was under greater strain, he awoke in the middle of the night to write a notebook entry of agonized love for Sara Hutchinson, coupled with his recognition that if there was anyone she loved it was Wordsworth – who already, he felt, was the object of quite enough feminine devotion. He ended his long note with the words: 'Awakened from a dream of Tears, & anguish of involuntary Jealousy ...'[78]

If one looks at the relationship in terms of an implicit, insidious power-struggle,[79*] it is evident that Coleridge had already admitted defeat, or rather refused a contest, but in any case it is hard to see the situation in that light, his problem being rather to understand how a love as intense as his for Sara could receive so little recognition, not merely from contemporary society but from the intimate friends he looked to for the fullest understanding. Already puzzled by the ignoble quality of his dreams,[80] he could not comprehend why the quality of a person's intent, far from resulting in a greater personal power, should if anything produce loss of identity. He was one of many victims of a belief in the power of human determination to overcome all psychic obstacles in its way, before psychoanalytic development encouraged human beings to regard all their impulses as natural, and 'unworthy' ones therefore as equally valid with those approved by the conscious self. He was too shrewd a self-observer not to be visited by suspicions that this might indeed be the case, yet that warred implacably with his Kantian belief in the supremacy of the human will and its potentialities.

His own position, moreover, had increasingly come to include an honouring of orthodox Christianity that seemed (despite Wordsworth's veneration for Milton) to be denied to his friend. He was still prepared to proclaim that Wordsworth's poetry at its best manifested 'THE VISION AND THE FACULTY DIVINE!'[81] but such statements need to be read alongside his own affirmations that the proper relationship between the human being and the Supreme Being would be one of proper humility, in accordance with Christian doctrine. Although he would continue to insist on the centrality of the sense of Being – the sense which reveals itself in the difference between saying 'I am' and 'It is'[82] – this did not mean that there was any scale on which one could compare the human 'I am' to the 'I AM' which was, in traditional belief, the hidden name of God. The furthest one might go in that direction lay in the realm of creative art, where acts of genius might be truly thought to relate the human to the divine, making the highest kind of imagination 'a repetition in the finite mind of the eternal act of creation in the Infinite I AM'; even here, however, he would remain uncertain.[83]

One direction in which his speculations concerning Being were moving was to transfer his sense of 'pure act', as found in works of genius such as those of Shakespeare, Milton or Giordano Bruno, to the work of God himself, readily defined as 'actus purissimus'.[84*] Another way in which they would extend in the following years is suggested by a note, dating probably from 1809, where he asks fundamental questions about human identity, in the form 'Where am I? What and for what am I? What are the duties, which arise out of the relations of my Being to itself as heir of futurity, and to the World which is its present sphere of action and impression?' There he compares the human soul to a ship's crew cast on an unknown island and the questions they would naturally ask about their current location and the possibilities of moving on, or away from it, continuing,

> The moment, when the Soul begins to be sufficiently self-conscious, to ask concerning itself, & its relations, is the first moment of its *intellectual* arrival into the World – its *Being* – enigmatic as it must seem – is posterior to its Existence –. Suppose the shipwrecked man stunned, & for many weeks in a state of ideocy or utter loss of Thought & Memory – & then gradually awakened.[85]

This controlling sense of human beings as basically asleep, needing to be wakened to the nature of their true Being, continues in the writings of subsequent years. *Aids to Reflection* contains among its early aphorisms a picture of the Christian as a pilgrim, 'awakened by the cockcrow' of some calamity or providential escape, which is constructed around an underlying faith that if his readers would only look sufficiently far into their own consciousnesses they would discover truths hidden there – truths of their own Being – which they would discover to be in correspondence with the doctrines of Christianity. One of his overwhelming tasks now was to hold together in his mind his sense of the unified identity of God with his sense of the Trinity as a threefold dynamic process within: he conducted various discussions, with diagrams, to show how this might operate, often using the Greek term for Being, to express the basic Divine.[86]

In the meantime the ideas of earlier years continued to haunt him, particularly when they offered to throw light on his own ills. His lamenting of the damage inflicted on his creative powers by exclusively attending to the analysing element in consciousness has already been mentioned. In a letter of 1811 he spelt this out more fully and specifically, using the very word 'under-consciousness':

> what I keep out of my mind or rather keep down in a state of under-consciousness, is sure to act meanwhile with it's whole power of poison on my Body ...[87]

This was not all. Renewed contact with Germany at the end of the Napoleonic wars brought news of an increased interest in ideas that had captivated him in the 1790s. Learning that Blumenbach now believed in hypnotic powers, he engrossed himself in recent treatises on the subject. The fascination lasted, with the result that he could be described by Thomas Carlyle in 1824 as 'a kind good soul, full of religion and affection, and poetry and animal magnetism'.[88*] His final, conclusion – or rather inability to reach a conclusion – was, however, set down in a rueful marginal comment:

Were I asked, what *I* think – my answer would be – that the evidence enforces Scepticism and a Non liquet. Too strong & consentaneous for a candid mind to be satisfied of its falsehood, or its solvibility in the supposition of Imposture or <casual> Co-incidence; – too fugacious and unfixible to support any Theory that supposes the always potential & under certain conditions & circumstances occasionally actual existence of a correspondent faculty in the human Soul. And nothing less than such an hypothesis would be adequate to the *satisfactory* explanation of the Facts – tho' that of a metastasis of specific functions of the nervous energy taken in conjunction with extreme nervous excitement, + some delusion, + some illusion, + some imposition, + (plus) some chance & accidental coincidence, might determine the direction, in which the Scepticism vibrated. Nine years has the subject of Zoo-magnetism been before me – I have traced it historically – collected a Mass of documents in French, German, Italian, & the Latinists of the 16th century – have never neglected an opportunity of questioning Eye witnesses, (ex. Gr. Tieck, Treviranus, De Prati, Meyer, and others of literary or medical celebrity) and I remain where I was, & where the first perusal of Klug's work had left me, without having advanced an inch backward or forward. Treviranus the famous Botanist's reply to me, when he was in London, is worth recording.... I have seen what I am certain I would not have believed on *your* telling; and in all reason therefore I can neither expect nor wish that you should believe on mine.[89]

If demonstrable evidence of a basis for zoomagnetism was unlikely to be forthcoming, however, what firm basis was there for thinking about Being? One solution was to contemplate the fact itself in a state of wonder. For Wordsworth, the ability of an individual human being to survive in solitude furnished the most impressive support for such an attitude. In a letter to Sara Hutchinson in which he tried to express the depth of feeling that he had been trying to express in 'The Leech-gatherer' – a poem which he had heard to his dismay that she found 'tedious' – he wrote:

What is brought forward? 'A lonely place, a Pond' 'by which an old man *was*, far from all house or home' – not stood, not sat, but *was'* – the figure presented in the most naked simplicity possible.[90*]

Wordsworth's desperate attempts to convey to a reader he respected what he found so impressive in the very fact of this man's determined

Being corresponds to the efforts that Coleridge would continue to make to awaken his readers to the contemplation of Being itself. In the 1818 *Friend* he fell back on traditional language of devotion:

> Hast thou ever raised thy mind to the consideration of EXISTENCE, in and by itself, as the mere act of existing? Hast thou ever said to thyself thoughtfully, IT IS! heedless in that moment, whether it were a man before thee, or a flower, or a grain of sand?[91]

In an appendix to one of his *Lay Sermons* he dwelt again on this power of objects to impress themselves by the very act of existing:

> I feel an awe, as if there were before my eyes the very same Power, as that of the REASON – the same Power in a lower dignity, and therefore a symbol established in the truth of things. I feel it alike, whether I contemplate a single tree or flower, or meditate on vegetation throughout the world, as one of the great organs of the life of nature.[92]

Shortly afterwards he argued that this feeling owed its power to a correspondence between the Being of contemplated objects and the Being of the observer:

> Without this latent presence of the 'I am,' all modes of existence in the external world would flit before us as colored shadows, with no greater depth, root, or fixture, than the image of a rock hath in a gliding stream or the rain-bow on a fast-sailing rain-storm.... The fact ... therefore, that the mind of man in its own primary and constituent forms represents the laws of nature, is a mystery which of itself should suffice to make us religious: for it is a problem of which God is the only solution.[93]

One cannot but admire the act of prestidigitation with which Coleridge conjures out of acknowledgement of a flower's existence a proof of the necessity for religion: it is a reminder of the magical quality that attended his earlier speculations. He could not, indeed, ever quite negate the effect that his earlier fascination with the levels of human consciousness had had in stimulating such speculations and, through them, his and Wordsworth's poetry.

An important, even an essential, part of their legacy was the element of elusiveness that characterizes their work at its best. Just as

Wordsworth could create fine poetry out of the fugitive cuckoo's song, so in *The Ancient Mariner*, just after the Mariner wakens to find to his relief that it has been raining, the effect is vivid:

> The upper air burst into life!
> And a hundred fire-flags sheen,
> To and from they were hurried about!
> And to and fro, and in and out,
> The wan stars danced between.

A similar unseizableness marks the activity of the water-snakes:

> Blue, glossy green, and velvet black
> They coiled and swam; and every track
> Was a flash of golden fire.

It is no accident that this is the moment in the poem when a 'spring of love' gushes from his heart, in an act of *unconscious* blessing. One virtue of such a conception was that it helped solve the problem of relationship between living beings, since it was otherwise hard to understand why each organism should not simply be a closed system, competing for survival with others, equally closed. The idea that at its inner Being was a core that could be expressed through light and energy provided the material for a conception of interlinking, each Being responding to others, however much the accompanying defensive system provided by more mechanical workings of the body might restrain them.

This, one might say, was close to the 'essential' Coleridge, the poet in whom his sense of Being was always linked to a lively, dancing consciousness. The activities of this consciousness were crucial to the health of Wordsworth's being, also, so that when their influence was withdrawn his poetry and thinking lost something essential: hence, no doubt, his plea that when Coleridge departed for Malta he should leave behind notes for 'The Recluse' – without which he evidently felt that the enterprise could not thrive. Hence too his dismay when Coleridge returned, no longer a 'fountain' at his 'fond heart's door', a fount of 'murmuring, sparkling, living love', but a 'comfortless ... hidden well'; hence, finally, his posthumous tribute to Coleridge's mind as a widely fertilizing one, its seed 'lavishly sown'.[94] In these images he showed awareness of his debt to Coleridge's intelligent consciousness as ensuring that his own strong identity did not freeze into stasis, a tacit acknowledgement of the validity of Coleridge's insistence on the need for an interaction between the primary consciousness that passively reflected Being and the play of active light and energies in the mind that actively nourished it.

As noted above, however, Coleridge's feeling for energy had gradually become restricted to its vegetable form. When he wrote how Being might be contemplated in 'a man, a flower or a grain of sand', his failure to mention insect or animal energy was telling, given that this was precisely the sphere where it became morally ambiguous. His optimism concerning the beneficence of the sensuous world, which had been at its height during the years of his co-operation with William and Dorothy Wordsworth, assisting the illumination and energy of his own best poetry, had been eroded by his own experiences in the world of sense until he would come to affirm that Nature was not a 'goddess in a petticoat' but a 'devil in a strait waistcoat', the 'devilish' element in nature evidently having to do with his sense of the degree to which animal energies could become perverted.[95]

This had not been so clear to him in 1804, however, when he left the Wordsworths, still enchanted with the vision of the natural world they all three shared, and embarked for Malta on the long sea-voyage which enabled him, among other things, to check the images and ideas of *The Rime of the Ancient Mariner* against immediate experience. There was one moment on the voyage which must have been particularly gratifying for its endorsement of his earlier poem: it came when he was aware of two modes of life on the sea. In the light there was a contrast with the vision of corruption in his earlier poem, when 'slimy things did crawl with legs', since he was now impressed by the comprehensive activity displayed: 'The path from the shore till within a good stone throw of the Vessel thickly swarming with insect life, *all* busy-swarming in the path, their swarming makes.' When the darker element in the scene exposed the inner essence of all this activity, on the other hand, it confirmed his earlier moment of vision by its vitality, its circular activity unfolding and folding again in an energy that was rewardingly illuminating and positive, yet which also succeeded in indicating a deeper level:

> But within the Shadow of the Ship it was – scattered at distances – scattered Os, rapidly uncoiling into serpent spirals – O how slow a word is to express the Life & time-mocking Motion of that Change, always O s before, always Spirals, coiling, uncoiling, *being*.[96]

In 1804, at least, it was still possible for him to feel that the true vision of Being might be a sublime version of the 'one Life' that linked human consciousnesses to other forms of Being. Already in these years, however, he had been overtaken increasingly by his sense of the need to link any sense of Being in nature to the Divine Being at the heart of Christianity, with all the moral demands that such an acknowledgment must involve. In subsequent years his writing would involve more and more the need to resolve the theological problems involved in trying to reconcile the demands of his two worlds: the world where appreciation of the growth and energies of life in nature was paramount and that of orthodox religion with its intellectual and moral demands.

The degree to which he believed himself to have succeeded would prove an important influence on young men who encountered him in the last phase of his life and contribute to the nineteenth-century picture of him as a significant religious thinker: this will be discussed in a later chapter. In the early years of his influencing, by contrast, the ideas of a link between the processes of natural life and the subconscious work of the human psyche in suggesting a radically new view of humanity and of true Being (not yet to be linked so firmly by him with established religion) set in motion ideas that would work potently in the minds of his young contemporaries, especially of those who heard his conversation. The magic of such thoughts would, in fact, continue to haunt his own work, for years to come, often giving it its unusual flavour, but now, because more immediately available, was most potent in its effect on the radical young writers of the new generation, Keats, Hazlitt, De Quincey, Byron and the Shelleys.

4
Keats and the Highgate Nightingales

The long journal-letter that Keats wrote to his brother and sister-in-law between February and May 1819, one of the most important documents of his career, includes crucial passages in his thinking about consciousness and the imagination – yet always, as it were, at one remove. The writing is dominated by its occasion: he is writing familiarly to two people who have gone to America, have not yet heard from him and have therefore been deprived of their customary intimacy for a very long period; as a result his writing contains swift transitions of thought which cannot readily be filled in by the reader. One moment Keats will be idling, talking what is apparently light-hearted nonsense, the next he will turn to his deepest thoughts of the moment.

During the previous period he had been increasingly engaged with Wordsworth's achievement, which he located primarily in his writing of a poetry of the human heart, referring to this (in a creative misreading) as 'the main region of his song'.[1] He went on to compare him with Milton as writers of long poems and to conclude (with a little hesitation) that Milton suffered from the comparison by reason of his willingness to accept the remaining dogmas and superstitions of religion and rest in them: 'He did not think into the human heart, as Wordsworth has done.' Here he was thinking more specifically of 'Tintern Abbey' and its emphasis on 'the burden of the mystery', but a few months previously he had referred to the recently published *Excursion* as one of 'three things to rejoice at in this Age'.[2] This too was a poem of the ' human heart': he was evidently most struck by the profundity of its feeling. He may well have responded strongly to some of the more visionary passages, also, notably those in Book Four, where the imaginative elements in Greek mythology play a strong part. This would help to explain why he chose to read the hymn to Pan from *Endymion* to Wordsworth when they met – to be greeted by the disconcerting response, 'A very pretty piece of Paganism'.[3] Whatever his feelings may have been, they were not sufficiently adverse to destroy his belief that Wordsworth was a great genius – a belief that was probably reinforced by more happy encounters while he remained in London.[4] He reiterated his praise of *The Excursion*, which may unwittingly have been coloured by the fact that some of the passages he was most drawn to had been written early and so likely to benefit strongly from the intercourse with Coleridge.

In any case Keats would already have known Coleridge's poetry well and have been particularly familiar with the combination of admiration and impatience shown by his friend William Hazlitt towards one whom he thought 'the only man he had ever known who answered to his conception of a man of genius' – and yet who had failed spectacularly to live up to radical expectations. An unusual interest, therefore, attaches to the occasion referred to in the same letter when he came across him, walking with his disciple J.H. Green, in a lane near Caen Wood in April 1819. 'After enquiring by a look whether it would be agreeable', he joined them and profited enough from what he heard to give a detailed account of the topics then broached:

> I walked with him at his alderman-after dinner pace for near two miles I suppose. In those two miles he broached a thousand things – let me see if I can give you a list – Nightingales, Poetry – on Poetical sensation – Metaphysics – Different genera and species of dreams – Nightmare – a Dream accompanied by a sense of touch – single and double touch – a dream related – first and second consciousness – the difference explained between will and Volition – so many metaphysicians from a want of smoking the second consciousness – Monsters – the Kraken – Mermaids – southey believes in them – southeys belief too much diluted – A Ghost story – Good morning – I heard his voice as he came towards me – I heard it as he moved away – I had heard it all the interval – if it may be called so.[5]

Most discussions of this report have been based on the assumption that this was little more than a catalogue of loosely connected topics, with the occasional addition that some of them might have suggested to Keats themes for subsequent poems. It tends also to be assumed that Keats's attitude was still dominated by Hazlitt's unsympathetic views. When he wrote his well-known comment, 'Coleridge, for instance, would let go by a fine isolated verisimilitude caught from the Penetralium of mystery, from being incapable of remaining content with half knowledge',[6] he was probably elaborating on an opinion heard from the lips of his older friend, with whom it would seem to have been a favourite sentiment, and who, in November 1811, for example, had concluded a long criticism of Coleridge in a literary company (reported by John Payne Collier) with the assertion that he

> was a man who had more ideas than any other person [he] had ever known, but had no capability of attending to one object, he was constantly endeavouring to push matters to the furthest till he became obscure to everybody but himself. He was like a man who instead of cultivating and bringing to perfection a small plot of ground, was attempting to cultivate a whole tract but instead of accomplishing his object dug up the ground only for the encouragement of weeds.[7]

Such contemporaries wrote as if Coleridge had an essentially butterfly mind, unable, despite his brilliance, to focus on one thing for more than a few moments before veering off on a new track, and no doubt there often was something of this effect, especially for casual listeners. De Quincey, on the other hand, insisted that where Coleridge was concerned, 'logic, the most severe was as inalienable from his modes of thinking, as grammar from the language'[8] and that his discourses, however much they might seem to ramble, always had a strong overall coherence. If he is correct, it is worth considering whether what Keats heard as he listened to Coleridge on this occasion was not an undisciplined stream of consciousness but the exposition of a skein of ideas, closely interlinked, that had long occupied his mind, developing the idea, (as outlined in the previous chapter) that what was normally regarded as consciousness was only secondary to a primary power in the human being, possessing a value of its own: sometimes existing in unison with what is thought of as normal consciousness, sometimes at odds with it, but always in any case to be regarded as closer to his or her true Being. An awareness of this level of consciousness, associated particularly with dreams and superstitions, was on this view necessary for a full understanding of the human mind. Those who neglected its existence could otherwise find their minds trapped into endless imprisoning cycles of analysis. Poets, by contrast, through their dealings with this primary consciousness, were closer to the truth of human nature than psychologists who simply analysed mental phenomena as if they existed in the human mind without any other layer. This radical view, inverting, I have argued, the common ranking between the conscious and the unconscious, can be seen to offer a binding conception behind the discourse Keats heard – which, we may suppose, retiring to a point behind Coleridge's more recent conservative-minded moral and social concerns to theories associated with his pre-Malta years – began with nightingales, maintaining that poets, hearing them with a richer consciousness than other people, were alive to what was permanently of value in their song,[9*] and then went on to make a connection with nightmare, where, he thought, the nature of the primary consciousness was most fully exposed – especially if at the same time an experience of touch was involved.

It may be suggested that Coleridge's willingness to revive and extend such theories at this time was affected in two ways. As mentioned above, his early interest in hypnotism, with its apparent scientific demonstration that areas of consciousness could exist in separation from one another, had evidently been dampened by Blumenbach's refusal to accept the validity of the phenomenon.[10*] But when, after the end of the Napoleonic wars, word reached him that Blumenbach had changed his mind, he began reading voraciously in works on animal magnetism, by now an important topic in Germany. So the man whom Keats heard discoursing was one who had recently recovered grounds for believing that the existence of more than one level of consciousness was scientifically demonstrable.

The other factor he mentioned to Keats – the difference between will and volition – bore on another area of his experience. In the moral sphere of his discourse this was a favourite subject; one may assume that he assigned 'volition' to secondary consciousness, regarding 'will' meanwhile as belonging to the primary, and so to central Being and arguing that if the human involved subsisted properly at that crucial level he or she would naturally perform good actions. Unfortunately, however, his own experience had often suggested otherwise. The failure of his attempts to act well was most notable in the matter of his opium addiction. Efforts of will to break himself of the habit might succeed initially, but would then be followed by withdrawal symptoms that drove him back to the drug again. In that respect, at least, his self-contradiction was enigmatic.

Keats no doubt glimpsed something of this, but it may also be suggested that he not only grasped the significance of the individual elements he mentioned in his letter, but understood something of the connections that Coleridge was making. If so, his reaction to the discourse he reports was not simply, as is often supposed,[11] a humorous wonderment at the garrulous dispersiveness of the ambling poet, but a deeper fascination on hearing for the first time the exposition of theories which gave some coherence and explanation to what he knew of Coleridge's writing and had heard of his ideas. His uppermost reaction afterwards was perhaps of bemusement: he was not able to decide whether he had been listening to a discourse that simply compounded the sense of Coleridge's ineffectuality as a figure of his time (Hazlitt's contention) or one that offered a crucial key to the nature of the human mind. All he could carry away from the encounter, therefore, was a memory ('I heard his voice as he came towards me – I heard it as he moved away – I had heard it all the interval – if it may be called so'), which left him haunted by the sense that he had heard things of importance.

If as time passed the effects of the discourse, and of Keats's understanding, went deep, it may further be argued that the important effect lay less in the introduction of new ideas into his mind than in a decisive new turn to trains of thought already in motion.[12*] Looking at Coleridge's portly frame as it trundled on, he could not have wanted to become what he saw him to be now: in that sense the older poet was a warning. Yet that simply made more impressive the impact of a range of thinking which was quite other, involving a preoccupation with ideas which could in themselves be said to draw for their existence on Coleridge's lasting awareness of the 'primary consciousness'. This, it can be argued, offered Keats a crucial new departure, even if an equivocal one.

What form had his thinking been taking before the meeting? The effects of his earlier medical studies on his thinking and writing up to this point have been seen by more than one scholar as crucial. Hermione de Almeida, in *Romantic Medicine and John Keats*,[13] explored many aspects of the ferment in medical thinking that had recently been taking place, including the controversies that had accompanied the thinking of John Hunter, and showed how Keats's interest in the figure of Apollo as creative god and healer could combine both his poetic aspirations and his medical interest; Alan Richardson's chapter on him in his *British Romanticism and the Science of the Mind*[14] dwells particularly on the effects of contemporary work concerning the physiology of the brain, demonstrating even more tellingly how knowledge of the intricate processes recently explored could show physiological references in the poetry and letters that might otherwise seem vague to be in fact very precise.

At the same time, it must be borne in mind that however exciting the study of such effects in the poems and letters may be, the most important recent movement in Keats's mind had been connected with his turning aside from medicine as a career and his urge to devote his energies rather to poetry, drawing on a reading of Wordsworth that suggested ways in which a great 'poet of the human heart' for his time might emerge. Soon he would be asserting that the reason for the English ability to produce the finest writers in the world lay in their capacity to treat them badly; a writer such as the Italian Matteo Boiardo, by contrast, had not been, for all his virtues, 'a miserable and mighty poet of the human Heart'.[15] Two centuries earlier, it would already have been possible to follow in the line of Shakespeare; now one might have the additional bonus of profiting from the precise and subtle knowledge of human physiology that recent work had made available. From Astley Cooper, his teacher at Guy's Hospital, he had learned, for example, of the close proximity of the heart and lungs to one another and the 'strict sympathy' that resulted: hence the close linking of the furious beatings of the one to the pantings of the other in the love-experiences of his own poems. Christopher Ricks, similarly, has drawn attention to hints of a connection between the rushing of the blood to the cheeks in blushing and to the phallus in erection. In the Romantic usages of the key word of the time, 'sensibility', the expansiveness of literary fashion could thus come together with the medical exactness of the medical school, offering richness of resonance. The evidence of his writing in such contexts is that Keats's attention was most intensely absorbed when such links involved the inter-working of biochemical and nervous functions. On the other hand, simply to stop short at clinical analysis of such workings might make them seem in themselves purely mechanical, leading to elimination of concepts such as the 'Soul' and to a materialism that might seem cold and even dead.

The argument to be presented here is that Coleridge's discourse seemed to offer a way out of such an impasse by way of insisting on distinctions such as those between will and volition, or between 'first and second consciousness', that challenged the supremacy of rational analysis. It stimulated, one may suggest, a mode of thinking that would persist through the subsequent months when the brilliant poetry of the Odes was being produced – even if a listener as acute as Keats, pressed increasingly by the burden of the actual, would necessarily remain unsure whether he had been offered a key to solve his intellectual problems or simply an attractive but delusive substitute.

The first impact of Coleridge's discourse may perhaps be discerned in a curious passage in Keats's continuation of his letter a day later. He had been looking over a correspondence that had taken place between his brother Tom, who had just died, and a woman, 'Amena', who had supposedly been in love with him. In point of fact, the whole thing had been an invention on the part of Keats's friend Charles Wells, who had maintained the fiction and corresponded with Tom under this name over a considerable period. Keats's bitterness of reaction is understandable, since he felt that the deception had played a part in bringing on Tom's fatal illness. Even so, however, his account of the matter is surprisingly melodramatic:

> I now see the whole cruel deception .... The instigations to this dia-bolical scheme were vanity, and the love of intrigue. It was not thoughtless hoax – but a cruel deception on a sanguine Temperament, with every show of friendship. I do not think death too bad for the villain. The world would look upon it in a different light should I expose it – they would call it a frolic – so I must be wary – but I consider it my duty to be prudently revengeful. I will hang over his head like a sword by a hair. I will be opium to his vanity – if I cannot injure his interests – He is a rat and he shall have ratsbane to his vanity – I will harm him all I possibly can – I have no doubt I shall be able to do so – Let us leave him to his misery alone except when we can throw in a little more.[16]

An influence from Shakespearean rhetoric is detectable here, particu-larly in the reference to 'ratsbane'.[17] Keats's charge of villainy, coupled with his awareness that the rest of the world would not think it such, suggests that he might have been applying Coleridge's ideas directly. According to those, the very fact that Amena's being was imaginary would make her *more* dangerous to Tom. A real woman who had treated him in this way could have been dealt with satisfactorily, since his whole personality would have been brought into operation. An illusory woman, on the other hand, who could never actually be encountered (Tom had once pursued her unsuccessfully as far as Paris), but who sent constant letters feeding his imagination with ideas of love – such a woman could not easily be dealt with at the conscious level, given that the encounter was taking place exclusively in the imagination, so creating an experience that sucked his life-blood like a vampire. There is a hectic quality about this – kept on a rein of irony, if at all, only by reminiscences of Hamlet's vengeful language.

That Keats was thinking on such lines is further suggested by a letter later in the year in which he wrote,

> Imaginary grievances have always been more my torment than real ones.... Our imaginary woes are conjured up by our passions, and are fostered by passionate feeling: our real ones are of themselves, and are opposed by an abstract exertion of mind.[18]

The point he was making rested on the assumption that the passions are closer than our conscious thoughts to our deepest nature, so that any work of the imagination which touches them will automatically resonate existentially.

Such a belief is likely to be more plausible to a sufferer from tuberculosis, who has less room for emotional manoeuvre. Keats recognized this in Tom and perhaps also in himself – hence his anger at Wells's trick. The affair may in addition throw light, for example, on 'La Belle Dame sans Merci', which appeared in his journal letter shortly after the encounter with Coleridge. The poem, with its description of a knight at arms, 'Alone and palely loitering', whose fatal meeting with and love for a woman has delivered him into a condition which, as he sees in a dream, corresponds with that of death – pale kings, princes and warriors all victims of the same charm – marks a striking departure in Keats's verse.

Literary precedents of this poem have been traced in Dante, Chaucer, Spenser and the ballads, among others.[19] What has been less noticed, surprisingly, is a likely source of the poem in Joseph Addison's essays on the imagination. Referring to the 'great Modern Discovery' that 'Light and Colours, as apprehended by the Imagination, are only Ideas in the Mind, and not qualities that have any Existence in Matter', Addison goes on,

> We are every where entertained with pleasing Shows and Apparitions, we discover Imaginary Glories in the Heavens, and in the Earth, and see some of this Visionary Beauty poured out upon the whole Creation; but what a rough unsightly sketch of Nature should we be entertained with, did all her Colouring disappear, and the several Distinctions of Light and Shade vanish? In short, our Souls are at present delightfully lost and bewildered in a pleasing Delusion, and we walk about like the enchanted Hero of a Romance, who sees beautiful Castles, Woods and Meadows; and at the same time hears the warbling of Birds, and the purling of Streams; but

upon the finishing of some secret Spell, the fantastick Scene breaks up, and the disconsolate Knight finds himself on a barren Heath, or in a solitary Desert.[20]

This passage was one that early Romantic writers must have found very striking. Wordsworth's Immortality Ode is, after all, an attempt to look at the same phenomenon from an opposite point of view, recognizing that the power of imagination may indeed be a transitory gift, fully endowed only in early childhood, yet arguing that so far from being a pleasing delusion, it is still a power associated with our deepest humanity, and a key to the meaning of existence. In Wordsworth's view it must necessarily fade with the years, but Keats's poem explores the same phenomenon on the assumption that the kind of desolation described by Addison might be the result of an over-intensity in the subliminal self. Once withdrawn, it would result in 'imaginary woes ... conjured up by our passions, and ... fostered by passionate feeling' – and therefore, on Keats's account of the matter, more tormenting, like Tom's thwarted, delusive love. Such speculations mark a new intensity in the extraction of 'the Romantic' from the romance tradition: it is not surprising, therefore, to discover the deep influence of the poem later on the Pre-Raphaelites, William Morris actually declaring that it was 'the germ from which all the poetry of his group sprang'.[21] There is something over-hectic about it, no doubt, and much to be associated with the sickness that affected both Keats and his brother; but allowing for that, a central preoccupation remains which throws its own light on the workings of the imagination.

Whether or not Keats's savage mood was affected by such view of the mind, as inherent in Coleridge's theories, those ideas may have worked at a still subtler level. He probably did not recognize the fact directly, but he was hearing in Coleridge's discourse a skein of ideas which Wordsworth himself had encountered twenty years earlier, providing, as mentioned above, an original stimulus to some of the most potent and attractive ideas in *The Excursion*.[22*] Having previously confronted and admired the poem, in other words, Keats was now receiving a deeper insight into processes behind passages which could in fact be regarded as a compound product of the two poets' minds. The notable lines that begin its final book, for instance, concerning the 'active principle' subsisting 'in all things', which 'circulates, the Soul of all the worlds' was drafted at an early stage, when the collaboration was close.[23] The lines, little altered from the first manuscript version, convey the sense of a power in the universe 'removed / From sense and observation' – relying for its apprehension, evidently, on a level of perception below normal consciousness. Wordsworth is using the sense of a hidden power, and of a secret means by which it can be grasped, to underwrite his doctrines – a device to be found more commonly in Coleridge's writings. When Keats heard Coleridge discoursing he was, by the same token, being offered a more direct access to the esoteric element in Wordsworth. The result was not the kind of excitement that had sometimes seized his mind as a young man. By now he had passed beyond such straightforward ecstasies – having been helped to do so, indeed, by Wordsworth's reflective poetry. The very sight and sound of Coleridge's portly, dreamy figure were enough to hold him back from a joyful sense of immediate, imitative inspiration. Yet it is probably true to say that the sense of double consciousness which haunted Coleridge's discourse gave new sharpness and definition to ideas already at work in his mind. 'La Belle Dame sans Merci' is a poem uneasy in its own intensity, and Keats's sense of the fact is shown by the joking way in which he wrote about the poem as soon as he had set it down for his brother and sister-in-law:

Why four kisses – you will say – why four because I wish to restrain the headlong impetuosity of my Muse – she would have fain said 'score' without hurting the rhyme – but we must temper the Imagination as the Critics say with Judgment. I was obliged to choose an even number that both eyes might have fair play; and to speak truly I think two a piece quite sufficient. Suppose I had said seven; there would have been three and a half a piece – a very awkward affair – and well got out of on my side ... [24]

Keats can retire nimbly enough from the heart-intensities of his poem to an ironic play that keeps open the lines of communication with his relatives; in the following months, however, he was to find ways in which the subliminal self could be at once expressed and contemplated sceptically within a poem – the most dramatic example being the 'Ode to a Nightingale', written a month later. The first version of *Hyperion* had ended with the dream of an Apollo who was about to be exalted by an immensity of knowledge which would, through the ministrations of Mnemosyne, 'pour into the wide hollows' of his brain

And deify me, as if some blithe wine
Or bright elixir peerless I had drunk
And so become immortal.

The 'Ode' begins with initiation into experience of a similar kind – though it is less what might be expected from a 'bright elixir' than that produced by a drug. In Apollo's mode, entry to the primary consciousness (if now interpreted in Coleridgean terms) would at once have taken in the secondary, so including all knowledge; admission to it in the human experience described in this new assay must be by temporary inhibition of the secondary consciousness. Before his heart can express itself properly a 'drowsy numbness' must pain his sense; yet by the same token, its expression when it comes will be ambiguous – an ache which is ecstatic because it enters totally into the nightingale's song, yet also a yearning ache, because bound by its very nature into its awareness of imprisonment in the flesh. ''Tis not through envy of thy happy lot', since the kind of consciousness that could envy is not in action. Rather, the over-response of the primary consciousness to the nightingale, reminding him of his own chains, renders him 'too happy in thy happiness'. The awareness, even negatively, of the restricted scope of the primary consciousness when tied, as it must be for a mortal, to its human condition, including the limitations of time and space, and, by knowledge of its own mortality, to the facts of life and death, sets him longing for a different sort of draught – an elixir which would actually liberate his primary self and release it into the bright world of Apollo, from which consciousness of the potentialities and limitations of human existence would be absent.

This different kind of 'heart-knowledge' involves him in his own mythology instead of allowing him to stand apart from it. At one level he has reached an impasse. The passiveness of the visionary experience leaves the heart aching with knowledge of its own limitations; an active visionary experience, total liberation into an Apollo-like world, is, on the other hand, impossible. But poetry offers a way forward by using language in a way that still keeps the secondary consciousness open to the operation of the primary. Keats finds the perfect correlative for this in an intermediate state of nature such as that of the moon at night surrounded by stars, an experience directly available to the senses in a way that a view of the sun, with its blinding and destructive power, is not; or – even more appropriately – the full sensuous experience of being in a wood, where if the secondary consciousness remains awake the modes of analysis that come most naturally to it are inhibited: since the eye cannot fully see, visual acuity is precluded. The chemical senses which are most directly in touch with primary consciousness and the subliminal self can therefore exert a stronger power.

This is necessarily a temporary state, nevertheless, since in a mortal sensuous pleasure must inevitably fade. The logic of the poem thus leads to an inclination towards death, a recognition that the only proper consummation of the experience would be the ultimate swoon that would make permanent this state of sensuous apprehension. A man who had reached a state where his primary consciousness was so dominant would then be able to die in peace, 'To thy high requiem become a sod'.

The next stanza expresses more fully Keats's sense of the nightingale's appeal in this context, that its song exists out of time:

> The voice I hear this passing night was heard
> In ancient days by emperor and clown:
> Perhaps the self-same song that found a path
> Through the sad heart of Ruth, when, sick for home,
> She stood in tears amid the alien corn ...

Any suggestion of simple historical process is immediately unrealized by the 'romantic' figures of emperor and clown. These suggest less a particular court in a particular place than embodiments of power and comedy belonging to ancient regimes which, even if they have actually disappeared from modern civilizations, retain their validity for the imagination. The figure of Ruth, equally, suggests biblical romance – tearing away any associations with formality and imposed moral law. Ruth, in tears amid the alien corn, expresses the dominance of a primary self, which is yearning and grieving – displaying an openness of heart which the nightingale can, by the same token, readily pierce. Finally the poem moves into a state where specific place is abolished: a world of pure magic. Here the casement that in previous poems opened 'to let the warm love in' or to 'let in the budding warmth and throstle's lay',[25] confirming the warm world of the sensuous, opens on to an 'organized infinity' – infinite, yet 'perilous' seas, suggesting the vulnerability of the primary consciousness when sharply aroused. In this scene, where the warmth of sensuousness is stressed by apprehension of danger, the nightingale's song transcends both. In 'The Eve of St Agnes' the lovers had achieved their ecstasy while hearing the hail beat on the 'casement high and triple-arched' ('in the trances of the blast', to adopt Coleridge's phrase); in this poem, where the casement is open, the trance is made perfect.

Even the distant hint of human suffering conveyed by 'perilous', however, is enough to restore Keats to awareness of his human condition and the impossibility of forsaking it. The overtones of the word, emerging at this moment in the poem, prolong the spell for a moment – only to break it immediately. In reminding the poet of one of Milton's most romantic lines it recalls also their sombre context. Adam, understanding that Eve has eaten the apple, resolves that without her paradise would nevertheless be unendurable:

> How can I live without thee? how forego
> Thy sweet converse, and love so dearly joined,
> To live again in these wild woods forlorn?

Keats's faery lands are likewise potentially 'forlorn' – a paradise which a mortal who wishes to retain his links with human society has no means of entering. So far as his existence among human beings is concerned he has not two selves but one, a realization which carries Keats back again out of the poetic world that he has entered:

> Forlorn! the very word is like a bell
> To toll me back from thee to my sole self!

For Keats the state of primary consciousness is not a 'self' in the normal sense; rather it involves an ecstasy, an identification with the nightingale and a movement beyond, which transcends the limits of selfhood.

It was, indeed, a part of Keats's dilemma that he had so little of an identifiable self: in his letters he sometimes dwelt on the fact that this was true of many good poets. 'As to the poetical Character,' he wrote, 'it is not itself – it has no self – it is every thing and nothing... It has as much delight in conceiving an Iago as an Imogen. What shocks the virtuous philosopher, delights the camelion Poet.' And as for himself, 'not one word I ever utter,' he went on, 'can be taken for granted as an opinion growing out of my identical nature – how can it, when I have no nature?'[26] Several times during the following winter he wrote of occasions when the identities of others pressed upon his own – which could be pleasurable enough in individual relationships, but when he was in a large throng caused him to feel annihilated.[27] By April, however, his thinking had progressed to the point where he could imagine the creation of an identity as an important and necessary stage in human development. Now he argued, as we have already seen, for a view of the world according to which human experience was organized so as to encourage the creation of each individual's identity through the proper action of mind and heart on each other: 'Not merely is the Heart a Hornbook, it is the Minds Bible, it is the Mind experience, it is the teat from which the Mind or intelligence sucks its identity – '[28]

Against the background of such meditations the 'sole self' to which he is returning in the 'Ode' has wistful connotations, marking a recognition that the sense of dual identity conjured by the nightingale's song is extremely fragile. He tries to reduce the emotional intensity by introducing a pair of banal lines:

> Adieu! the fancy cannot cheat so well
> As she is fam'd to do, deceiving elf.

Yet a note of nostalgia creeps in, a yearning after the fading nightingale's note. Whatever the sole self may be, it continues to follow the nightingale into the next valley-glades, retaining not a certainty of deception but an ambiguity:

> Was it a vision, or a waking dream?
> Fled is that music: – Do I wake or sleep?

Which, after all, is the reality? Keats's question recalls Caliban's account of his dreams:

> The clouds methought would open, and show riches
> Ready to drop upon me; that when I waked,
> I cried to dream again.[29]

Keats can neither positively affirm the existence of a primary self nor ignore the powerful attractions of the realm which 'Fancy' (the term which a rationalist would be most likely to ascribe to the faculty) opens up. What he now sees more clearly than before, however, is the importance of the Imagination's role for an understanding of the full working of the human psyche.

The resulting complexities are explored still further in his 'Ode on a Grecian Urn', where (in Coleridgean terms again) the reader is continually reminded of the alternations between the formal external shape of the urn, which presents itself to the spectator's straightforward vision (or the secondary consciousness) as beautiful, and the effects of the tale told by the figures on the urn, which, by invoking the primary consciousness, awakens the imaginative powers.

The concluding stanza of the poem, with its famous 'Beauty is Truth, Truth Beauty' along with the accompanying comment 'That is all | Ye know on earth, and all ye need to know', has given rise to considerable critical debate – a debate which is little assisted by resort to the manuscript versions[30*] and which is further muddied by the later history of the phrase, quoted repeatedly and in isolation towards the end of the century and so linked with the rise of the Aesthetic movement and the cult of 'art for art's sake'. Opposition to such thinking gathered momentum during the First World War, when any attempt to identify the full truth of what was actually happening as beautiful seemed obscene. It might even be assumed then that the kind of sloppy idealism which was capable of such a mistake had actually contributed to the stupidities and horrors of those events.

The two main contenders among the possible significances of the lines are those which would see the final words as addressed by the urn to mankind or by the poet to the figures on the urn. According to the choice one makes, the weight of the last line is changed. As an utterance to mankind, it is weighty, firm, reassuring; addressed to the figures it becomes rueful, yearning, wistful. And there are elements in Keats's writing which can be adduced in support of either reading. If it is a maxim for mankind it falls in with statements such as 'What the imagination seizes as Beauty must be truth'.[31] If it is being said to the figures, on the other hand, it is in continuity with the lines describing

> the weariness, the fever and the fret,
> Here, where men sit and hear each other groan

in the 'Ode to a Nightingale'. In the latter case Keats exhibits his knowledge that the whole truth is not beautiful, while implicitly asserting that figures associated with ideal beauty in art do not, fortunately for them, need to be aware of that.

So long as the poem is read in these alternative contexts it is hard to resolve the debate. Indeed, the most attractive reading of the poem might well be one which would regard both meanings as applicable – needing to be viewed not in any kind of counterpoint that could ultimately be harmonized but strictly as meanings that could only be held as alternating messages in the mind, never both at the same time.

Nowhere does the impact of Coleridge's skein of ideas seem more present, finally, than in 'Lamia'. When he wrote 'The Eve of St Agnes' Keats no doubt had in mind the opening scene of 'Christabel', with its heroine living in a castle which is, like that in Keats's poem, a place of death, a castle altogether at odds with the drama that is constructed in its walls. But although the scenes resemble one another in some ways, with Madeleine's chamber reminiscent of Christabel's, Keats's drama is simpler, moving in linear fashion to a consummation lacking the ambiguity of the encounter between Christabel and Geraldine.

If one is looking for possible effects of Coleridge's ideas it is better, indeed, to look at 'Lamia', where it may be suggested that Keats, newly enlightened by what he had heard from him, returned to the 'Christabel' story with a different perception of its significance. Geraldine could after all be said to be an embodiment of the primary consciousness as Coleridge had painted it, with Christabel's father, Sir Leoline, a master of the secondary consciousness in his obsession with the world of death. The Lycius of Keats's poem has some affinities with the Lyca of Blake's *Songs of Innocence and of Experience*: both are essentially innocent. Lyca has all the possibilities of experience before her, however; Lycius, by contrast, is already a grown man, a passive figure, a devotee of religion. Keats's description of him as 'like a young Jove with calm uneager face' should not be overlooked: in his universe, it is the eager who are more likely to find approval. And the calmness of Lycius is deceptive, since he is at the mercy of his own consciousness, ready to be initiated by Lamia into the delights of a luxurious life but lacking the ardour that might waken his primary consciousness more positively. Just as mankind may easily be enslaved to

> that false secondary power by which
> In weakness we create distinctions, then
> Deem that our puny boundaries are things
> Which we perceive, and not which we have made[32]

so with Lycius, if he attends too exclusively to his master. Under the warm eye of love the forces of primary consciousness expand and burgeon, but once the eye of the secondary fastens upon them they shrivel correspondingly, and warp – which is precisely what happens when Apollonius fixes Lamia with his eyes.

Although Lamia's behaviour has a palpable resemblance to that of Geraldine in Coleridge's poem, and although the world of death may be said to enter with the figure of Apollonius, there are fewer echoes of Coleridge's poem than in 'The Eve of St Agnes', the relevance here lying rather in the allegorical method. The Miltonic echoes this time are not with the Hell of *Paradise Lost* but with the building of Pandaemonium in that poem. The house built by Lamia for her wedding feast is a more benevolent and florid version of the palace built by Satan and his followers. Just as in Milton

> The hasty multitude
> Admiring entered, and the work some praise
> And some the architect [33] –

so in 'Lamia'

> each guest, with busy brain,
> Arriving at the portal, gaz'd amain,
> And enters marvelling.

Pandaemonium, like Apollo's temple created to music, has been converted by this Romantic mind into an emblem of the mysterious workings of the creative imagination: what Milton ascribed to demons becomes for Keats part of a daemonic enterprise wholly akin to the artistic.

The poem as a whole replies to Milton in another respect. Where the Second Brother in the *Masque* of Comus exclaimed,

> How charming is divine philosophy!
> Not harsh and crabb'd as dull fools suppose,
> But musical as is Apollo's lute,
> And a perpetual feast of nectar'd sweets,
> Where no crude surfeit reigns.[34]

Keats is careful to distinguish such 'divine philosophy' from the sort represented by Apollonius, unmusical, harsh and a destroyer of 'nectar'd sweets':

> Do not all charms fly
> At the mere touch of cold philosophy?
> There was an awful rainbow once in heaven;
> We know her woof, her texture; she is given
> In the dull catalogue of common things.[35]

True to the assertion, Lamia loses her charm, fading to a ghost, and Lycius is destroyed. When the primary consciousness figured in Lamia and the secondary consciousness represented by Apollonius confront one another, the secondary is likely to triumph, 'brow-beating her fair form'. (One is reminded, by contrast, of Coleridge's describing Mary Wollstonecraft's easy playfulness in her responses to William Godwin as an example of 'the ascendancy which people of imagination exercised over those of mere intellect'.[36])

As with 'The Eve of St Agnes', this poem has a double structure: a plot of death and, at its heart, a growth-point of life. But whereas the previous poem begins and ends in coldness and death, transcended in the middle by the warmth of the lovers, 'Lamia' ends in the death of the warm lovers, to be transcended only by the energy of the reader's own vision. The crucial lines are those which precede the tragedy:

> What wreath for Lamia? What for Lycius?
> What for the sage, old Apollonius?
> Upon her aching forehead be there hung
> The leaves of willow and of adder's tongue;
> And for the youth, quick, let us strip for him
> The tyrsus, that his watching eyes may swim
> Into forgetfulness ...

The 'quick, let us ...' gives the key. *We* have, potentially, the kind of energy, to *us* is assigned the humane activity and eagerness that Lycius lacked; accordingly we can be spared his fate, if we so wish – perhaps not come near it in the first place. At the same time, we see the enactment of a process which Keats has come to believe is always going on in the human psyche: the struggle between the rational consciousness which corresponds to the Coleridgean secondary and the imaginative element subsisting in the primary, easily to be destroyed by over-busyness of the rational power, but the true source of Being.

In the period after he met Coleridge, Keats was passing through the most critical period of his career: his disease was gaining on him, without having yet begun to assume total mastery, and he was producing poetry of an unrivalled intensity. Had he followed the lead of Blake he might have been ready to find more open expression for one important conflict in his psyche, dramatizing the struggle between the deathly stasis of the rational and a delight in free-running energy. Indeed, he was to succeed in making one notable statement of the kind in the 'Ode to Autumn', where stillness and energy were wonderfully – however temporarily – reconciled. But in *Hyperion* energy does not have an absolutely positive status – despite mention of the 'young God of the Seas with his chariot 'foamed along | By noble winged creatures he hath made'. The energy of Hyperion displays itself rather in wrath:

> His palace bright,
> Bastioned with pyramids of glowing gold,
> And touched with shade of bronzed obelisks,
> Glares a blood-red through all the thousand courts,
> Arches, and domes, and fiery galleries;
> And all its curtains of aurorean clouds
> Flush angerly ...

This god, oppressed by 'horrors portioned to a giant nerve', his taste vitiated by 'savour of poisonous brass and metals sick', is still capable of expressing rage; indeed, in the last glimpse of him as he rushes by: 'His flaming robes streamed out beyond his heels'.

How such movements of his thought and imagery might have developed if Keats had lived, we cannot know. His successors, unaware of the full, complex process of his development, would simplify what he was saying, appropriating elements for their own use while ignoring the rest, and so providing works which would be less satisfactory because less responsive to the whole range of human experience.

Already in the great Odes, however, Keats had faced the main objection to a theory of the primary consciousness which had apparently been felt also by Wordsworth – and, to a lesser extent, by Coleridge himself. To cultivate the sense of Being by exploring the workings of the subliminal powers (we have already noticed that Keats would have fought shy of regarding them as a kind of firm identity) was to distance oneself from the tribe,[37] where suffering was an experience to be coped with continually and where everyday life allowed little opportunity for the cultivation of luxury. He allowed the question to dominate the revised version of *Hyperion*, which, instead of working towards a culmination in godlike knowledge, challenged the poet's pretensions to knowledge, in the person of Moneta.

Moneta's speeches provide a new centre for the poem, challenging the poet's status in relation to his own creation. Their impact is accompanied by an intensification in the sombre tone of the whole, concluding now with the portrait of Hyperion mentioned above: as before, a figure imprisoned by his own energy but now more ominously. It may be that, just as the Indian maiden and the moon goddess merged into a single benevolent figure at the end of *Endymion*, so in this poem Hyperion and his rage were to have been superseded by a new version of the Apollonian power which, like that of Osiris in Egyptian mythology, would temper heat with light, embodying the new humane spirit Keats thought he could discern at work in the contemporary world.

That he did not succeed in concluding his poem may be ascribed to two factors. First, Keats was viewing himself in Hyperion's condition rather than in that of a transcending poet. In such circumstances indeed, as has already been suggested, he had come to be wary of the effects of his own ardour. The man who had written in March 1818 that 'probably every mental pursuit takes its reality and worth from the ardour of the pursuer' was by August 1819 writing to Fanny Brawne,

> Forgive me for this flint-worded Letter – and believe and see that I cannot think of you without some sort of energy – though mal a propos. [38]

Second, the dilemma in which Keats found himself is traceable to a deeper level. Against the flaring energy of Hyperion is to be set the image of Thea, coming to Saturn in despair:

> One hand she pressed upon that aching spot
> Where beats the human heart, as if just there,
> Though an immortal, she felt cruel pain ...

She speaks to Saturn, but does not even wish to wake him in their misery: the result is that they remain in the same postures:

> The frozen God still bending to the earth,
> And the sad Goddess weeping at his feet.

This vision of a world alternating between cold stasis and an angry flaring motion, with human suffering enacted between, seems increasingly to have haunted Keats: it was the world into which he had been delivered by his determination to live physically and emotionally by the human heart. That which began in a universal aspiration had ended in an increasingly intense yet imprisoning commitment to a single woman.

What might happen when the subliminal self was located in and identified with the heart and its workings was never seen more painfully, perhaps, than in a poem which H.W. Garrod related to the Coleridgean discourse Keats had heard, pointing out that it might have been prompted by the phrase 'a dream accompanied by a sense of touch':

> This living hand, now warm and capable
> Of earnest grasping, would, if it were cold
> And in the icy silence of the tomb,

So haunt thy days and chill thy dreaming nights
That thou would wish thine own heart dry of blood
So in my veins red life might stream again,
And thou be conscience-calm'd – see here it is – [39]

What to Garrod was the simple use of a romantic theme turns out to be more subtle if we relate Keats's thinking to Coleridge's theory as a whole. 'When I am dead,' he seems to be saying,

there will only be one level of reality by which I exist – the icy coldness of the grave, and one might think that that would be the end of me for you as well. In your primary consciousness, on the contrary, I shall continue to be active. It may not then be altogether pleasant to think of me in the grave while you are awake, but it will be far worse when you are asleep, for my hand, now fully alive and capable of giving you a pledge of my whole being will then, if it touch you in your dreams, do so with a 'single touch'[40] that must freeze your blood with terror. Now, at least, I can offer it to you in its warmth, its 'earnest grasping' to be taken with the double-touch of shared physical acceptance. This is the difference between death and life, between the refusal of love and its full acceptance. Not only that, but if you accept it in that spirit you will automatically find 'single touch', stripped of its horrors, no longer a nightmare but an ecstasy, transforming the segregated consciousness into completeness of Being.

Garrod points to another phrase in a poem of 1819, 'Touch has a memory' and relates it to the same topic in the Keats-Coleridge conversation, 'A dream accompanied by a sense of touch'. 'Touch has a memory in dreams,' he comments.[41] But in fact the lines in question seem to refer not to a dream but to a real incident: it is only at the end of the poem that the poet takes such refuge. He begins,

What can I do to drive away
Remembrance from my eyes? for they have seen,
Aye, an hour ago, my brilliant Queen!

The next line, which begins with the words 'Touch has a memory', continues

say, love, say,
What can I do to kill it and be free
In my old liberty?

> When every fair one that I saw was fair,
> Enough to catch me in but half a snare,
> Not keep me there:
> When, howe'er poor or particolour'd things,
> My muse had wings,
> And ever ready was to take her course
> Whither I bent her force,
> Unintellectual, yet divine to me; –
> Divine, I say! – What sea-bird o'er the sea
> Is a philosopher the while he goes
> Winging along where the great water throes?[42]

In Coleridgean terms everything here can be related to the 'primary consciousness' of the poet, which was normally free like a bird (recalling the 'pigeon tumbling in clear summer air' of 'Sleep and Poetry'[43]). Such a realm had nothing to do with space–time (it was 'unintellectual'). But in the love he describes the primary consciousness is enthralled, robbed of its freedom and its sense of infinity. 'Touch has a memory'; this love by contrast is consuming. Seizing the primary consciousness through the senses it binds it back into the time-process.

Keats proceeds to paint the hell which he fears as a result of his new bondage – not the fiery hell of popular tradition but the frozen Tartarus of enslaved man:

> Where shall I learn to get my peace again?
> To banish thoughts of that most hateful land,
> Dungeoner of my friends, that wicked strand
> Where they were wrecked and live a wretched life;
> That monstrous region, whose dull rivers pour
> Ever from their sordid urns unto the shore,
> Unowned of any weedy-hairèd gods;
> Whose winds, all zephyrless, hold scourging rods,
> Iced in the great lakes, to afflict mankind;
> Whose rank-grown forests, frosted, black, and blind,
> Would fright a Dryad; whose harsh-herbaged meads
> Make lean and lank the starved ox while he feeds.
> There bud flowers have no scent, birds no sweet song,
> And great unerring Nature once seems wrong.

These lines could refer either to the despair of the rejected lover or the frozen state of hebetude belonging to the married state awaiting the accepted. The ambiguity is perhaps deliberate. Keats is preoccupied

first and foremost by a state in which he should lose his creative liberty
for the bonds of marriage, where love might freeze, leaving only material demands, and the frozen wastes of despair.

The poem continues with the agonized longing for renewed physical
contact:

> Oh, let me once more rest
> My soul upon that dazzling breast!
> Let once again these aching arms be placed,
> The tender gaolers of thy waist!
> And let me feel that warm breath here and there
> To spread a rapture in my very hair –
> Oh, the sweetness of the pain!
> Give me those lips again!

and concludes

> Enough! Enough! It is enough for me
> To dream of thee!

The unrestrained sensuousness of these lines mark the impossible situation to which Keats had now arrived, caught in the agony of an
unfulfillable physical aspiration. It was the logical end to a more general
attitude that had been inspired initially by Wordsworth's mediating
devotion to the human heart. For the most part this was a benign strategy, equipping him to attend humanely to the pains and sorrows of
others without regard to their social class. The problem came when (as in
the case of Coleridge's love for Sara Hutchinson) his philosophy of the
human heart led to the cultivation of a single love for an individual
woman. There was much to be said in favour of a concept of Being
which allowed one's conduct to be dominated by the heart rather than
the head; particularly since the mores of the age forbade any fuller
freedom. This was, after all, the beginning of an age which would, in its
full flowering, be the Victorian. But when it led to the painful intensity
of his love for Fanny Brawne and the agonizing despair of his last letters
to her it must also be questioned. 'A man's life of any worth,' he once
wrote, 'is a continual allegory.'[44] His own career fulfilled the saying by
displaying to its extreme the effect of focusing his Being in the heart.
What was originally learnt from Wordsworth as an emphasis became
finally a total stance by which he would be destroyed and – eventually –
remembered. His final existence, in other words, was as an energy concentrated in his own heart that would be unforgettably emblematic for
all who sought to live by the heart.

This was not, however, the only form Being might take. I have already suggested that by his glimpse into Coleridge's thinking in 1819 Keats had been initiated into a sense which would enable him to explore all his potentialities as a poet, aware of the different kinds of consciousness at play. His letters show how well prepared he already was. His well-known remarks on 'negative capability'[45] demonstrate a developing ability to 'let the mind be a thoroughfare for all thoughts' and not a 'select party'.[46] The aspiration aligned him with Shakespeare – and with Coleridge himself, for that matter, though in his case likewise, a falling equally under the spell of Wordsworth meant that he was inhibited from achieving the kind of freedom such a conception of Being offered. In Keats's psyche was played out again the struggle between Coleridgean consciousness and Wordsworthian identity, which he endeavoured to resolve, as both poets had done before him, by drawing on the heart as a mediating resource.

Coleridge, another seeker after a stable identity, once wrote to Wordsworth that when in his alienated state he felt torn between two states of mind: 'a wish to retire into stoniness & stir not, or to be diffused upon the winds & have no individual Existence'[47] – and if it had ever come to that extremity, one can easily suspect which course he would have taken. In the end Keats was enough of a Coleridgean to have elected diffuseness of identity also – and for his name, as he put it in his own epitaph, to be 'writ in water',[48] with all the ambiguities that later readers would discover in that phrase. Gone was the carefree stance that could, when he chose, turn any situation to light-hearted occasion for play. As Christopher Ricks has shown, he would retain to the end a superb courtesy which could turn even recognition of his awkward bow into a graceful inclination,[49] but shot through even that was the in-tensity of his heart-drive, destined eventually to be all-consuming.

Other poets and thinkers who would in turn feel the need to develop their sense of the potentialities of consciousness by positing the existence of a Being supplementary to it would learn that they too would be wise not to risk following his fate by similarly identifying that Being so closely and immediately with the directings of the 'human heart'. At the same time Coleridge's recurring attempts to find in the work of the imagination the best clue to the nature of that Being would prove his most rewarding gift to his creative successors. They might well remember that the thrust of his own poem on nightingales, written in Somerset at the height of his delight in the 'universe of life',[50] had been an insistence that their note was one not of melancholy but of joy.

5

De Quincey and the Dark Sublime

Although the idea that there could be a state of Being in humanity which included, but was not contained by, consciousness began to be current in the Romantic period, it was not always formulated precisely in those terms. It had nevertheless been foreshadowed variously in the previous period. Evidence of discontent with current psychological views can be found in the margins, at least, of eighteenth-century literary discourse, where existing terms that did not fit the scheme of the rationally ordered mind but could sometimes still be offered as aesthetic were offering themselves for reinterpretation. Two of the prime examples, 'sublimity' and 'pathos' – encouraging the expression, respectively, of states of elevated spirit and indulged sentiment – were to be radically transformed with the advent of those new Romantically-minded writers who made the transition from a publicly conditioned social consciousness to a more private sense of engaged Being. The concept of sublimity, which had hitherto been indulged by way of detached contemplation, could now be considered in a more ecstatic mode, almost as a passing out of oneself into possession by a superior power. The sense of pathos, similarly, turned from a state of pitying external contemplation into an empathy aiming to enter the psyche of the suffering victim more fully.

It was his sense of a new kind of profundity, perhaps, that first attracted the young Thomas De Quincey to Wordsworth, who seemed not simply to entertain his ideas, but to live by them. In the eyes of later readers Coleridge, deep in dreams, fantasies and 'facts of mind', might have seemed the more natural forerunner, given the nature of De Quincey's later career, but when he ran away from Manchester Grammar School in 1802, his first impulse was to go to Grasmere. Writing a letter to Wordsworth a year later about his failure to reach him on that occasion, he allowed his feeling for Coleridge to emerge briefly in the conclusion, saying that he would not have written in such terms to any man on earth 'except yourself and one other (a friend of your's)'.[1]

By then, certainly, Coleridge was for him a strong presence. When he thought of him, it was as 'a compound of Ancient Mariner and Bath concert room traveller with bushy hair',[2] and when he tried to figure a sublime character for himself, the same poem returned to his mind: '"What shall be my character?" ... wild – impetuous – *splendidly* sublime? dignified – melancholy – *gloomily* sublime? or shrouded in mystery – supernatural – like the "ancient Mariner" – *awfully* sublime?'[3] He had not, of course, met Coleridge yet, and when he did, four years later, the decline had already set in: the ebullient preacher of earlier years had turned into the more fixedly meditative man whose conversation – that conversation of which Carlyle was to say, even so, 'no talk, in his century or in any other, could be more surprising'[4] – was now less like a pulsing spring than a majestic river in flood.

Even if Coleridge's presence in the flesh did not live up to De Quincey's more romantic imaginings, however, it was still portentous; and as he came to know him better, he must have become aware of the similarities in their early upbringing. In one of his essays he commented sympathetically on Coleridge's plight as a child who, having been the darling of his father and mother, was separated suddenly from both by the death of his father and precipitated into the wilderness of a London school.[5] He would presumably have seen further resemblances in the fact that Coleridge, like himself, had suffered the early death of a beloved sister. His description of Coleridge as a 'flower unfolding its silken leaves only to suffer canker and blight'[6] may well reflect a sense of failed promise in his own career.

Some of De Quincey's twentieth-century critics have reinforced the sense of similarity by tracing in him an existential weakness, which could be ascribed to his early circumstances. Hillis Miller has discussed the traumatic effects of his sister Elizabeth's death, while more recently A.S. Plumtree has argued that if we are seeking the root of De Quincey's anxieties we should look back still further, to his relationship with his mother.[7] Drawing on the ideas of R.D. Laing, Plumtree claims that Mrs De Quincey's frigidity towards her child, as described by De Quincey himself, led to an existential lack to be traced throughout his career. This insight, however, important as it is, does not tell the whole story, as may be discovered from the description of the 'morning parade', during which Mrs De Quincey would inspect her children until they could be 'pronounced to be in proper trim'. Then, her son continues, we were dismissed, but with two ceremonies that to us were mysterious and allegorical – first, that our hair and faces were sprinkled with lavender-water and milk of roses; secondly, that we received a kiss on the forehead. The mystery in this last instance regarded the place; because we little silly people in the nursery never planted our kisses on foreheads, but sprang right at the lips.[8]

This passage may fairly be read, as it is in Plumtree's study, with De Quincey's preceding description of her:

Figure to yourself a woman of admirable manners ... distinguished by lady-like tranquillity and repose, and even by self-possession, but also freezing in excess. Austere she was in a degree which fitted her for the lady president of rebellious nunneries. Rigid in her exactions of duty from those around her, but also from herself; upright, sternly conscientious, munificent in her charities, pure-minded in so absolute a degree that you would have been tempted to call her 'holy', – she yet could not win hearts by the graciousness of her manner. That quality which shone so brightly in my sister, and the expansive love which distinguished both her and myself, we had from our father.[9]

Although this lack at the centre of De Quincey's childhood may have been responsible for many personal problems, an interpretation of them in terms of an absolute frigidity on the part of his mother misses some of the subtleties involved. For if there was a lack of direct physical cherishing and reassurance in Mrs De Quincey's relationship with her son, there was, accompanying it, a deep and anxious concern, evident in her many letters and remonstrances. Within the politics of the family the relationship of a parent towards a child may often encompass a power-seeking that masks itself as love or compensates for a personal lack by unreasonable calls for a loving self-denial. One very striking feature of Mrs De Quincey's letters, by contrast, is her lack of such emotional demands. Nor should we ignore the 'lavender-water and milk of roses', which must have left an impression of sensuous love puzzlingly at variance with the detachment of the kisses themselves. De Quincey's problem seems to have been that his mother, despite her coldness, never gave him any reason to hate her, nor any indication that her motives were other than disinterested, while in subliminal ways (as through the perfume) she offered oblique signs of affection.

For a better understanding, we perhaps need to read not only the writings of R.D. Laing but also the *Confessions* of St Augustine, setting De Quincey among that select class of men who respond in the end to their mother's desire for their career – but not necessarily by the course that that mother had wished, endeavouring instead to reconcile the mother's (not ungratifying) sense that her child is a chosen human being with their instinctive sense that the life of self-abnegation proposed would also be suffocating. St Augustine fulfilled this task largely by way of postponement: he did what his mother would have wished, but only after exploring other possibilities. Romantic writers, caught up in a world less readily explicable in terms of orthodox Christianity, tried to work the reconciliation without referring to traditional religious forms. Indeed, De Quincey's passage about opium, easily dismissed as a whimsical flight of fancy, is susceptible of a more serious reading. 'This is the doctrine of the true church on the subject of opium,' he writes, 'of which church I acknowledge myself to be the only member, – the alpha and omega.'[10]

In all this, it could be said, De Quincey was seizing upon one side of Coleridge's enterprise – his exploration of the dynamics of the human subconscious in the hope of discovering universal truths – and taking that to a logical conclusion, while neglecting the other side of what Coleridge had to say concerning the moral imperative. Against the latter he had been anaesthetized by his mother's very insistence; this did not mean, however, that it was dead.

If his mother's behaviour and her demands upon him remained a dark enigma, there was no such problem about his feeling for his sister. Here he found a quickness of affection and a support for his emotions which were to be remembered as idyllic. Like others in that age he found in such a relationship of the heart qualities which seemed to him to transcend sexual attraction. Love of this order, which might, it was hoped, provide a way forward for mankind generally, seemed also to provide a permanent resource for the individual. A love, he wrote many years later, 'which is altogether holy, like that between two children, is privileged to revisit by glimpses the silence and the darkness of declining years'.[11] This love, we may suppose, also gave him the chief link with the poetry in *Lyrical Ballads*, in which he found 'the ray of a new morning'.[12] The note which runs through that volume, from the awakening of the Ancient Mariner as a spring of love gushes involuntarily from his heart to Wordsworth's Wye Valley meditations on the growth of the affections, is of a faith in the power of the human heart, as such, to illuminate one's sense of humanity at large.

This strain of thinking was so congenial to many minds, as a viable way of mediation between established rigidities and the perils of unrestrained freedom, that many took to it without even analysing closely what was meant by the 'heart'. There were those who found such a way of life dangerously self-indulgent and even narcissistic, their opposition reproducing in a subtler form the eighteenth-century polemic of the 'man of reason' against the 'man of sensibility'. Others found the new development positively exciting, interpreting the heart commonly as a metaphor for affectionate experience. Shadworth Hodgson, writing about 1880, declared that a constellation of poets at the beginning of the century had made it what it was in literature and philosophy: 'They are the fathers of that reaction, that reconstruction, that revival of the heart as the unifying principle against the dispersing, criticising understanding, as the end or telos of all action and of all thought.'

Of the six poets he named, Hodgson singled out Wordsworth and Coleridge as paramount. He also designated two orders of individual minds: 'minds genial, flexible, and imaginative, on the one side, minds ungenial, inflexible, ratiocinative, on the other; minds that seem to be Nature's offspring and inherit her spontaneity, and minds that seem to be her handiwork and perform her tasks.'[13] (Hodgson's categories, it will be noticed, correspond to the division between the Coleridgean 'primary' and 'secondary' consciousnesses.[14]) Wordsworth and Coleridge he saw as exemplars of his first kind. De Quincey he also aligned with it, but not in the first rank: his mind, being illuminating rather than creative like theirs, on the other hand, could be classified as 'subtle' rather than 'acute'. In pursuing his argument, Hodgson quoted a telling passage by De Quincey himself on the education of the sensibilities through their experience in life and literature:

> When speaking of man in his intellectual capacity, the Scriptures speak not of the understanding, but of 'the understanding heart', – making the heart, i.e. the great intuitive (or non-discursive) organ, to be the interchangeable formula for man in his highest state of capacity for the infinite.[15]

This passage, posing as it does 'the heart' as the organ through which man communes with infinite powers, is a central reflection of the strain fostered by Wordsworth. Coleridge and Keats in Romantic thought.

As with Wordsworth and Coleridge, moreover, De Quincey's cultivation of the heart's affections did not rest in detached observation of the behaviour of other people, but led naturally to emotional commitment, recalling the intensity of his affection for his sister years before. Whether or not he knew of the deep love which Coleridge focused on Sara Hutchinson is hard to say – quite probably not. It is doubtful, equally, whether he fully grasped the intensity of William and Dorothy Wordsworth's affection for each other. But De Quincey could hardly live in close association with these people, as he did from 1808, or read their poetry for that matter, without picking up implications of a love of the heart which seemed to transcend sexual desire. He had, after all, known a love of the same kind, not only with Elizabeth but also with Ann, the young Oxford Street prostitute whom he befriended. And it was fully in consonance with this cultivated feeling that he should have fallen in love, equally sexlessly, with Catherine, the Wordsworths' three-year-old daughter. After her sudden death, he was overcome by a fierce 'convulsion of grief'.[16] Eventually, after he had indulged in his frenzy of loss for much of the summer, he was overtaken by a debilitating 'nervous malady';[17] finally, an opposing process set in. The most remarkable feature of his recovery was that 'all grief for little Kate Wordsworth, nay, all remembrance of her, had, with my malady, vanished from my mind. The traces of her innocent features were utterly washed away from my heart; she might have been dead for a thousand years, so entirely abolished was the last lingering image of her face or figure.'[18]

De Quincey's grief over Catherine's death, and his subsequent need to work through the emotion again and again until the final cathartic illness cleared it from his mind, could hardly have been an isolated process, detachable from everything else that had been happening to him during these years. Indeed, the destruction of his love may have eliminated along with it many of the associations and emotional tensions that had been accumulating during his sojourn in Grasmere. If so, this would help explain the incompleteness of his later reminiscences, including his apparent inability to communicate what he had earlier found so overwhelming in the writing and ideas of the two poets he admired.

The theory to be suggested here is that when De Quincey, sharing many of Coleridge's abilities and anxieties, was attracted to Wordsworth as by a 'deep deep magnet',[19] it was for reasons similar to those that had drawn his speculative predecessor. After the initial excitement of ideas which opened up the human unconscious as an unknown territory ripe for new discoveries, a young man might easily find instead that he was afloat on an unknown sea where bearings were easily lost. In a situation of that kind a welcome resource was to be found in a strength such as Wordsworth's, with the sense he gave of someone existing in what Coleridge would call 'the dread Watch-Tower of man's absolute Self'.[20] But if that strength had been simply a solidity, it would have been little more than another version of dead eighteenth-century formulations. The impressive feature of Wordsworth's poetry was its ability to suggest further layers of meaning: intimations of dark fear, indications of mysterious love, often most readily to be traced when a suffering human being experienced initiation into what seemed another sphere of existence: 'Suffering is permanent, obscure and dark, I And shares the nature of infinity'.[21] Hearing Wordsworth read the drama in which those lines first appeared, Coleridge had been impressed by its '*profound* touches of the human heart',[22] just as in hearing 'Guilt and Sorrow' he had been struck by the 'union of deep feeling with profound thought'.[23] De Quincey evidently felt much the same.

Wordsworth's poetry appealed to elements in the psyche that had been excited, but not previously stirred so deeply, by the new ways of thought abroad; it also seemed to be calling for personal commitment. If it was true that 'we have all of us one human heart',[24] the cause of humanity could surely be advanced both by behaving towards all human beings as equals and by cultivating intense personal relationships. Coleridge, falling in love with Sara Hutchinson, or De Quincey, falling in love with Kate Wordsworth, could feel that they were fulfilling the Wordsworthian ideal as much as Wordsworth himself in the intensity of his affection for Dorothy. With the withdrawal of Sara and the death of Kate they were left 'like men betrayed' – and certainly without guidance from Wordsworth himself, whose marriage had represented a move towards more conventional forms of human relationship. So Wordsworth remained an enigma: even if he no longer spoke or acted like a prophet, something in the man still conveyed intimations of a dark sublime which could communicate with more positive potencies in the human heart.

While Wordsworth was always wary of approaching the hiding places of his power, Coleridge and De Quincey were ready to attempt a direct assault – even to the extent of exploring drug experiences. Although opium was obviously a major point of contact between the two, it is not altogether clear how far De Quincey grasped the extent of Coleridge's addiction at the time when they were first acquainted. De Quincey's contention that opium led to a failure of the creative principle in his later work is reminiscent of Coleridge's account of a similar state of mind in 'Dejection', but although the poem fascinated De Quincey as a representation of 'extinguished power',[25] he did not, openly at least, make the further connection. Certainly, his enslavement to opium became fearful to him only when the addiction was very advanced; he was then forced – like Coleridge again – into desperate straits to try to free himself. While he could not but acknowledge the harm he had received, he continued to be drawn back to the revelatory power of experiences which had seemed to unlock secrets of his own being.

The question is complicated by later bitterness, coupled with a certain ambiguity and even confusion in the attitudes of both men to their addiction. They could concentrate on either the 'pains' or the 'pleasures' of opium, but it was hard to hold both in the mind simultaneously. In view of this, it is less surprising that De Quincey's career sometimes parallels his predecessor's so closely, features which characterized one phase in Coleridge's being re-enacted in a more extended form in De Quincey's. Writing to a friend in 1810, Dorothy Wordsworth had spoken of Coleridge's irregular habits: 'He lies in bed, always till after 12 o'clock, sometimes much later; and never walks out – Even the finest spring day does not tempt him to seek the fresh air; and this beautiful valley seems a blank to him.' She also expressed her fear that if he were not under their roof he would be 'as much the slave of stimulants as ever', asserting that 'his whole time and thoughts, (except when he is reading and he reads a great deal), are employed in deceiving himself, and seeking to deceive others'.[26] De Quincey, likewise, came to spend more and more time studying far into the night and sleeping much of the day. When he speaks of himself as sitting with a decanter of laudanum and a volume of German metaphysics,[27] the resemblance to Coleridge is particularly striking. Nor is this simply a matter of drugs. Whether or not a direct influence is to be traced, De Quincey's intellectual dilemma was similar: he too wanted to investigate and establish the correspondence of the inner mind with the inwardness of physical nature; he too found himself torn between the intellectual stringency of Kant's logic and the subtler, different revelations afforded by opium.

Although the two men drifted apart after Catherine's death, certain ideas which he shared with Coleridge continued to haunt De Quincey, particularly those that helped him interpret his sometimes nightmarish experiences under opium. They also enabled him to understand madness better. He came to claim, indeed, that insanity was normally based on a disorder of the liver, recalling that, as opium came to affect his own, 'the whole living principle of the intellectual motions began

to lose its elasticity, and, as it were, to petrify'. He thus 'began to comprehend the tendency of madness to eddy about one idea; and the loss
of power to abstract ... or to exercise many other intellectual acts, was
in due proportion to the degree in which the biliary system seemed to
suffer'.[28] This description of the effects where the 'living principle' is
negated probably owed something to Coleridge, who also speaks of the
tendency of madness to 'eddy' round a single obsession.[29] It also links
itself with the whole section concerning 'The Pains of Opium' in the
Confessions of an English Opium-Eater, where the title itself echoes that
of Coleridge's poem 'The Pains of Sleep' (the imagery of which clearly
relates to his opium-taking). On the other hand, as Alethea Hayter has
pointed out,[30] the actual obsessions which fixed his mind during his
opium addiction belonged to a period before he began taking the drug
in any large measure: that of his wanderings in Wales and London
during the years 1802–3, when he befriended Ann of Oxford Street and
came to know something of the abyss of human misery. Just as images
from school and university haunted Coleridge's dreams,[31] so images
that visited De Quincey during his opium visions (crowds of faces, the
sacrificial girl child) dated from those early years.

The fact that his experiences of misery preceded his opium addiction
helps to explain an element in his thought which we shall encounter
again. Great as was his relief at having escaped from his Manchester
predicament, De Quincey evidently felt that his time in Wales and
London was one of the most 'real' periods of his life. Among other
things the sense of heightened realism may well account for his obsession with the 'pariah' state in humanity, ranging from individuals
whom he had known, such as Ann of Oxford Street and the daughters
of Samuel Hall,[32] to oppressed races such as the gypsies and the Jews,[33]
and including Oedipus and Antigone.[34] Through such references runs a
supposition that 'pariahs' (of which he counted himself one) are
admitted to a knowledge not available to ordinary, comfortably placed
human beings. It is a recurrent theme, connected with that of the Dark
Interpreter in *Suspiria de Profundis*. There is also a link with the
'Introductory Notice' to that work:

> The machinery for dreaming planted in the human brain was not
> planted for nothing. That faculty, in alliance with the mystery of
> darkness, is the one great tube through which man communicates
> with the shadowy. And the dreaming organ, in connection with the
> heart, the eye and the ear, compose the magnificent apparatus
> which forces the infinite into the chambers of a human brain, and

throws dark reflections from eternities below all life upon that *camera obscura* – the mirrors of the sleeping mind.[35]

Coleridge, similarly, could write at the crisis of his opium-taking: 'O infinite in the depth of darkness, an infinite craving, an infinite capacity of pain and weaknesses', and 'O I have had a new world opened to me, in the infinity of my own Spirit!'[36]

So far as the original experiences were expressed, however, it was rather to Wordsworth that De Quincey turned as one who more deeply understood the human issues involved. I have already quoted the lines concerning suffering as 'permanent, obscure and dark', and sharing 'the nature of infinity'. When Wordsworth repeated them in his epigraph to *The White Doe of Rylstone*, he added a further passage, beginning, 'Yet through that darkness (infinite though it seem l And irremoveable) gracious openings lie', which link his sentiments still more closely with those of the younger writer. De Quincey could find in Wordsworth a figure whose philosophy and poetry provided a humane framework for his own thinking. Where Coleridge's speculations offered keys to the unlocking of the positive subliminal powers, Wordsworth seemed to understand more fully the connection between these powers and states of suffering and love.

The extent of De Quincey's devotion to Wordsworth throughout his career is manifested not merely by the testimony cited earlier, but by the number of occasions on which he introduces – often, it seems, unconsciously – Wordsworthian phrases into his writing. Such usages suggest not just 'influence', in the simple sense, but shared preoccupations. We may take, for example, two passages involving a similar run of phraseology. In describing his feelings after Ann disappeared, De Quincey remembers his wish that

> the benediction of a heart oppressed with gratitude ... might have power given it from above to chase, to haunt, to waylay, to pursue thee into the central darkness of a London brothel, or (if it were possible) even into the darkness of the grave, there to awaken thee with an authentic message of peace and forgiveness, and of final reconciliation.[37]

The words 'to chase, to haunt, to waylay' look strangely at odds with the rest of the passage, suggesting as they do a language of sexual pursuit. A similar usage occurs in a passage concerning Coleridge's self-withdrawal from nature, which De Quincey interprets as having been possibly due to the painfulness now associated with scenes that had formerly surrounded experiences of strong emotion:

> Phantoms of lost power, sudden intuitions, and shadowy restorations of forgotten feelings, sometimes dim and perplexing, sometimes by bright but furtive glimpses, sometimes by a full and steady revelation, overcharged with light – throw us back in a moment upon scenes and remembrances that we have left full thirty years behind us. In solitude, and chiefly in the solitudes of nature, and, above all, amongst the great and enduring features of nature, such as mountains, and quiet dells, and the lawny recesses of forests, and the silent shores of lakes, features with which (as being themselves less liable to change) our feelings have a more abiding association – under these circumstances it is that such evanescent hauntings of our past and forgotten selves are most apt to startle and to waylay us.[38]

The 'startle' and 'waylay' at the end, like the 'to chase, to haunt, to waylay' of the other passage, hark back to the opening stanza of Wordsworth's 'She Was a Phantom of Delight':

> She was a Phantom of delight
> When first she gleamed upon my sight;
> A lovely Apparition, sent
> To be a moment's ornament;
> Her eyes as stars of Twilight fair;
> Like Twilight's, too, her dusky hair;
> But all things else about her drawn
> From May-time and the cheerful Dawn;
> A dancing Shape, an Image gay
> To haunt, to startle, and way-lay.

Tracing the phrases to Wordsworth changes their effect in the passage about Ann, while also suggesting something about the underlying complex of thought involved. The very fact that De Quincey takes words which for Wordsworth characterized his wife when he first knew her and uses them to describe himself in pursuit of Ann suggests that he sees the imagery as transcending female beauty, emblematizing a love of the heart between human beings. For the same reason he believed that he would be able to awaken Ann, if ever he found her, with a 'message of peace and forgiveness, and of final reconciliation'. The second of the echoes, on the other hand, moves back from the more affirmative belief (which was, after all, cheated when he failed to rediscover her) to psychological wonderment over the phenomenon involved in the ability of feelings to revive instantly, abolishing a gap of many years.

The implication of this reference and many others is that De Quincey found Wordsworth's poetry distinguished not only by an unusual feeling for humanity, but also by its ability to describe certain unusual states of nature and of the human spirit in a way that suggested the existence of a correspondence between them. It was in Wordsworth's transmutations of Coleridge's ideas, however, that De Quincey's most acute focus of interest lay. Just as Hazlitt, having encountered the younger, more radical Coleridge, creamed off his enthusiasm for the heart's imagination and developed that to a higher intensity in the service of the liberal cause, so De Quincey's more conservative temperament found itself drawn to Wordsworth's balancing of the visionary against the mundane.

In the case of 'She Was a Phantom of Delight', his feeling for the poem as a whole, with Wordsworth celebrating an equivalent balance of virtues in his wife, develops more fully into his own fictional picture of such a woman:

> This double character, one aspect of which looks towards her husband and one to her children, sits most gracefully upon many a young wife whose heart is pure and innocent; and the collision between the two separate parts, imposed by duty on the one hand, by extreme youth on the other, – the one telling her that she is a responsible head of a family and the depositary of her husband's honour in its tenderest and most vital interests; the other telling her, through the liveliest language of animal sensibility and through the very pulses of her blood, that she is herself a child, – this collision gives an inexpressible charm to the whole demeanour of many a young married woman, making her other fascinations more touching to her husband and deepening the admiration she excites; and the more so, as it is a collision which cannot exist except among the very innocent.[39]

This is not just a reconciliation of opposites. A Coleridgean combination of the organic and the vital[40]* is drawn into service on both sides of the balance: it is there in the responsible self that looks after her husband's honour 'in its tenderest and most vital interests'; it is there, equally, in the juxtaposition of the 'liveliest language of animal sensibility' with the 'very pulses of her blood'. On both sides sensibility and vitality are set in apposition as equal participants in the twin qualities that constitute her charm.

De Quincey pursued the Coleridgeo-Wordsworthian idea still deeper, seeing at the heart of the child-like sensibility and pulsing vitality he describes a link with the subliminal source of vision described in the Immortality Ode, where the light of the sun becomes the direct image of an intimation of immortality that is 'not to be put by'.[41] A similar identification of the immanent powers of childhood with those of the sun underlay his deep love for Kate Wordsworth, so that her death seemed all the more a violation of his deepest beliefs.[42] A more abstract version of the same imagery is used in connection with the Wordsworths themselves. Of Dorothy he wrote, 'The pulses of light are not more quick or more inevitable in their flow and undulation, than were the answering and echoing movements of her sympathizing attention.'[43] And of her brother, 'he did not cease for years to wear something of the glory and the aureola which, in Popish legends, invests the head of superhuman beings'.[44] The one other place where he uses this image of an 'aureola' is in his description of his own sister, 'around whose ample brow, as often as thy sweet countenance rises upon the darkness, I fancy a tiara of light or a gleaming aureola in token of thy premature intellectual grandeur'.[45] Wordsworth had, it seems, become for him a supreme guarantor of the world into which he felt himself to have been initiated by his early relationship with Elizabeth, a different world of Being.

Where it occurs, this light imagery, though not common in De Quincey's writings, runs deep. It expresses, essentially, his idea of God:

> God must not proceed by steps and the fragmentary knowledge of accretion ... God must see; he must intuit, so to speak; and all truth must reach him simultaneously, first and last, without succession of time or partition of acts; just as light, before that theory had been refuted by the Satellites of Jupiter, was held not to be propagated in time, but to be here and there at one and the same indivisible instant.[46]

The old theory of light, he is implying, was closer to the true conception of God than the one now enforced by experimental observation. And this concept of God in terms of a supernatural light-filled vision, seeing all in one, he elsewhere holds to be a property of human consciousness in certain extreme states – notably in the moment of death. De Quincey was particularly impressed by the account of an old lady concerning what had happened to her when she almost drowned at the age of nine:

At a certain stage of this descent, a blow seemed to strike her; phos-phoric radiance sprang forth from her eyeballs; and immediately a mighty theatre expanded within her brain. In a moment, in the twinkling of an eye, every act, every design of her past life, lived again, arraying themselves not as a succession, but as parts of a coexistence ... Her consciousness became omnipresent at one moment to every feature in the infinite review.[47]

The same story is told in a note to the *Confessions*, where it is further asserted that 'she had a faculty developed as suddenly for comprehend-ing the whole and every part',[48] and it is there associated with a similar quality in certain of his experiences under opium. That powerful expe-riences under the influence of drugs do sometimes take such a form is supported by other testimony, but it was the evidence concerning equivalent experiences in moments of extremity given by people who did not resort to drugs that was the more welcome to De Quincey, sug-gesting as they did the possession of a vitality independent of chemical accident. Wordsworth's Immortality Ode, coming from a man who was not addicted to drugs, had a similar importance for him.

But why, in that case, did De Quincey not write more openly about Wordsworth's visionary powers, leaving it instead to hover in echoes from the poetry? Part of the answer, as suggested earlier, may well have lain in the death of his memory of the tragic young Catherine, which may be thought to have carried away in its passing some of the visionary light that had surrounded all the Wordsworths. But a strange ambiguity had also been detectable in Wordsworth himself, a failure to live up to the vision of his own poetry, which De Quincey found disturbing. In a note to his essay on 'Walking Stewart' he dis-cusses Wordsworth's pride and his unwillingness to discuss certain subjects (including even the beauties of nature!) outside his immedi-ate family circle, or to allow an acquaintance to indulge in self-justify-ing argument[49] – behaviour which must have been bewildering to a man who had first been drawn to Wordsworth by the general feeling for humanity displayed in *Lyrical Ballads*. And his puzzlement was undoubtedly brought to a head by the Wordsworths' opposition to his relationship with Margaret Simpson, whom they considered beneath him.[50*]

That someone who had written so eloquently on the universality of the human heart should object when De Quincey put that principle into practice must have been not only socially wounding, but intellec-tually bewildering.

It is not difficult to see the Wordsworths' attitude in a different light. De Quincey's marriage to Margaret came after a period of growing depression and his first addiction to opium, which in turn followed the crisis of Kate Wordsworth's death and his response to it. We may suppose that his relationship to the Wordsworths had already been affected by that death, while his opium addiction would have roused in them memories of Coleridge's fate not long before. Their concern at what seemed to them an improvident marriage, on that reading of the matter, may not have been snobbery so much as the culmination of a growing disquiet associated with his current condition.

By the time this happened, however, De Quincey had invested too much emotion in the Wordsworthian position, as he conceived it, to find an easy alternative. Just like Wordsworth himself, stranded intellectually when the French Revolution showed its harsh side – or indeed as Coleridge would soon be, following the quarrel with his friend – so now De Quincey found himself isolated, forced to find a new basis for his life. There was no firm ground in the past to which he could return; emotionally, his career had been a steady development along lines to which Wordsworth and Coleridge beckoned. If he were to find ways of existing outside that development, it would involve something like a reinventing of himself.

We see a hint of the underlying problem in a passage about opium to which John E. Jordan has drawn attention. When the opium-eater is in 'the divinest state incident to his enjoyment', says De Quincey, 'crowds become an oppression to him; music, even, too sensual and gross. He naturally seeks solitude and silence, as indispensable conditions of those trances, or profoundest reveries, which are the crown and consummation of what opium can do for human nature.'[51] As Jordan points out,[52*] the essential Wordsworthian nature is here transposed into a fitting background for the drug-taker. This would have been offensive to Wordsworth himself, whose devotion to solitude and silence and receptiveness to profound reveries were always accompanied by an element of strenuousness, always deliberately undrugged. Yet, while De Quincey's growing addiction would have been a matter of anxiety for Wordsworth, particularly after the melancholy example of Coleridge, De Quincey in his turn must have found Wordsworth's unwillingness to go beyond a certain point in his inner explorations of the psyche a timidity – even a betrayal of his own insights.

De Quincey's sense of Wordsworth as a great visionary was by no means simple or straightforward, moreover. Just as it accorded with the Gothic tradition that there was something terrible in the nature of any true seer (Coleridge's Ancient Mariner and his figure of genius in 'Kubla Khan' are again relevant), so De Quincey sensed a darker side to Wordsworth. On one occasion he described him as having a 'natural resemblance to Mrs. Ratcliffe's [*sic*] Schedoni and other assassins roaming through prose and verse'.[53] The reference, though made lightly enough, suggests a serious comparison at some level with Schedoni, as described in the novel:

There was something in his physiognomy extremely singular, and that can not easily be defined. It bore the traces of many passions, which seemed to have fixed the features they no longer animated. An habitual gloom and severity prevailed over the deep lines of his countenance; and his eyes were so piercing that they seemed to penetrate, at a single glance, into the hearts of men, and to read their secret thoughts; few persons could support their scrutiny, or even endure to meet them twice.[54]

Ann Radcliffe's comment on the play of passions and severity in Schedoni's face certainly corresponds to some descriptions of Wordsworth: his eyes, according to Leigh Hunt, were 'like fires, half burning, half smouldering, with a sort of acrid fixture of regard'.[55] The Schedoni description also suggests the image of Cain, popular at the time, whose ravaged features bore witness to misapplied energies yet who still carried with him the dark memory of a lost paradise.[56] The 'mysterious character'[57] who haunted De Quincey's youthful imagination no doubt owed a good deal to such accounts of Gothic and biblical characters.

If De Quincey's glancing reference to Schedoni hints at an ambiguity in his attitudes to Wordsworth, it also suggests that the fascination which he continued to find in him was associated with a sense that his upright and kindly philosophy was backed by deeper subliminal powers. He would have found ample food for such speculation in *The Prelude*, where Wordsworth's belief that his growing love for humankind had been assisted both by the growth of a powerful organic sensibility and by the passionate experiences of his childhood was a major theme. It was, after all, a poem that he was one of the few persons permitted to read during Wordsworth's lifetime. That he could remember lines from it many years later[58] without, apparently, having a manuscript from which to refresh his memory is evidence of the profound impression it made. De Quincey also had unusual knowledge of Wordsworth's own interpretation of the experiences which he termed 'spots of time'. He describes how on one occasion when they had walked up to Dunmail Raise, hoping to intercept news of the Peninsular War, Wordsworth, who had been putting his ear, Indian-fashion, to the ground in the hope of hearing distant wheels, rose from the effort and simultaneously caught sight of a bright star. Seen at that moment of relaxation, the star according to Wordsworth 'penetrated my capacity of apprehension with a pathos and a sense of the infinite, that would not have arrested me under other circumstances'. 'Pathos and a sense of the infinite': these were twin factors of the typical Wordsworthian experience in which an expansion of spirit was closely associated with a response in the depths of the heart. Wordsworth went on to illustrate how the phenomenon was described in 'There Was a Boy', the lines about his boyhood experience of blowing 'mimic hootings' to the owls by Windermere where he noted how sometimes

> a gentle shock of mild surprise
> Has carried far into his heart the voice
> Of mountain-torrents; or the visible scene
> Would enter unawares into his mind.

De Quincey, quoting the passage from memory, foreshortens it: in his account it is simply the 'complex scenery' which is 'carried *far* into his heart'. Although this throws an interesting light on the processes of his own remembering, it does not greatly affect the point he goes on to make: 'This very expression, "far", by which space and its infinities are attributed to the human heart, and to its capacities of re-echoing the sublimities of nature, has always struck me as with a flash of sublime revelation.'[59] Whether conceived audibly or visually, the impressive point for him was that the word 'far' linked the sublime in nature to the pathos of the heart.

Wordsworth's ability to make such a collocation evidently impressed Coleridge equally. Of the same lines he remarked that if he had 'met them running wild in the deserts of Arabia he would have instantly screamed out "Wordsworth!"'[60] Yet the very unusualness of the collocation meant that there was no ready public mode for its expression. To combine an esoteric sense of the sublime with the private feelings of the heart might create no more than an area of embarrassment. Yet the compulsiveness of the idea, once engaged in, also made it difficult for the writer to extricate himself easily. Indeed, in a converse of the 'spot of time' revelation, he might find himself drawn into an involuted private vortex where the workings of the heart's affections were exacerbated into intensity by reinforcement from unconscious primary powers. Coleridge and Sara Hutchinson, Hazlitt and Sarah Walker, Keats and Fanny Brawne – most intensely and impossibly, De Quincey and Kate Wordsworth: in each case an intense cultivation of the heart's affections enfolds the writer into a nympholepsy from which he seems powerless to escape except by way of trauma or death. For Coleridge, expression of his love had to be confined to his notebooks; Hazlitt's account was first published anonymously, Keats's left in private letters. De Quincey's story was perhaps the most openly told, yet his impulses to reveal were still tangled with a strange reticence about his other Grasmere experiences, a reticence which may involve a genuine amnesia but also seems to reflect an uncertainty about their true significance. When he reprinted his reminiscences in book form, even the seminal account of Wordsworth and the star was removed.

After nearly two centuries it is hard to grasp the traumatic power of such experiences, since inability to consider seriously the idea of the heart as a centre of emotional life blocks apprehension of the complex as a whole. At the time, however, the effect was to leave the writer in a labyrinth from which it was difficult to escape. Marriage might provide a solution, as it did for Wordsworth. De Quincey found a similar mediating affection in a wife whose benignity matched Mary Wordsworth's, yet in his case the resolution was less complete. He was disappointed at Wordsworth's failure to extend the insights of *The Prelude* into his later poetry (or, as we have seen, into his dealings with other people), yet remained fascinated by the balance of forces which his more profound poetry had earlier held in tension.

Wordsworth's final position enshrined wisdom of a different kind from De Quincey's. Unwilling to stimulate or revive his visionary power by resort to drugs of any kind, he had opted instead for a secure domestic happiness and a mediating role in his society, even if this involved a turning away from his more directly passionate powers. One reason, no doubt, was his fear of the betrayals which those passions could bring about, another the perception that his visionary powers had always been best brought into play, as at Dunmail Raise, through an *intermission* of energy or attention. This made him unwilling to compromise with less strenuous methods of invocation. De Quincey eventually reached a similar position, but only many years later. It was not until his third opium crisis in 1844, in fact, that he discovered a counterbalance to opium and a means of successful withdrawal by way of almost preternatural bouts of energy. Then he actually set himself an exercise range of 44 yards in a circuit; treading it constantly, he was able in ninety days to cover 1,000 miles.[61]

Even so, De Quincey could not achieve a comprehensive relationship between energy and vision. As Coleridge may have done at times, he believed that vision might be experienced directly, given the right means or stimulus. Yet he evidently remained fascinated by Wordsworth's recordings of such experiences when they combined the resources of energy and pathos – supervening most characteristically in moments of transition between energy and peace. The most directly communicable of these, moreover, seemed to take place at night, rather as if the nearest approach to total pathos or sublimity was a kind of negative experience – a dark pathos, a dark sublime. We may think of his night-time meeting with the discharged soldier, when the mildness of the man's utterance helped enforce a sense of human interdependence, or the revelation on Snowdon, when his sudden awareness of the mild light of the moon, accompanied by sounds of hollow roaring, counterpointed the simple light by a suggestion of infinite energies.[62] These emblems of a dark profundity were, on one interpretation, negative images: as in the case of the moon, which at once revealed and hid the sun's power, they suggested the existence of a harmonious vision beyond, linking all human beings.

The sense of a possible hidden sublime, unavailable to reason but answering to the human sense of grandeur and the numinous, continued to haunt De Quincey – the more so, one suspects, because it provided a possible answer to the emotional lack in contemporary religious thinking. Hillis Miller has claimed him as his first great example of a man confronting the disappearance of God in the nineteenth century, arguing that the crucial event in De Quincey's development was the early loss of his sister and, with her, the one positive and sustaining relationship with another human being that he had known: this, which had been the one spiritual value to be put in the place of a disappeared God, could henceforth be recovered only in memory.[63] On the reading developed in the present discussion, the case was more complex. The Christian God had not exactly disappeared from De Quincey's world; it would seem more accurate to suggest that the divine presence was for him real but ambiguous – and mirrored with strange precision by the behaviour of his own devout mother. In the name of that Christian God she had called for his spirit to refine itself in holiness while insisting that her demand was being made in the name of love, a love which in her remained inaccessible.

Like several other early Romantic writers, therefore, De Quincey's attitude was governed not by a persuasion that God had vanished but by uncertainty about the nature of a God who *could* so successfully hide himself. As with his mother, he had the sense of a love which was implicit yet could not declare itself directly. His expansive experiences under opium might be said in this sense to have had an obliqueness similar to that of the 'lavender-water and milk of roses' of his childhood. The effects of his bewilderment stand out prominently in his mind and writing. There is, on the one hand, an element of neurotic anxiety; on the other, the sense of life as being a process in which mystery underlies everything. 'What is life?' asks the narrator in 'The Household Wreck', and then replies to his own question:

Darkness and formless vacancy for a beginning, or something beyond all beginning; then next a dim lotos of human consciousness, finding itself afloat upon the bosom of waters without a shore; then a few sunny smiles and many tears; a little love and infinite strife; whisperings from paradise and fierce mockeries from the anarchy of chaos; dust and ashes, and once more darkness circling round, as if from the beginning, and in this way rounding or making an island of our fantastic existence.[64]

The view is tailored to the pessimism of the tale that is about to unfold, but the intellectual precision of the imagery suggests that De Quincey found such a view persuasive – at least at one extreme of his moods. On the alternative view, the 'lotos of human consciousness' would prove to be a manifestation of the one life, the love and smiles by which it was from time to time blessed being direct manifestations of the true underlying order, while the 'tears' and 'strife' were no more than dark interpreters of that truth. De Quincey was fairly caught between these conflicting versions of the world, his neurotic pursuit of facts being coupled with the sense of being involved in an overall maze, which required an utmost subtlety of mind for its negotiation.

All in all, the surprise is not that De Quincey said so much about labyrinths but that he did not devote a separate study to the subject. The experience was perhaps so innate a feature of his own career that it was difficult for him to contemplate it in detachment. We may compare his image of taking the 'wrong turning' in the Bath maze, 'pathetically shadowing out the fatal irretrievability of errors in early life',[65] with a sentence or two in the revised *Confessions*.

Oh heavens! that it should be possible for a child not seventeen years old, by a momentary blindness, by listening to a false, false whisper from his own bewildered heart, by one erring step, by a motion this way or that, to change the currents of his destiny, to poison the fountains of his peace, and in the twinkling of an eye to lay the foundations of a life-long repentance![66]

The passage refers not to his first taking of opium but to his escape from Manchester Grammar School. At the same time it was to this escapade that he dated the frame of mind in which he had allowed himself to fall into the addiction; his whole career during those years had, he felt, been of a piece. The excerpt is itself curiously labyrinthine, moreover. The moral implication of the surface text is clear and seems to be confirmed by certain literary echoes. The 'false, false whisper' from the 'bewildered heart' reminds us of the 'wicked whisper' that made the Ancient Mariner's heart as dry as dust, while the 'motion this way or that' suggests Wordsworth's *Borderers*, where such action is said to leave a feeling of betrayal. Yet these allusions need only to be examined further to raise possible counter-indications. For the Ancient Mariner the 'wicked whisper' was later to be matched by the 'spring of love' that reawakened the power of the heart. De Quincey's further references to the 'currents of his destiny' and the 'fountains of his peace' suggest that he may be recalling at another level the use of river and spring imagery in Wordsworth and Coleridge to describe the hidden, positive state of man.

The subsequent period of his life would, indeed, include a chain of episodes about which his feelings would remain profoundly ambivalent. He might deplore his decision to run away from Manchester, yet the subsequent experiences had proved crucially important. The friendship with Ann of Oxford Street had provided an introduction to his lifelong awareness of the 'pariah worlds' of humanity, worlds that furnished their inhabitants with knowledge of a kind not available in ordinary life. De Quincey's feelings about opium were similar, as when he seems to switch from self-blame to self-congratulation. Indignation with Coleridge for suggesting that he took up opium as a voluptuary and insistence that his original resort to it was, like Coleridge's, for the relief of severe pain is followed, in almost the same breath, by the statement that if he had known of the drug's properties to tranquillize irritations of the nervous system, to stimulate the capacities of enjoyment and to sustain unusually extended exertion he would have entered on his career 'in the character of one seeking extra power and enjoyment'.[67]

The contradictions begin to make sense, however, when we see them as a function of his own divided consciousness. Those faculties by which De Quincey related himself to the world of society, objectively and morally, could not but urge him to look back in disgust at his addiction; yet his subliminal self remained attached and fascinated, aware of the activity to which it had been stirred by those effects. Such experiences were of the same ambiguity as those in the labyrinth: nightmarish or golden by turns, bewildering yet opening out a place of security at the heart of the maze. So for the rest of his life he would remain fascinated by them, returning again and again by way of auto-biographical reminiscence.

A good example of the way in which he was pursued into later years by an inability either to comprehend or to abandon the feelings that had been aroused in him during those years is to be found in the essay 'On the Supposed Scriptural Expression for Eternity'.[68] Although the greater part is portentously digressive, the essay has a point, and one particularly interesting in terms of words already used above. De Quincey argues that when the Bible speaks of 'eternal punishment' the word used is 'aeonic', which means not an infinite length of time, but a duration appropriate to the entity in question. Thus the aeon of an individual man would be something on the order of threescore years and ten; that of the Tellurian race, probably millions of years. The aeon of evil, it follows, is not meant to be compared with that of good, which is necessarily eternal; the duration of 'eternal' punishment, therefore, will not be of the same order but corresponds simply to the proper nature of evil.

The full point of De Quincey's interest in the matter, however, emerges only when the essay is placed alongside his references to the figure of Memnon. Writing of the wind which he heard after his sister's death and had often heard on hot days, he describes it as 'uttering the same hollow, solemn, Memnonian, but saintly swell: it is in this world the one great audible symbol of eternity'.[69] In a note explaining the word Memnonian by the story of the Egyptian statue, which suppos-edly gave out a musical note when touched by the first ray of the rising sun at dawn, he refers also to the statue of Memnon in the British Museum as 'that sublime head which wears upon its lips a smile co-extensive with all time and space, an Aeonian smile of gracious love and Panlike mystery, the most diffusive and pathetically divine that the hand of man has created'.[70] This description should be read in con-junction with his other account of the same statue in his 'System of the Heavens'. When he first saw it about 1812, he says, it struck him as the 'sublimest sight' he had ever seen. It was to be regarded not as a human but a symbolic head, symbolizing:

1. The peace which passeth all understanding. 2. The eternity which baffles and confounds all faculty of computation; the eternity which *had* been, the eternity which *was* to be. 3. The diffuse love, not such as rises and falls upon waves of life and mortality, not such as sinks and swells by undulations of time, but a procession – an emanation from some mystery of endless dawn.[71]

This passage brings out the fuller implications of De Quincey's conception of the aeonic; it was a quality which he had presumably found shadowed forth in his best experiences under the influence of opium but which he believed to have a further, metaphysical authenticity.

The word 'aeon' which so attracted De Quincey corresponds, of course, to the one that was found appropriate above to describe some aspects of Wordsworth's visionary experiences.[72] In post-Renaissance society actions that could be thought of as perfectly suited to their occasion, in the mode of *kairos*, became more difficult to achieve. Hamlet is here a prophetic figure, all the more so since one of the most undeniable of such fulfilling acts might, paradoxically, be an efficient murder, a point recognised perhaps within the irony of De Quincey's own essay 'On Murder Considered as One of the Fine Arts'. De Quincey was also aware that the experience of *aion* might in certain circumstances involve betrayal of a potential *kairos*. The key text here is the culminating episode of *The English Mail-Coach*. The sense of disjunction which Wordsworth felt after the death of his brother John – the sense that cultivation of aeonic experience might be dangerous to one's humanity, leaving one 'housed in a dream, at distance from the Kind'[73] – was enacted equally powerfully for De Quincey when his release from the oppressions of organized time and space, which had been assisted by a customary dose of laudanum, was broken in upon by an immediate demand that found him powerless to prevent the mail-coach in which he was travelling from colliding with a light gig, containing a man and a woman, which lay in its path. What kind of trust could, after all, be placed in an aeonic state which, for all its seductive sense of realisation, had so little to do with the vicissitudes that can beset simple humanity?

This sensed moral ambiguity at the core of things has many ramifications. The figures of the Whispering Gallery and the echoing hall[74] embody, respectively, his nightmares of being in a room beset by hostile whispers or in a large chamber toward which hostile footsteps are approaching, experiences which find one apotheosis in the essay 'On the knocking at the gate in Macbeth'.[75] Yet that is simply the obverse of his delight in being safe in the cell at the heart of a labyrinth.[76] And he never lost his hope that at the heart of that cell was an Ariadne thread that might connect him with the meaning of the universe at large. We are reminded again of his childhood love for the story of Aladdin in the *Arabian Nights*, where the magician who searches for a child with the power to find the enchanted lamp in its underground cell hears from 6,000 miles away the steps of the child Aladdin and recognizes in them 'an alphabet of new and infinite symbols' or 'secret hieroglyphics uttered by the flying footsteps'.[77] Even in the midst of his deepest miseries De Quincey believed that such experiences could serve as talismans for the discovery of important truths. Of the power of eidetic vision in some children he wrote: 'There is in the dark places of the human spirit – in grief, in fear, in vindictive wrath – a power of self-projection not unlike to this ... There are creative agencies in every part of human nature, of which the thousandth part could never be revealed in one life.'[78]

If we want to see the forms under which such agencies might be imaged, on the other hand, we may turn to a passage such as that where he refers to Wordsworth's description of birds wheeling in the air[79] and continues: 'So also, and with such life of variation, do the primary convulsions of nature – such, perhaps, as only primary formations in the human system can experience – come round again and again by reverberating shocks.'[80] The Coleridgean sense of a 'primary' link between the essence of nature and the essence of man, set forward so guardedly in these words, is for him by its very nature almost impossible to communicate in prose or in a system of philosophy. If there is any such possibility, it is to be sought in images and energies which he tries to elicit through the subjects and powers of his own description. So in a passage about his friends the Lloyds he describes the chanting sound of the river Brathay, which he had often listened to with Lloyd, commenting that he has sometimes heard in it the implied message 'Love nothing, love nobody, for thereby comes a killing curse in the rear';[81] but goes on to say that he has sometimes also heard, in the very early morning

> in that same chanting of the little mountain river a more solemn if a less agitated admonition – a requiem over departed happiness, and a protestation against the thought that so many excellent creatures, but a little lower than the angels, whom I have seen only to love in this life – so many of the good, the brave, the beautiful, the wise – can have appeared for no higher purpose or prospect than simply to point a moral, to cause a little joy and many tears, a few perishing moons of happiness and years of vain regret![82]

There was then, perhaps, at the heart of the stream's noise, a more hopeful hint of correspondence between the destiny of man and the grandeur of his endowments.

Faced with this possibility, De Quincey found it once again natural to invoke Wordsworth, who had approached the question from a different point of view. In the Convention of Cintra pamphlet, which De Quincey saw through the press for him, Wordsworth lamented that the true tragedy of man lay not in the failure of the mind of man but in the fact that 'the course and demands of action and of life so rarely correspond with the dignity and intensity of human desires'.[83] Yet in his own celebration of a 'little mountain river', the sonnets dedicated to the River Duddon, he had faced the same query that De Quincey raised concerning 'the good, the brave, the beautiful, the wise' in words which De Quincey seems in fact to be echoing. Wordsworth's 'Afterthought' concludes:

> While we, the brave, the mighty, and the wise,
> We Men, who in our morn of youth defied
> The elements, must vanish; – be it so!
> Enough, if something from our hands have power
> To live, and act, and serve the future hour;
> And if, as toward the silent tomb we go,
> Through love, through hope, and faith's transcendent dower,
> We feel that we are greater than we know.

His solution takes up the tentative sense of a correspondence between the potentialities of mankind and some hidden principle in nature into a more practical sense that in the service of the future, at least, there is scope for the exercise of love, hope, and faith. The conclusion to *The Prelude* makes clearer the indispensability of that tentative faith for Wordsworth's backing of any practical programme. In the same way, De Quincey, describing what he means by the 'literature of power', characterizes it as that 'exercise and expansion to your own latent capacity of sympathy with the infinite, where every pulse and each separate influx is a step upwards, a step ascending as upon a Jacob's ladder from earth to mysterious altitudes above the earth'.[84]

About the ultimate metaphysical status of such ideas there must inevitably be dispute. It was Wordsworth's implicit contention that the final truth about them could not in this life be known: it was the role of human beings to live under the perpetual shadow of such possibilities, not to imagine that they would ever be physically enacted.

For Wordsworth it was enough if men could feel that they were 'greater than they knew'. De Quincey, on the other hand, believed that final revelations might sometimes take place, for example, in dreams. There are at least two climaxes in his works where such a transmutation is seen in action. The first is in 'The Affliction of Childhood', where the dream echoes ten years later take up all the elements of his former vision of endless suffering and transpose them into a vision of hope:

> And now all was bound up into unity; the first state and the last were melted into each other as in some sunny, glorifying haze. For high in heaven hovered a gleaming host of faces, veiled with wings, around the pillows of the dying children. And such beings sympathise equally with sorrow that grovels, and with sorrow that soars. Such beings pity alike the children that are languishing in death, and the children that live only to languish in tears.[85]

The other is in the 'Dream-Fugue' appended to *The English Mail-Coach*. As in that dream the carriage bringing the news of victory bears down inevitably on a fairy chariot bearing a baby, the dynamics of the scene are suddenly reversed: everything that had been in motion is frozen, while the dying trumpeter sculptured on a stone comes to life and blows three times. At the third blast all the forms which had been in their turn frozen to a bas-relief are released again, but this time into a beneficent scene from which the baby has disappeared: 'The seals were taken off all pulses; life, and the frenzy of life, tore into their channels again; again the choir burst forth in sunny grandeur, as from the muffling of storms and darkness; again the thunderings of our horses carried temptation into the graves.'[86] Sublimity turns to pathos: the baby, now grown to a woman, is elevated high above the scene, gesturing in terror and despair, while at her side her better angel pleads for her deliverance and wins. This vision is then itself cast back into a final all-inclusive sublimity, as the deliverance which he had witnessed for the lady in the gig is wrought up, again and again, into something more like cosmic event:

> A thousand times in the worlds of sleep have [I] seen thee followed by God's angel through storms, through desert seas, through the darkness of quicksands, through dreams and the dreadful revelations that are in dreams; only that at the last, with one sling of His victorious arm, He might snatch thee back from ruin, and might emblazon in thy deliverance the endless resurrections of His love![87]

In such experiences the dialectic between stasis and frenzy within which the subliminal self normally works in the fullest intensity of its states, is transposed into visionary terms, a process where *kairos* is no longer impermanent, having become the truly *aionic*.

This indicates the relevance of De Quincey's thinking to the major theme of this study. Although he was as moved as Keats by Wordsworth's poetry of the human heart he did not follow him to the extent of seeking in that heart an ultimate key to the sense of Being; he was even more aware of the ambiguities involved. For him in the end such a sense, and of its relationship to consciousness, was, like Wordsworth's at crucial points of *The Prelude*, founded rather in a deep sense of mystery, taking in the process a strong colouring from Coleridge's psychological speculations and his interest in subliminal experiences.

It was appropriate, therefore, that opium dreams, with their extremes of pleasure and terror, their ability to expand and contract the normal perceptions of time and space, seemed to provide one touchstone for him by which to question conventional orderings; other examples were provided by experiences of delirium in high fever and by an extraordinary vision at the moment of apparent death which had been reported to him in matter-of-fact fashion by the lady who had experienced it. He refers to all three in a single brief formula. Describing how griefs and joys inscribe themselves successively on the brain 'like the annual leaves of aboriginal forests, or the undissolving snows on the Himalaya, or light falling upon light', he goes on: 'But by the hour of death, but by fever, but by the searchings of opium, all these can revive in strength.'[88]

Whether or not one treats the visionary coherence of what was experienced on such occasions as marking access to a truer reality than that apprehended by normal sense-experience or simply as unusually vivid examples of fantasy is, of course, a matter for debate. There is a strange appositeness in the report of De Quincey's own death, nevertheless, which for him was apparently the scene of another such revelation, involving first his mother and then his sister:

> Twice only was the heavy breathing interrupted by words. He had for hours ceased to recognise any of us, but we heard him murmur, though quite distinctly, 'My dear, dear mother. Then I was greatly mistaken'. Then as the waves of death rolled faster and faster over him, suddenly out of the abyss we saw him throw up his arms, which to the last retained their strength, and say distinctly, and as if in great surprise, 'Sister! sister! sister!'[89]

That he should have felt himself reunited with his sister is appropriate enough, but the account also suggests that this perception was preceded – perhaps made possible – by a perception to the heart of his mother's treatment of him, so that he understood, as he had never done before, how it could have been the dark manifestation of a love which had, in spite of everything, been warm and immediate. If so, the deepest of the ambiguities that had haunted him throughout his life was resolved for him in the moment of death, as the dark sublime of his Being opened once again, to reveal a visionary core.

6
Tennyson, the Cambridge Apostles and 'Reality'

Metaphorical invocation of the sea as a symbol of Being certainly did not end with Wordsworth's 'Listen! The mighty Being is awake...' It would continue to appear in nineteenth-century literature when writing there approached ultimate issues of human existence. From Matthew Arnold, enisled in his own secure identity yet sensing between himself and others an 'unplumbed, salt, estranging sea',[1] to Tennyson, whose Ulysses heard the deep 'moan round with many voices', but led his comrades forth manfully, not knowing his future fate, it was a proving image, testing human pretensions and themes. Even those who turned to historical religion for security in a time of trouble saw the Church, in terms of Old Testament typology, as the ark which would convey them through the waves of intellectual questioning that were beginning to beat higher and higher in their civilisation. Was the sea truly a symbol of faith, as Arnold assumed,[2] or rather, in Wordsworth's terms, a metaphor of Being itself, with all its vicissitudes?

Coleridge, a Victorian doubter before the event, had also noted the appropriateness of the image. His own metaphorical use has already been quoted:

> Doubts rushed in; broke upon me *'from the fountains of the great deep'*, and fell *'from the windows of heaven'*. The fontal truths of natural religion and the books of Revelation alike contributed to the flood; and it was long ere my ark touched on an Ararat, and rested.[3]

For the rest of his life he would seek to find an island in the deep which might, as the waters of doubting receded, reveal itself, after all, to be a visionary mountain-top from which the true nature of the universe could be seen. His general account of his condition when he began to perceive how far the truths of science and the truths of revelation might be at odds with one another bears an obvious resemblance to many records by Victorian thinkers of the state in which they found themselves in the middle of the following century. The general problem was present throughout the intervening years, however. The argument to be advanced here is that Coleridge's long struggle to 'reconcile personality with infinity', far from being carried out in isolation, was known to some of his successors, and had an important effect on the group which came to be known as the Cambridge Apostles. In this way, by an oblique route, it reached the poetry of Tennyson.

To establish a connection between Coleridge the thinker and Tennyson the poet might at first sight seem to be an unrewarding enterprise, given Tennyson's own reticence on the subject. In his biography, Hallam Tennyson mentions Coleridge only as someone 'for whose prose my father never much cared, but to whose poetry, especially *Kubla Khan*, *The Ancient Mariner* and *Christabel*, he was devoted'.[4] And if one looks through the other records one fares little better. William Allingham, for example, records a brief conversation:

> W.A.   Did you ever meet Coleridge?
> T.   No, I was asked to visit him, but I wouldn't.
> W A.   Coleridge was a 'noticeable man, with large grey
>   eyes'.
> T.   Oh yes.[5]

This is hardly promising, but Tennyson did have a grievance against Coleridge, whose remark that he had 'begun to write verses without very well understanding what metre is' was sometimes quoted to tease him.[6] The poems named by his son must after all have been some of the most important influences on him as a poet. There is also a further possibility: that Tennyson did not like talking about Coleridge because the name brought back too vividly memories of conversations with Arthur Hallam, reviving the agonizing ambiguities that had surrounded his death.

Tennyson's silence about Coleridge would be less surprising were it not for the fact that he was a member of the society known as the Cambridge Apostles and that, at the time when he joined, Coleridge's was a name to be conjured with. We now know more about the Apostles, thanks to several important studies.[7*] A point which all make clear is that in the early years, when it evolved from its foundation as the Cambridge Conversazione Club, it was not a particularly secret society, though the members no doubt exercised a certain reserve. Even after the rule of secrecy began to be imposed, it was not always fully observed. When Roger Fry was admitted in 1887, he lost little time in breaking it. In one of his letters he stated (incorrectly as it happens): 'It was started by Tennyson and Hallam I think about 1820, and has always considered itself very select.'[8] A short while later he wrote, 'Tennyson, I think I told you, is still a member and there are references to the society in *In Memoriam* which none but the duly initiated can fully understand.'

A great deal of documentation about individual Apostles survives, particularly if they became sufficiently famous to merit substantial biographies. Many, too, referred retrospectively to the society's activities in letters and diaries. Fry's account, however, is one of the few that suggests the existence of an esoteric element. For the most part those who wrote about it in the nineteenth century were intent on describing its spirit and what that had meant to them.

Of the three main accounts, each comes from a different phase and singles out a different quality as the most characteristic; a certain consistency of spirit over the years emerges, nonetheless. The most succinct is in a marginal note by Jack Kemble, a contemporary of Tennyson and Hallam, and runs, 'No society ever existed in which more freedom of thought was found, consistent with the most perfect affection between the members; or in which a more complete toleration of the most opposite opinion prevailed.'[9] A later account by Sir Arthur Helps, who had been elected in 1833, dwelt on the personal qualities required of an Apostle:

> A man to succeed with us must be a real man, and not a 'sham', as Carlyle would say.... He was not to talk the talk of any clique; he was not to believe too much in any of his adventitious advantages; neither was he to disbelieve in them – for instance, to affect to be a radical because he was a lord. I confess I have no one word which will convey all that I mean; but I may tell you that, above all things, he was to be open-minded. When we voted for a man, we generally summed up by saying, 'He has an apostolic spirit in him,' and by that we really meant a great deal.[10]

The longest account was given by Henry Sidgwick, who also dwelt on their open-mindedness:

I can only describe it as the spirit of the pursuit of truth with absolute devotion and unreserve by a group of intimate friends, who were perfectly frank with each other, and indulged in any amount of humorous sarcasm and playful banter, and yet each respects the other, and when he discourses tries to learn from him and see what he sees. Absolute candour was the only duty that the tradition of the society enforced. No consistency was demanded with opinions previously held – truth as we saw it then and there was what we had to embrace and maintain, and there were no propositions so well established that an Apostle had not the right to deny or question, if he did so sincerely and not from mere love of paradox. The gravest subjects were continually debated, but gravity of treatment, as I have said, was not imposed, though sincerity was. In fact, it was rather a point of the apostolic mind to understand how much suggestion and instruction might be derived from what is in form a jest – even in dealing with the gravest matters.[11]

Sidgwick belonged, of course, to a later, mid-Victorian, generation and his account shows the marks. While continuing the points established by Kemble and Helps, it sharpens them. Kemble's 'freedom of thought' becomes Sidgwick's 'pursuit of truth with absolute devotion and unreserve', his 'perfect affection' Sidgwick's 'group of intimate friends, who indulged in any amount of humorous sarcasm and playful banter' and Helps's demand that an apostle be not a sham, Sidgwick's insistence that he argue 'sincerely and not from love of paradox'. Sidgwick's account makes his generation sound at one and the same time more earnest and more bantering than their predecessors. It opens the way to the spirit of Bloomsbury, where the banter would be still more evident while the earnestness dropped away in favour of a more generally valued 'seriousness'. Nevertheless it displays a marked agreement with the earlier spirit as described by Kemble and Helps, a consistency which survives in accounts much later than Sidgwick's.

While the accounts quoted give a clear account of the spirit in which meetings of the Apostles were conducted and throw light on cross-currents of earnestness and humour that can be traced in Tennyson himself, they do not explain Fry's allusion to 'references to the society in *In Memoriam* which none but the duly initiated can fully understand'. Contemporary readers, particularly those fresh from reading about activities of the Apostles in the 1930s, might well suppose that a cult of homosexual love was being referred to. This is doubtful, however. It is unlikely to have been in the mind of Fry himself, who was writing to his mother when he made the statement; in any case, the nineteenth-century Apostles were a very different group from their successors in the early twentieth century, when Lytton Strachey became a dominant presence. This is not to suggest that nothing of the kind ever went on; if so, it would presumably have been kept very quiet: there is no indication that it played any part in the acknowledged activities of the Society as such.

Extravagant language was, on the other hand, common among young men at the time, a spirit of high sentiment being dominant.[12*] Henry Hallam, as is well known, was disturbed about the possible effects on his son's reputation if further constructions were placed upon such affectionate statements, and altered some of his manuscripts before publication.[13] He also sent out a coded message on the subject in his discussion of Shakespeare's sonnets in his *Introduction to the Literature of Europe*, whereupon Tennyson commented, 'Henry Hallam made a great mistake about them; they are noble.'[14]

If clues survive concerning Fry's mysterious reference to the duly initiated, they should be looked for not in the written accounts, but in the strange jargon which the Apostles adopted when talking about themselves and their activities. Some are obvious enough: they would refer to themselves as the Brethren, or the Elect, or the 'wise and good', while those who did not share their views were known as 'unapostolic', or, if more blatantly philistine, as 'Stumpfs'. The trunk in which the records of the Society were kept was known as the 'Ark'.[15*] There was also a whimsical, self-deprecating element in their development of such jargon: the anchovies on toast which formed their traditional fare were known as 'whales', while when a member gave one of the regular Saturday night papers which were the staple of their discussions, he was said to be 'called to the hearthrug'.[16] Such coinages witness to their desire not to take themselves too solemnly.

Other usages, however, suggest a further possible depth. Those who had shown that they could be particularly profound in discussion were called 'illumers', at least in the early days.[17*] Those who were undergoing the process of vetting and discussion before being deemed worthy to become a member were known as 'embryos', and induction into the society was known as 'birth', while when the time came for one of the brothers to resign from formal membership in order to make way for new ones to be elected he was said to have 'taken wings' and to have become an 'angel'. In a more unusual formulation the Society and its doings were known as 'Reality' or 'Noumena', while everything else in the world was referred to as 'Phenomena'.[18] Such formulations have an obvious Kantian flavour; in the strangest of all the terms, one who had been admitted as a member of the Society was said to have attained 'the category of Being'.[19]

The metaphor of taking wings can be associated loosely with Coleridge, who was attracted by the fact that, in Greek, 'psyche' meant both soul and butterfly and used the idea of progression from the larva to describe the spiritual development of individuals.[20] But although the same idea is inherent in Apostolic discourse the precise image is different. It is the last word, 'Being', that suggests a Coleridgean origin. The only other English writer of the time (apart from Wordsworth) who seems to have used the word with anything approaching the same emphasis was Shelley; for him, however, it primarily expresses the wholeness of personality, the full sincere identity – which is not the same.

Although Coleridge's views came much closer to orthodox Christianity in his later years, we have already seen signs that he never quite abandoned his early speculations, however cautious he may have become in expressing them publicly. He was more likely to speak freely, if at all, in private notes and conversations, confining himself in his published works to hints, particularly in footnotes and asides. For this reason, if someone is said to have been influenced by the later Coleridge in his later years, it is pertinent to ask which 'Coleridge' he or she was responding to: whether his published works, private writings or the conversation of the man himself.

In appraising the impact of Coleridge upon the Cambridge Apostles these questions are particularly crucial, since some had privileged access to the man himself. Detailed chronology is also important, since in the early, formative period their major preoccupations could alter sharply from one three-year undergraduate generation to another. The period during which they began to take on their distinctive character was in the mid-1820s, when the proceedings were dominated by Frederick Denison Maurice, joined shortly afterwards by John Sterling. Maurice in particular achieved a lasting respect: in 1834 he was toasted by the London Apostles as the true 'author' of the club.[21] At the time when Maurice arrived in Cambridge, in 1823, Coleridge's reputation as a prose-writer was confined mainly to *The Friend,* a work in which he urged the need for a return to fine principles in public affairs and the recovery of a more enlightened view of the human mind. In the 1820s he turned increasingly to religious questions. When his influential *Aids to Reflection* was published in 1825, Maurice had already been up at

Cambridge for two years. Since Maurice claimed that before he went to Cambridge he had already read and received much influence from Coleridge, he must have been thinking of *The Friend*, and perhaps the *Lay Sermons*, which emphasized the need to distinguish the Reason from the Understanding, assigning a higher and more absolute status to the Reason as an organ for apprehending truth intuitively. Doctrines of this kind were felt to be particularly timely in an age when respect for the doctrines of utilitarianism seemed to some to be undermining the nobility of human nature.

Neither Maurice nor Sterling met Coleridge during their undergraduate days, and Maurice never did. When Sterling went down, on the other hand, he met Coleridge shortly afterwards and wrote of him with some familiarity in his contributions to the *Athenaeum*. By this time he had attended some of the evening gatherings which were held at the Gillmans. Carlyle, describing them in his life of Sterling, quotes Sterling's own account as follows: 'Our interview lasted for three hours, during which he talked for two hours and three quarters.'[22] Carlyle then goes on to give his own hostile account of Coleridge's conversation and the frustration of being forced to listen for so long. He does not, however, quote the rest of Sterling's account, which runs: 'It would have been delightful to listen as attentively, and certainly easy for him to speak just as well for the next forty-eight hours.'[23]*

Sterling's concerns at this time were primarily social, and his records of Coleridge's conversation dwell on that aspect: he quotes, for example. Coleridge's remark, 'The division of labour has proceeded so far even in literature, that people do not think for themselves; their review thinks for them.' Sterling and Maurice alike were turning increasingly to such questions, in the context of which the figure of Coleridge seemed portentous. Soon the *London Magazine* was apparently complaining that the *Athenaeum* was in the hands of 'dreaming, half-platonic half Jacob Behmenite mystics';[24] Trench, a fellow Apostle, wrote sympathetically, meanwhile, of their 'Platonico-Wordsworthian-Coleridgean-anti-Utilitarian principles'.[25] Contributing to the number for 1828, Sterling wrote the first of a series of essays purporting to be by a visiting Swede, this one being devoted to his impressions of London. Viewing the city from the top of St Paul's, he contemplates its multiplicity, the thousands who are 'to moral purposes, dead and decaying', the few hundred who are prompted to a 'higher aim of being':

But, above all, there may be even now moving among those undistinguished swarms below me, or dwelling upon that dim eminence which rises in the distance, some great and circular mind, accomplished in endowment, of all-embracing faculties, with a reason that pervades like light, and an imagination that embodies the essence of all truth in the forms of all beauty, – even such a one as C – , the brave, the charitable, the gentle, the pious, the mighty philosopher, the glorious poet.[26]

Like Sterling, Maurice saw Coleridge as a beneficent moral presence in a world that seemed increasingly in need of his guidance. His desire to link such a lofty view of humanity with solid and practical concerns intensified as he went on to become one of the initiators of Christian socialism.

Although Maurice and Sterling were to maintain strong associations with the Apostles, they had both left Cambridge in 1827. By the autumn of 1828, the point at which both Hallam and Tennyson arrived in Cambridge – to be elected to the Society during the following year – they may have been regarded as fatherly presences but were not present in the flesh to influence discussion.

The social concern they had shown was increasing, nevertheless – general enthusiasm for liberty being coupled with a growing awareness of the problems created by new economic and industrial conditions. For young men, such concerns could still be linked with enthusiasm for the poetry that had recently been written by the second generation of Romantics. A group based primarily on Trinity College could hardly fail to be aware of the effect created in Europe by Byron's support for the cause of liberation, while members such as Hallam, who came up from Eton, would be similarly conscious of Shelley's doctrines. When he arrived in Cambridge, Hallam was still in fact suffering as a result of his love for Anna Wintour, which had a strong Shelleyan element. In his first year he was active in promoting a published version of *Adonais* and his early poems betray the influence everywhere. During the summer immediately preceding his arrival in Cambridge, however, it was Coleridge he was reading. Although his first reaction was to describe his work as 'strong meat' and to wonder whether it did not require a stronger stomach than his own, he was soon exploring it more fully,[27] stimulated no doubt by his new ambience, which was receptive to recent American influences. 'The ascendant politics are Utilitarian,' he wrote to Gladstone in November, 'seasoned with a plentiful sprinkling of heterogeneous Metaphysics. Indeed the latter study is so much the rage, that scarce anyone here above the herd does not dabble in Transcendentalism, and such like.'[28] By December, he was asking his friend John Frere, a nephew of John Hookham Frere, Coleridge's friend, whether he could get from Coleridge clear definitions of 'Reason, Understanding, Imagination, as he understands the words'.[29] In the same letter he reported that his father had been attacking the ideas of Coleridge and Shelley, lamenting that while they were read, John Locke and Francis Bacon would not be. He himself was determined to work out his own metaphysical creed for himself, and could not share his father's condemnation of Coleridge (having recently been trying to buy *The Friend*).

It was R.J. Tennant, apparently, followed by Hallam and Monckton Milnes, who introduced the Society to the side of Coleridge's thoughts that bordered on and sometimes seemed to pass over into mysticism. Tennant himself is unfortunately one of the least documented of the Apostles.[30]* Hallam, however (who was actually proposed for membership by Tennant), described him in December 1829 as 'the calm earnest seeker after Truth – who sat for months at the feet of Coleridge, and impowered his own mind with some of those tones, from the world of mystery, the only real world, of which to these latter days Coleridge has been almost the only interpreter'.[31] Two or three years later, Blakesley, telling a friend that he had been seeing old friends in London, reported: 'Tennyson had his sister with him, to whom Tennant was doing the amiable in a very open way for a mystic. She is really a very fine looking person, although of a wild sort of countenance, something like what Alfred would be if he were a woman and washed.'[32] This casual reference to him as a 'mystic' provides further evidence of the way that Tennant was regarded by his friends. Hallam had written the previous year that he was keeping his authorship of the pamphlet on Professor Rossetti's Dante theories a secret, having 'no wish to earn the reputation of an Atheist or a Mystic'.[33]

It may have been through the good offices of Frere and his uncle or of Tennant, who had attended Christ's Hospital, Coleridge's school, and had been visiting him for two or three years past, that Hallam actually met Coleridge at this time. Monckton Milnes records that he and Hallam both went to call on him – to be received, he said, rather as they might have been by Goethe or Socrates, and to be told that as young men they ought to be going to America: 'I am known there,' said Coleridge. 'I am a poor poet in England, but I am a great philosopher in America.'[34]

Hallam had certainly met Coleridge, and probably more than once, by the spring of 1829, since it was then that he wrote a poem in competition for the Cambridge prize – which Tennyson in fact won – on the subject 'Timbuctoo'. In the course of it he pictured an ideal society and then continued with lines which he glossed in a footnote as follows:

These characters are of course purely ideal, and meant to show, by way of particular diagram, that right temperament of the intellect and the heart which I have assigned to this favored nation. I cannot, however, resist the pleasure of declaring, that in the composition of the lines 'Methought I saw,' &c., my thoughts dwelt almost involuntarily on those few conversations which it is my delight to have held with that 'good old man, most eloquent,' Samuel Coleridge.[35*]

The lines in question run:

Methought I saw a face whose every line
Wore the pale cast of Thought; a good old man,
Most eloquent, who spake of things divine.
Around him youths were gathered, who did scan
His countenance so grand and mild; and drank
The sweet, sad tones of Wisdom, which outran
The life-blood, coursing to the heart, and sank
Inward from thought to thought, till they abode
'Mid Being's dim foundations, rank by rank
With those transcendent truths, arrayed by God
In linked armor for untiring fight,
Whose victory is, where time hath never trod.[36]

We have no further direct record of Coleridge's doctrines as heard by Hallam and Milnes, but it is not unlikely that in the course of his exposition he referred to Heraclitus as the Greek philosopher who, with his dualism, had come closest to the truth, since we know from other sources that this was a favourite topic in his more esoteric moments.[37] When Monckton Milnes was set to write a Latin declamation in that same year, he chose for his theme (to the amusement of Julius Hare, his tutor) 'The Truth of the Essential Dualism of Heraclitus', commenting to his family, 'as this subject penetrates to the very foundations of Coleridgian philosophy it will give me some hard Fagging'.[38]

Hallam's mention of 'Being's dim foundations' suggests that he had seen further into Coleridge's larger purposes than had those who simply read his later published works. Coleridge's emphasis on the

importance of Being was, however, always available to attentive
readers. Maurice, in his 1842 dedication to *The Kingdom of Christ*, spoke
of his debt to him for having made him aware that 'a knowledge of
The Being is the object after which we are to strive'.[39] This version of
Being seems for Maurice to have been conceived in objective terms,
truly to be discovered in the Supreme Being, but to be considered primarily in the light of more practical concerns. A young man such as
Hallam, on the other hand, who had steeped himself in the poetry of
Shelley, where the word 'being' is a favourite one to describe human
personality, would be likely to respond to the Coleridgean hints that a
further depth was involved, and that there was in human nature, if
one looked devotedly, an inward being which actually corresponded to
that of the divine.

A particular virtue of this approach for some was that it could be
regarded as Christianizing the thoughts of Shelley, whose more general
idea of being was so extensive as to authorize an idea of the Supreme
Being which might claim superiority to the Christian version.
Coleridge's, by contrast, anchored the idea in the Christianity promulgated in St John's Gospel. The following of this line of thought had
indeed enabled him to return to the Church in which he had been
brought up.[40] In Carlyle's hostile and mordant phrasing, he had found
himself able to 'say and print to the Church of England, with its singular old rubrics and surplices at Allhallowtide, *Esto perpetua* [may it last
for ever]'.[41] For young men such as Hallam, on the other hand, whose
delight in the new romanticism was combined with a respect for the
faith of their fathers, Coleridge's thought pointed to a possible solution
for current dilemmas.

The supposition that a process of this kind took place in Hallam's
mind, grafting Coleridgean ideas of Being on Shelley's, seems necessary
to account for the shape of his thinking during the subsequent period;
it can also be supported by a number of his statements, including
some apparent echoes from Coleridge himself. At the same time, his
moods were volatile, alternating between depression and exaltation,
with some fears of insanity. By the autumn of 1829 his father was
deeply concerned, urging him to turn his mind from 'the high metaphysical speculations, and poetic enthusiasm that were sapping its very
foundations'.[42]

There are signs nevertheless that it was Coleridge's idea of Being
that Hallam continued to be particularly interested in. By the beginning of 1830 he had read his new book *On the Constitution of the
Church and State,* which contains the statement '... even the 'O 'ΩN,

the Supreme Being, if it were contemplated abstractly from the Absolute Will, whose essence it is to be causative of all Being, would sink into a Spinozistic Deity'. The following year, in *Theodicaea Novissima*, he wrote of Christ, 'He is God, not in that highest sense in which the Absolute, the 'O 'ΩN is God: but as the object of the Infinite Being's love.'[43] While the term 'O' ΩN for 'Being' or God comes from the Greek version of the Old Testament, it was rarely used in Hallam's time; the version 'the 'O 'ΩN', which with its double article is particularly Coleridgean, suggests that Hallam was still paying attention to what he had to say about the nature of Being.

Two further apparent echoes from Coleridge both, as it happens, resonate into Hallam's relationship with Tennyson. The first comes in *Aids to Reflection,* when Coleridge, passes into one of his occasional gnomic passages, suggesting that there is further esoteric wisdom that he could divulge if he had a mind to. After a long discussion of the problem of Redemption, Coleridge argues that the causative act is 'a spiritual and transcendent Mystery, "that passeth all understanding"' and that to define it by analogy with ordinary human acts of redemption is to fall into error. He continues:

I will merely hint, to my more *learned* readers, and to the professional Students of Theology, that the origin of this error is to be sought for in the discussions of the Greek Fathers, and (at a later period) of the Schoolmen, on the obscure and *abysmal* subject of the Divine *A-seity* and the distinction between the θηλημα and the βουλη, i.e. the absolute Will, as the universal Ground of *all* Being, and the Election and purpose of God in the personal Idea, as the Father. And this view would have allowed me to express (what I believe to be) the true import and scriptural idea of Redemption in terms much more nearly resembling those used ordinarily by the Calvinistic Divines, and with a conciliative *show of* coincidence.[44]

Discussing the same question in the *Theodicaea,* Hallam writes,

I believe that redemption is universal, in so far as it left no obstacle between Man and God, but man's own will: that indeed is in the power of God's election, with whom alone rest the abysmal secrets of personality, but as far as Christ is concerned, his death was for all ...[45]

Without going fully into the intricacies involved, we need simply to look at the word 'abysmal', used in a similar sense to Coleridge's 'the *abysmal* subject of the Divine *A-seity*' – where his italics suggest that he is at one and the same time being ironically self-deprecating and intimating profundity. It links with other statements of Coleridge about the abyss-like nature of God, which suggest that when we are most aware of the abyss within ourselves, we are in a state which may link us to that within which God is most likely to be found. This particular correspondence between Hallam's point and Coleridge's is all the more striking since, although the idea of God as containing an abyss within himself which is also source of the fountain of life can be found elsewhere in Christian theology,[46] it is hard to find a writer other than Coleridge who uses the word 'abysmal' in this way. Hallam's phrase 'the abysmal secrets of personality' was used in an adapted form by Tennyson a few months later in 'The Palace of Art', moreover, at the point where the soul, in the middle of her triumphing, is suddenly struck down. Tennyson continued,

> Lest she should fail and perish utterly,
> God, before whom ever lie bare
> The abysmal deeps of Personality,
> Plagued her with sore despair.[47]

The point here seems to follow Coleridge's: in the very act of sinking into the depths of despair, the soul was delivered into the abyss of her own personality – which, being linked to the abyss of the divine, made redemption possible.

Tennyson was deeply impressed by *Theodicaea Novissima*: it was he who put to Hallam's father the case for including it among Hallam's *Remains*.[48] It is also clear that the philosophy of love which was expounded in it corresponded closely to the idea of noble love which he was to expound in *In Memoriam*. That philosophy is also to be found in other essays by Hallam such as those on Dante, Tennyson's debt to which has been explored by others.[49] The point to be made here has to do not with the idealization of love, which is clear enough, but with the link between that idea of love and the idea of Being outlined above which, I have contended, comes primarily from Coleridge. In the *Theodicaea*, Hallam maintains that the passion of love is grounded on a conviction of similarity, 'as though we had suddenly found a bit of ourselves that had been dropt by mischance as we descended upon earth'.[50] This is Platonic and Shelleyan; but it also raises the question whether there may be other respects in which the Being of a person could be said to be related to the Being of the divine. Hallam seems to have left this issue behind him after his Cambridge days, but there are signs that during that earlier period it went deep, while still remaining subject to his Apostolic scepticism. In April 1830, for instance, when he met Emily Tennyson at Somersby for the first time, he wrote to Blakesley, 'I feel a new element of being within me – don't laugh ...' [51]

There is a further cluster of references which may throw light on the origin of a phrase that was to become famous. Writing about the veil of the Law as discussed by St Paul, Coleridge asks, 'What was the great point of which this Law, in its own name, offered no solution? the mystery, which it left behind the veil?'[52] The mystery, he suggests, was that of redemption. The Bible itself does not use the phrase 'behind the veil' but 'within the veil'. When Hallam met Emily Tennyson and felt 'a new element of being', the experience can be connected with his use of Coleridge's version of the Pauline phrase in a poem dated by his editor in December 1829:

> Art thou not She
> Who in my Sais-temple was a light
> Behind all veils of thought, and fantasy,
> A dim, yet beautiful Idea of one
> Perfect in womanhood, in Love alone,
> Making the earth golden in hope and joy?[53]

Hallam's editor persuasively traces the image of the Sais-temple to a story by Schiller, where the temple contains a veiled statue of Truth, which a young man is forbidden to lift. If that was Hallam's source, it would link almost inevitably with Shelley's 'Lift not the painted veil' and still more with the traditional figure of the veiled Isis. In his essay on Cicero he comments that his load of prepossessions was a disadvantage to him: they were 'as the veil of the temple of Sais, hiding impenetrably "that which was, and had been, and was to be"'[54] – a clear reference to Isis. The image which expressed most naturally his awakening love for Emily was, in other words, one that extended to the nature of Being itself. Hallam's sudden death just before he could marry Emily cast a shadow of grim irony over such imagery for those who survived him. In *Maud* Tennyson wrote, 'For the drift of the Maker is dark, an Isis hid by the veil ...';[55] and when he wrote in *In Memoriam* about the cruelty of Nature, with her apparent disregard for the transience of all life – whether individuals or types – and how she showed herself 'red in tooth and claw', his final question: 'What hope of answer, or redress? I Behind the veil, behind the veil'[56] carries an added plangency if it is seen to involve Hallam's own use of the veiled goddess for a Shelleyan harmony at the core of the creation corresponding to his own feelings of love. Yet there is also a suggestion that the Coleridgean echo would reinforce – that there might in the depths of divine mystery be a purpose that escapes the eye of questioning human beings.

That this delicately poised ambiguity should then have been transposed into one of the easiest of Victorian platitudes is one of the sadder ironies of Tennyson's career. The process may have begun with Edward FitzGerald's use of the phrase in *Omar Khayyam* 9: 'When you and I behind the Veil are past'.[57*] By the end of the century, at all events, it had become a common phrase (whether as 'behind', 'within', or 'Beyond' the veil) to describe the process of death which it had not been, apparently, when Tennyson wrote.

It is not to be suggested that Hallam became a total devotee of the Coleridgean philosophy, but that some of the ideas in it – and notably those about 'Being's dim foundations' – deeply engaged him in ways he could reasonably be expected to discuss later with Tennyson. Back in 1828–9, he had been in a volatile state: unsettled, subject to moods of despondency. It was natural that he should turn from the imponderables of Coleridge to the more substantial-seeming poetry of Wordsworth. By September he was quoting to Gladstone lines from *The Excursion*, which set the word 'Being' in a readily acceptable context:

> One adequate support
> For the calamities of mortal life
> Exists, one only; an assured belief,
> That the procession of our fate, howe'er
> Sad or disturbed, is ordered by a Being
> Of infinite Benevolence and Power,
> Whose everlasting purposes embrace
> All accidents, converting them to good.[58]

It had not always been so. Two years before he had been fined by the Eton Society for annotating one of Wordsworth's lines irreverently.[59] Now, in the summer of 1829, it was a source of grief to him that, in spite of expounding to her the manner in which Wordsworth was 'on all objects of our double nature, Inward and outward, shedding holier light', he could not convert his friend Anne Robertson to that philosophy.[60] His enthusiasm for the Romantic poets generally was running high during the following academic year – particularly for Shelley.[61] Sterling believed that they were wrong to promote this particular hero, writing disapprovingly:

> I believe he has in his time done many of us a good deal of harm. I scarcely hold fast by anything but Shakespeare, Milton and Coleridge and I have nothing to say to any one but to read the 'Aids to Reflection in the formation of a Manly Character' – a book the more necessary now to us all because except in England I do not see that there is a chance of any men being produced any where.[62]

Events were moving rapidly in these years, engendering a sense of crisis. Those Apostles who argued for the pursuit of true Being in the depths of human consciousness were likely to encounter the argument that this was a dangerously indolent occupation when so many practical problems called for direct action. Those who proclaimed the gospel of Shelley, equally, might be met with claims for the more active Byron, and this indeed seems to be precisely what happened during the summer of 1830 when, as Kemble and Trench took up the cause of the Spanish exiles and went to Gibraltar, Tennyson and Hallam visited the Pyrenees, using the occasion apparently to convey to the rebels some money that had been subscribed for them. The return of Kemble and Trench after several months was followed by a calamitous conclusion at the end of 1831 when the exiles landed in Spain, fell immediately into an ambush and were all executed.[63]

In England, meanwhile, social unrest was growing, along with the agitations that gave rise to the Reform Act. Hallam was present in Cambridge in December 1830 when local rick burnings gave rise to highly coloured fears that the town itself was due to be attacked.[64] His own writings several times contain phrases such as 'the times that are coming on us';[65] his instincts were with those who thought that the new reforms would bring disaster. So far from developing further any of his metaphysical speculations, his concern was now to create a synthesis which would reconcile the new with the old. In a letter to Edward Moxon in July 1831, when the latter was taking over *The Englishman's Magazine*, he wrote of a plan entertained by some of his friends to start a periodical 'with the double purpose of maintaining Conservative principles in politics, and those of the New Poetical

School in literature'.[66] (He was disappointed to learn that the journal
was on the side of reform.) In a review of Tennyson's 1830 collection
of poems for the same journal he sought to bring out his originality,
maintaining that 'his thoughts bear no more resemblance to Byron or
Scott, Shelley or Coleridge, than to Homer or Calderon, Ferdusi or
Calidas'.[67] He was also increasingly wary concerning cultivation of personal affection and attempts to link it with the divine. A fortnight after
his letter to Moxon he wrote to Monckton Milnes disclaiming that he
had any friendship, in the more lofty sense of the word, for him, and
by the following May was dissociating himself from Milnes's religious
beliefs. 'I believe the only transcendental Knowledge possible for man
is to be deduced from the written Word of God,'[68] he claimed.

Coleridge's ideas were not subject to such an interdict, however,
since he had explicitly attempted to link them with 'the Word of God'.
One which Hallam may well have picked up from his conversation was
that, from the limited point of view possible to human perception,
God acquired his Being through the son. In a letter of 1826 Coleridge
had twice made this point with reference to a quotation from St John's
Gospel in the original Greek describing the son as 'the being in the
bosom of the father'.[69] This is close to the kind of discussion that
Hallam initiates in *Theodicaea Novissima*.[70] In 1829, when he was listening to Coleridge, it would have been particularly timely, enabling
him to turn to account, by universalizing, the love that he had felt for
Anna Wintour; his despair at the loss of her thus opened the way both
for further love and for devotion to Dante. When Tennyson opened *In
Memoriam* with the line 'Strong Son of God | immortal Love...', adding
the laconic note 'This might be taken in a St John sense'[71] which may
well have been what he had in mind, particularly when one recalls
that the next lines, 'Whom we, that have not seen thy face, | By faith,
and faith alone, embrace ...' could also be associated with the same
verse of St John – which reads in full, 'No man hath seen God at any
time; the only begotten Son, which is in the bosom of the Father, he
hath declared him'.[72*] The theology of *In Memoriam* may, in other
words, be more fully and intricately thought-out than it is sometimes
taken to be.

In Memoriam is not primarily a theological poem, however, nor was it
for theological ideas that Tennyson primarily remembered Hallam.
When the Apostles discussed the question of Being, similarly, not all of
them were thinking in Christian terms. What was likely to be exciting
about the idea was that it offered a more profound way of approaching
their own experiences as human beings, suggesting that in heightened

states of love, and even of suffering, they were initiated into an order of reality which made better sense of their experience as a whole than did theories such as those of utilitarianism, based on a straightforward rationalist interpretation of common human experience. Such a view was as appealing to Monckton Milnes, whose cultivation of high sentiment led in the direction of homoerotic attachments, as it was to Hallam, with his attempts to reawaken ideas of Christian nobility.

For Tennyson, such discussions must have struck further chords. There were elements in his personality that were particularly open to the idea that human experience could not be limited to the 'common-sense' evaluation of the everyday, since from an early age he had been familiar with states of mind in which his ordinary consciousness was overtaken by an impersonal state of vision. The best-known account is the one recorded in his son's *Memoir*, where he recalls

> a kind of 'waking trance' (this for lack of a better word) I have frequently had quite up from boyhood when I have been all alone. This has often come upon me through repeating my own name to myself silently, till all at once as it were out of the intensity of the consciousness of individuality the individuality itself seemed to dissolve & fade away into boundless being – & this not a confused state but the clearest of the clearest, the surest of the surest, utterly beyond words – where Death was an almost laughable impossibility – the loss of personality (if so it were) seeming no extinction but the only true life.[73]

Robert Bernard Martin quotes another statement of Tennyson's in which he felt himself to be the only thing alive in a dead world: 'through excess of realising my own personality I seemed to get outside of myself.'[74] As Martin comments, these trances could be terrible as well as joyful: if they were ecstatic they were so in the strictest sense of the word. Yet they were at least fulfilling Coleridge's desire of reconciling personality with infinity.

The poetry suggests that his more trance-like moments had a twofold quality. On the one hand, he seems to experience the sense of Being centrally as a sense of flowing, like the flowing of a stream. There may also be in this the suggestion of a correspondence between the flowing of the human bloodstream and the flowing of streams in the world that one notices also in the linking language and imagery of Wordsworth's 'Tintern Abbey'.[75] The other is a sense of pulsing – again as if the beating of the human heart might be related to some basic rhythm in the universe at large. Tennyson's interest in flowing things is too obvious to need illustration; his sense of pulsings emerges as early as in the adolescent poem 'Armageddon', where first he records,

> ...I held
> My breath and heard the beatings of my heart

and then at the end of the poem, after the vision of the Angel Mind, concludes,

> There was a beating in the atmosphere,
> An indefinable pulsation
> Inaudible to outward sense, but felt
> Through the deep heart of every living thing,
> As if the great soul of the Universe
> Heaved with tumultuous throbbings on the vast
> Suspense of some grand issue.[76]

As Christopher Ricks has pointed out, this image is picked up, though apparently in a quite different mode, in the lines 'An Idle Rhyme', where Tennyson forswears discussion of literary fashions in favour of a more blissful and indolent state reminiscent of Keats in some of his moods,

> As stretched beside the river clear,
> That's round this glassy foreland curled,
> I cool my face in flowers, and hear
> The deep pulsations of the world.[77]

Against this sense of inner being as pulsing and flowing, wheels and wheeling are a more ambiguous phenomenon. The wheeling of the planets can be a sublime conception, but it may also be an intimation of necessity, linking with the idea of the Wheel of Fortune or the circling of the planets and producing no more than a depressed sense of what Blake called 'the ratio of all things', repeating 'the same dull round' until it becomes 'a mill with complicated wheels'.[78] One can find simple examples of the contrast involved in 'Locksley Hall', where the hero's reason for asking his cousin to trust him is that 'all the current of my being sets to thee' whereas his imagery of rejection takes the wheeling form 'Let the great world spin for ever down the ringing grooves of change' and 'Better fifty years of Europe than a cycle of Cathay'.[79]

The early emergence of such images into Tennyson's poetry, and the weight he gave them, makes it likely, to say the least, that if he heard his friends discussing the idea of Being as displaying a correspondence between the profundity of the divine and the 'abysmal secrets of personality', or heard them expounding a Heraclitean dualism which suggested a fluency at the heart of things, such discussions made contact with the strange states of mind he had known when personality passed into impersonal vision, and with the sense of the abysmal, or of pulsing, or of flowing that he found characteristic of such states.

It is also possible that a more roundabout connection with Coleridge's poetry is involved: for whatever the latter may have been saying about the nature of Being at the time when Hallam heard him discoursing, he had been investigating the question in a more radical and free-ranging fashion thirty years before when he wrote the poem which Tennyson valued so much, *The Ancient Mariner*. A debate at the Union late in 1828 on the subject 'Will Mr Coleridge's poem of the Ancient Mariner or Mr Martin's acts, be most effectual in preventing Cruelty to Animals?' was opened, according to Milnes, by some 'very deep poetical criticism' from R.J. Tennant,[80] who, as Hallam reported, had been imbibing Coleridge's doctrines from the man himself. It is hard to see how debate on the poem could proceed very far without its being seen to involve questions that went far beyond that of 'cruelty to animals' in the simple sense.

It must still be borne in mind, however, that while Tennant may have been expounding a mysticism based on what he had heard from Coleridge, the debates of the Apostles were characterized by that interplay of earnestness with light scepticism that was to remain their most lasting characteristic; and this too comes across in Tennyson's writing of the time.

Only rarely has one the chance to see the collection that Tennyson published in 1830, *Poems, Chiefly Lyrical*, in its original form, and many of the poems in it were subsequently dropped from later collections, but when read together they are not only seen to contain some of the ideas outlined above, but to approach them with varying degrees of seriousness. In the poem 'A Character',[81] for example, Tennyson depicts in adverse terms the character of one of the Apostles, Thomas Sunderland, who was acknowledged to be one of their most brilliant orators, but who seemed to Tennyson and others to lack the true Apostolic spirit of fellowship. Worse, he had taken over the doctrines of Wordsworth only to make them a vehicle for his own separatist philosophy. Monckton Milnes and Blakesley complained of his zest for 'perfect solitude' and for direct contemplation of the absolute'.[82] Tennyson put it more brutally: whenever his character discoursed on the life in dead things or similar Wordsworthian therapy he was 'looking as 'twere in a glass':

> With lips depressed as he were meek,
> Himself unto himself he sold:
> Upon himself himself did feed:
> Quiet, dispassionate, and cold,
> And other than his form of creed,
> With chiselled features clear and sleek.[83]

At the other extreme, an outreaching to embrace all existence could, for all its attractiveness, seem damagingly vague. In a poem 'The Idealist',[84] not published but written into manuscripts for his friends Allen and Heath, the identification of the philosopher with the whole of existence is rehearsed ('I am the earth, the stars, the sun, I I am the clouds, the sea') with the conclusion, 'I am all things save souls of fellow men and very God!' The irony that seems to lurk here is akin to that of Jack Kemble, who was heard to remark during a meeting of the Apostles that the universe was one thought and he was thinking it.[85] More acutely, the 1830 collection contains a poem entitled in Greek 'Hoi Reontes'[86] ('the flowing ones'), which is about the Heraclitean philosophers and their belief that everything existed in a state of flux. Its refrain is 'For all things are as they seem to all, I And all things flow like a stream'; it also contains the lines 'All men do walk in sleep, and all I Have faith in that they dream'. The pay-off comes in the comment that follows the poem: 'Argal – this very opinion is only true relatively to the flowing philosophers'. The poem gains force from this lightness and its hint of possible self-criticism. Tennyson is intensely drawn to things that flow and to the question of movement through time, just as he is to dreams and their relation to reality, yet he is also fully aware that this kind of speculation, if given a free rein, would be likely to end in a total relativism, far from the rock-like certainty that he, like his contemporaries, wants to find. He cannot, nevertheless, renounce his interest in flowing, or in the compulsive power of dreams at their most intense, as he shows in another, less sceptical poem of the time entitled 'The Mystic', describing human vision and its power to impress images of eternity against the transience of human experience. This includes the lines:

> He often lying broad awake, and yet
> Remaining from the body, and apart
> In intellect and power and will, hath heard

> Time flowing in the middle of the night
> And all things creeping to a day of doom.[87]

Other poems in the collection, such as the pair 'Nothing Will Die' and 'All Things Will Die',[88] are written more lightly, in the tradition of rhetorical antithesis, putting the case for and against the idea as seen within the order of time.

Poems such as these, along with the 'Supposed Confessions of a Second-rate Sensitive Mind Not in Unity With Itself',[89] show Tennyson in tune with the current state of mind of the Apostles in 1829 to 1830; the cut-and-thrust of argument, including light-hearted banter, as sustained by the majority of them, is shot through by the vein of metaphysical questioning introduced by Tennant and Hallam, which had sometimes spoken very directly to him when seeming to correspond with – and even to explain – abnormal experiences of his own.

The fact that Hallam not only shared his speculations, but in his own personality seemed to provide an actual example of noble being, opened the issues out into a further dimension, however, which some-times thrust scepticism into the background. Watching him work through his doubts and evolve his philosophy, Tennyson found his own world making sense in a new way. His most vivid account of the process was inspired by standing outside a room in Trinity College and hearing the noise of glasses being smashed at a rowdy party – which aroused the contrary memory of a different society (almost certainly the Apostles, where much tobacco was smoked but no wine was taken) and of Hallam in action in that same room.

> Where once we held debate, a band
> Of youthful friends, on mind and art,
> And labour, and the changing mart,
> And all the framework of the land;
>
> When one would aim an arrow fair,
> But send it slackly from the string;
> And one would pierce an outer ring,
> And one an inner, here and there;
>
> And last the master-bowman, he,
> Would cleave the mark. A willing ear
> We lent him. Who, but hung to hear
> The rapt oration flowing free

From point to point, with power and grace
And music in the bounds of law,
To those conclusions when we saw
The God within him light his face,

And seem to lift the form, and glow
In azure orbits heavenly-wise;
And over those ethereal eyes
The bar of Michael Angelo.[90]

The idea of the God within him lighting his face involves the constant Romantic preoccupation with genius, inspiration and illumination, beginning with Edward Young's assertion, in his *Conjectures on Original Composition,* that 'Genius is that God within'.[91*] It also conveys Tennyson's sense that there were times when, in the full energy of discussion, Hallam seemed transported to another dimension, more akin to direct inspiration. And there are signs that this sense was one which was sustained among the Apostles: that it was not just the cut-and-thrust of candid debate that was valued, or the openness of friendship, or the sense of brotherliness that sprang up among them, but that sometimes in the height of discussion they felt themselves to be in the grip of a transcendent experience.

The doctrine of Being could issue in many forms of behaviour, acting at one extreme as a possible defence of Christianity, at the other as a more general energizing power in poetry. It was of the nature of such Being that it might be revealed most readily in suffering. 'I have suffered such an extinction of Light in my mind,' wrote Coleridge, it will be recalled, 'I have been so forsaken by all the *forms* and *colourings* of Existence, as if the *organs* of Life had been dried up; as if only simple BEING remained, blind and stagnant.'[92] In some of the most haunting lines of *In Memoriam* Tennyson used a simpler, if differing, image to describe his more depressive moods. Section I originally opened:

Be near me when the pulse is low,
When the blood creeps, and the nerves prick
And tingle; and the heart is sick,
And all the wheels of Being slow.[93]

He then revised the imagery to take in the image of light which Coleridge also had used, so that the opening line read 'Be with me when my light is low'; this expanded the conception, setting up a link with the sign of hope given at the end of the section by the returning light of the physical world:

> ... on the low dark verge of life
> The twilight of eternal day.

In these verses Tennyson's sense of Being, closely related as we have seen to pulsations and a sense of flowing (with wheeling and cycling as a more ambiguous form of movement) opens out into that imagery of glimmering or glowing light that is his most constant resource.

The last word to be introduced into this cluster is one that may or may not come directly from Coleridge and Hallam but is closely associated with the range of preoccupations we have been discussing. 'Aeonian', with its suggestion of an element which is beyond or out of time, comprehending time and even cancelling consciousness of its workings at the height of its operation, has already been discussed above in connection with both Wordsworth and De Quincey. Where the idea of Being is used in conjunction both with the word 'Æonian' and with an imagery of light one should be particularly alert to the possibility that a Coleridgean complex of ideas is at work, in view of his influence on both writers. (George Macdonald, also, uses the word later in his supernatural writings.[94])

Tennyson's invocation of a similar cluster of images comes at one of the crucial moments of *In Memoriam*, when he is rereading some of Hallam's former letters:

> A hunger seized my heart; I read
> Of that glad year which once had been,
> In those fallen leaves which kept their green,
> The noble letters of the dead:
>
> And strangely on the silence broke
> The silent-speaking words, and strange
> Was love's dumb cry defying change
> To test his worth; and strangely spoke
>
> The faith, the vigour, bold to dwell
> On doubts that drive the coward back,
> And keen through wordy snares to track
> Suggestion to her inmost cell.

So word by word, and line by line,
   The dead man touched me from the past,
   And all at once it seemed at last
His living soul was flashed on mine,

And mine in his was wound, and whirled
   About empyreal heights of thought,
   And came on that which is, and caught
The deep pulsations of the world,

Æonian music measuring out
   The steps of Time – the shocks of Chance –
   The blows of Death. At length my trance
Was cancelled, stricken through with doubt.[95*]

In one sense this is the climax to Tennyson's remembrance of Hallam in the poem. He later changed 'His living soul' to 'The Living soul' and 'mine in his' to 'mine in this', saying that the first reading troubled him as perhaps giving a wrong impression;[96] but he had let it stand for twenty years and it is clear that that, in his own terms, is what he meant. On the other hand, the visionary experience could not last. When the trance was 'cancelled, stricken through with doubt', all that was left, as before, was the external illumination of the dawn to act as mediator between internal and external. In the same way he could rest with the more down-to-earth reflection 'I felt and feel, though left alone, | His being working in mine own, | The footsteps of his life in mine'.[97*] There was also hope of a more conventional kind for the future in the promise of a newborn child to renew the pattern of nobility: 'A soul shall draw from out the vast | And strike his being into bounds'.[98] But while the concluding statements of the poem are formulated to meet the gaze of its more sceptical readers, the subterranean work of the poem continues through rhythms of pulsing and flowing. The movement of *In Memoriam* as a whole is that of a great eddying stream. Even the separation into short sections, each self-contained, is countered by the distinctive rhyme-scheme, in which the insistent falling-back upon the opening rhyme in each verse creates a continuous but unobtrusive eddying motion throughout the section and beyond.

A simple eddying motion would not be enough to achieve the full effect that Tennyson needs at the conclusion of his poem. As he reaches it a strong and insistent pulsation rises in the final stanzas to suggest portentousness and even apocalypse: the last eleven stanzas progress in fact without a single full stop, culminating in the lines:

> Whereof the man, that with me trod
> This planet, was a noble type
> Appearing ere the times were ripe,
> That friend of mine who lives in God,
>
> That God, which ever lives and loves,
> One God, one law, one element,
> And one far-off divine event,
> To which the whole creation moves.

Tennyson may well have felt that in writing *In Memoriam* he had done all he could in trying to reconcile the contradictory tides of his own personality and that from now on he must find other modes of expressing himself. It is only occasionally in his later writing that one finds speculations coming to any kind of overt statement, even if flowings and pulsations continue to provide some of his most characteristic effects. In the second half of the nineteenth century the idea that it might be possible to solve the universe in a manner that reconciled science with traditional morality was recoiling under the blows of Darwinism in its various forms. There are occasional poems in which Tennyson revives the task of mediation, however, usually in an oblique manner. The three most notable, 'The Ancient Sage', 'Akbar's Dream' and 'De Profundis'[99] have associations with Benjamin Jowett, who had long been encouraging him to write a visionary poem on the theme that 'All Religions are One'.[100]

Both 'The Ancient Sage' and 'Akbar's Dream' transfer the discussion of Tennyson's unusual trance-experiences to the Far East, where the traditional experiences of great sages allow for their inclusion. 'De Profundis', on the other hand, written on the birth of Hallam Tennyson, draws on the English tradition more directly. The imagery of flowing follows that of Wordsworth's Immortality Ode, human life being seen as like a stream that draws out of the deep, returning eventually to it. In this poem Tennyson is again wrestling explicitly with Coleridge's problem of reconciling personality with infinity as he describes

> the pain
> of this divisible-indivisible world

> Among the numerable-innumerable
> Sun, sun, and sun, through finite-infinite space
> In finite-infinite Time – our mortal veil
> And shattered phantom of that infinite One[101]

– lines which, although subtle and precise in thought, are hardly likely to be remembered as great poetry.

The Apostles, meanwhile, continued to meet, keeping alive their traditions with extraordinary consistency. It was not until the first years of the twentieth century that the temper of the society began to shift to that of Bloomsbury. The word used by them most frequently in the latter part of the century was not 'Being' but 'Reality'. Sidgwick, for instance, recalls: 'it came to seem to me that no part of my life at Cambridge was so real to me as the Saturday evenings on which the apostolic debates were held';[102] Forster, similarly, who was a member at the turn of the century, dedicated his novel *The Longest Journey to* them ('Fratribus') and tried to convey something of the apostolic spirit in his first chapter, where the question of Reality is central both to the opening scene and to the novel as a whole.[103] The word 'being' did not vanish altogether from view. Virginia Woolf, for instance, who had known some of the Apostles by way of her brother Thoby and found some of them insufferable, could still honour their spirit at its best, as when she writes in her autobiographical fragments of the experiences which she calls 'moments of being'.[104]

The most striking evidence of such continuity comes in the typescript of a speech which Donald MacAlister, who had been elected in 1876, made at the Apostles dinner in 1908, when he rose to propose the toast of those who could not be present. Absent members, he declared, would still turn fondly to the 'hearth-rug' which was the symbolic locus of their weekly meetings, for it was there that each member

> learned to contemplate pure being.... There with eyes undimmed, even by tobacco smoke, he beheld the vision of absolute truth .... There he mastered the art of reconciling by a phrase the most divergent of hypotheses, the most fundamentally antagonistic of antinomies. There he grew accustomed to differ from his comrades in nothing but opinion. There, upborne by the ethereal atmosphere of free and audacious enquiry, he mewed his budding wings, and discovered to his delight that, towards midnight on Saturday, he too

could soar. Others might find the medium but a vacuum.... But he was no chimaera, for he felt his reality and knew that he was alive.[105]

At the end of the section of *Idylls of the King* entitled 'The Holy Grail', King Arthur deplores the waste of effort by some of his knights in going after the Grail when they might have been doing more practical things. Although man's duty is to undertake direct and mundane tasks during the day, however, things, he concedes, are different by night:

> the King must guard
> That which he rules, and is but as the hind
> To whom a space of land is given to plow.
> Who may not wander from the allotted field,
> Before his work be done; but, being done,
> Let visions of the night or of the day
> Come, as they will; and many a time they come,
> Until this earth he walks on seems not earth,
> This light that strikes his eyeball is not light,
> This air that smites his forehead is not air
> But vision – yea, his very hand and foot –
> In moments when he feels he cannot die,
> And knows himself no vision to himself,
> Nor the high God a vision, nor that One
> Who rose again: ye have seen what ye have seen.'[106]

'So spake the King', concludes the narrator, in a Browningesque gesture; 'I knew not all he meant.' By the end of the nineteenth century the intervention of Darwinian theories had undermined hopes that a firm rock for Christian faith might be found by seeking the ground of Being within human consciousness and the Apostles were beginning to turn away from metaphysics altogether. Such things do not easily vanish in their totality, however, and the evidence of McAlister's speech is that even as late as 1908 his fellow Apostles would have recognized a language that was far from unfamiliar.

7
Byron and Shelley: Polarities of Being

In 1829 – during the early days when they were still known as the Cambridge Conversazione Club – three of the Cambridge Apostles had journeyed to Oxford to further their desire for debate. Richard Monckton Milnes, Arthur Hallam and Thomas Sunderland debated with members of the Oxford Union the relative merits of Lord Byron and Percy Bysshe Shelley. Paradoxically, the Oxford debaters plumped for Cambridge's Lord Byron, carrying the day by a large margin against their visitors, who were supporting the claims of the Oxford-educated Shelley. The paradox is less pointed, however, when it is recalled that the first two, at least, of the Cambridge men had been taught the virtues of Coleridge by their tutor Julius Hare and so given some basis for sympathizing with Shelley's views. And although their friend Tennyson, himself as an adolescent, had been so devastated by the news of Byron's death that he immediately carved the words 'BYRON IS DEAD' on a rock, his brother had told him shortly after about the existence of an even finer poet, quoting a line from *The Revolt of Islam*.[1]

The early political thinking of the group round Tennyson had taken inspiration from Shelley's proclaimed principles, though the fate of the Spanish expedition[2] had acted as a sad check on their unworldliness.

For young poets growing up about 1810 and less readily checked by the knowledge of such harsh realities, disinterestedness had seemed a more achievable goal, even while the literary scene appeared stultified. The conservative reaction that set in at the turn of the century had been strengthened by international events that called for patriotism and solidarity against the French – who only a few years before had seemed to embody the chief hope for mankind. The literary offerings of Southey, Coleridge and Wordsworth were now dismaying to those who had seen them as prophets of reform: cultivation of principle and at best programmes of limited retrenchment seemed now to be the order of the day. If more of their manuscript work had been available, such as Coleridge's notebooks and the full text of Wordsworth's *Prelude*, the course of their progress might at least have been more comprehensible; as things were, it was all too easy for Byron, in *English Bards and Scotch Reviewers*, to pick off the easiest targets – devotion to asses and glowworms, for example – to suggest that his chief Romantic predecessors were namby-pamby sentimentalists. This was by no means a permanent or even a fully considered view, however; on the contrary, he wrote of Wordsworth in 1816 as a 'great poet ... of whom there can exist few greater admirers than myself'.[3] A note of strong enthusiasm is detectable in the summer of that year, when he was constantly in touch with Shelley. It was then that he added praises of Rousseau, and Rousseau's power to associate scenery with the feelings of his Julie, to new stanzas for *Childe Harold*, including a note shot through with Wordsworthian and Shelleyan philosophy:

> the feeling with which all around Clarens, and the opposite rocks of Meillerie, is invested, is of a still higher and more comprehensive order than the mere sympathy with individual passion; it is a sense of the existence of love in its most extended and sublime capacity, and of our own participation of its good and of its glory: it is the great principle of the universe, which is there more condensed but not less manifested; and of which, though knowing ourselves a part, we lose our individuality, and mingle in the beauty of the whole.[4]

By the autumn, however, he could write of his inability to gain such benefits from nature, despite his love and admiration for her:

> neither the music of the Shepherd – the crashing of the Avalanche – nor the torrent – the mountain – the Glacier – the Forest – nor the Cloud – have for one moment – lightened the weight upon my heart – nor enabled me to lose my own wretched identity in the majesty & the power and the Glory – around – above – & beneath me...[5]

He was in fact experiencing something of the same loss of feeling that Coleridge had described when he produced his Dejection ode.

Whatever political disenchantment Shelley may have felt, he was more perceptive than Byron concerning the writings of his two major predecessors, tracing, among other things, the metaphysical streak lurking there – particularly as far as Coleridge was concerned. This probably owes much to connections with his own researches. Like Coleridge, he had read deeply in the esoteric works available at the time and seen that a clever thinker might relate, say, the Neoplatonist texts then being popularized in the translations of Thomas Taylor to the most advanced scientific thinking of the time, by paying attention to subtle electrical and chemical forces that had been ignored by those who based their scientific thinking primarily on Newtonian physics and a simplified economy of the universe. The idea of an 'active' universe, an inviting concept for contemporary French *philosophes*, had already attracted Wordsworth, while Coleridge had explored wider speculations similar to those just mentioned:[6] the results could be traced even in the limited amount of their published work that was available. Shelley also, reading the Platonists and carrying out chemical experiments, was evidently looking for discoveries that might transform the sense of what it was to be human. In one sense he was taking Rousseau's philosophy to another level, in which the claim that human beings were born free might be developed by demonstrating the existence of an inner human nature that transcended the instincts and passions.

In the principles that guided the careers of Shelley and Byron we can trace in at least ghostly form the presuppositions of their respective classes. Shelley was taking to an extreme certain qualities to be associated with the eighteenth-century ideal of the gentleman, while Byron tried to bring to a fine point that feeling for action traditionally associated with an aristocratic way of life. There was, however, in both men an intensity that took them beyond the bounds suggested by such generalizations. Their quarrel with existing society and its conventions took them in each case beyond the modes of conscious thinking fostered by their respective backgrounds, delivering them into the uncharted territory of Being.

The questions involved in that transit could take more than one form, as they had in the previous generation. In my earlier discussion of Wordsworth and Coleridge, I dwelt on the degree to which their fascination with the issue of Being had involved attention to its interplay with the subjective consciousness, sometimes working unconsciously or subconsciously itself, sometimes fusing with the very sense of life. Wordsworth's investigations in *The Prelude* returned frequently to the question, while Coleridge's investigations allowed him to build a whole religious position on the supposition that the ability to say I AM might set one in alignment with the God for whom this was his secret name. I also gave some attention to the relationship between the Beings – or identities – of the two individuals concerned, the one mercurial and changing, the other firm and consistent, I concerned myself less, however, with another question, also touched on by Coleridge:

> Hast thou ever said to thyself thoughtfully, IT IS! heedless in that moment whether it were a man before thee, or a flower, or a grain of sand? ... If thou hast indeed attained to this, thou wilt have felt the presence of a mystery, which must have fixed thy spirit in awe and wonder ...[7]

This question, involving the relationship between consciousness and external, objective form, was considered by him less frequently, yet its implications pressed strongly on him from time to time, as when he embarked on a walking holiday in the Cumbrian mountains during the summer of 1802. Climbing on Scafell, he had an alarming experience, finding himself crag-fast while coming down from a height, with nothing but two fearful drops available for further descent. Yet in these circumstances he also found himself surprised by his lack of terror: curiously, he found it a relief to be so close to the solid form of the mountain, with only his human faculties to rely on:

> O God! I exclaimed aloud – how calm, how blessed am I now / I know not how to proceed, how to return / but I am calm & fearless & confident / if this reality were a Dream, if I were asleep, what agonies had I suffered! what screams! – When the Reason & the Will are away what remains to us but Darkness & Dimness & a bewildering Shame, and Pain that is utterly Lord over us ... [8]

This account was written only a week after he had repeated his suspicion of there being a radical difference between himself and Wordsworth; it was followed soon afterwards by the composition of his 'Hymn before Sun-rise', the genesis of which he described following an assertion that poetic feelings, despite their ability to exert tempest-like power, could still retain a core of organic stability – that they

> Yet all the while, self-limited, remain
> Equally near the fix'd and parent Trunk
> Of Truth & Nature, in the howling Blast
> As in the Calm that stills the Aspen Grove...

That this is deep in our Nature, I felt when I was on Sca' fell – I involuntarily poured forth a Hymn in the manner of the Psalms, tho' afterwards I thought the Ideas &c disproportionate to our humble mountains – & accidentally lighting on a short Note in some swiss Poems, concerning the Vale of Chamouny & it's Mountain, I transferred myself thither, in the Spirit, and adapted my former feelings to these grander external objects.[9]

As critics have pointed out, this was a disingenuous account so far as it concerned the relation between the 'Hymn' and Friederike Brun's poem on Chamounix, a much shorter but still recognizable source.[10] The fact should not, however, divert attention from the full significance of what the composition involved in terms of Coleridge's thinking at this time. He continued by saying how he had come to see the Psalms as offering an answer to those who think the God of the Old Testament to be no more than a personal and national god like those of the Greeks. In contrast, he affirmed, the Hebrew poets displayed true imagination, by which 'each Thing has a Life of it's own, & yet they are all one Life'.

Whatever view is taken of this as criticism, it can be said to mark an important point in the development of Coleridge's thought, especially the transference of his thinking about the 'one Life' from nature to Hebrew poetry. This is matched by the devotional quality of the 'Hymn before Sun-rise', where the whole of nature is seen as joining in the praise of God. The writing of the 'Hymn' may also suggest some development of his recent criticisms of Wordsworth, in whom he had noted, 'here & there a daring Humbleness of Language and Versification, and a strict adherence to matter of fact, even to prolixity, that startled me'.[11] The high-flown quality of his writing in the 'Hymn' could demonstrate in contrast, he must have hoped, a poetry that need not be the subject of such censure.

Wordsworth, for his part, did not altogether like the 'Hymn'. He might be prone to the 'matter of fact', but he was equally disturbed by what might be called Coleridge's 'riddling fantasy'.[12*] With reference to the 'Hymn' he asserted that his friend was 'not under the influence of natural objects', adding, 'A remarkable instance of this ... is his poem, said to be "composed in the Vale of Chamouni". Now he never was at Chamouni, or near it, in his life.'[13] He also spoke about the poem to Coleridge himself, who recalled the criticisms in a later letter:

I described myself under the influence of strong devotional feelings gazing on the Mountain till as if it had been a Shape emanating from and sensibly representing her own essence, my soul had become diffused thro' 'the mighty Vision'; and there

As in her natural Form, swell'd vast to Heav'n.

Mr Wordsworth, I remember, censured the passage as strained and unnatural, and condemned the Hymn in toto ... as a Specimen of the Mock Sublime. It may be so for others; but it is impossible that I should myself find it unnatural, being conscious that it was the image and utterance of Thoughts and Emotions in which there was no mockery.[14]

As he goes on to develop the point, it becomes clear that it was one of the main areas of the dissociation from his associate that he had been sensing in 1802. To believe it a natural act of the imagination to project oneself into total empathy of form with what was being looked at was not, he had found, an experience that Wordsworth shared, or was likely to share.

At the same time, Wordsworth's unease probably reflected a sense that Coleridge's verse had strayed from the simple gift for natural description that had characterized his meditative verses of a few years before, There was about the rhetoric in the 'Hymn before Sun-rise' something which must have struck him as overblown, a retreat from what then been effortlessly achieved.

Yet a poet of the new generation would not necessarily have a problem with this mode. The outward-going Shelley, from the beginning an enthusiast for Coleridge's poetry, seems to have had little difficulty in appreciating the kind of enterprise just described, though he could not follow his predecessor to the point of adjoining it to conventional religious affirmation. Such conjunctions of sentiment were not, of course, unfamiliar to him: by the time he himself visited Mont Blanc the Alps had already been annexed as a site for religious enthusiasm. Thomas Gray had written to a friend from the Grande Chartreuse in 1757: 'There are certain scenes that would awe an atheist into belief without help of other arguments';[15] according to A.C. Swinburne, a visitor just before Shelley had given vent to 'an outbreak of overflowing foolery, flagrant and fervid with the godly grease and rancid religion of a conventicle; some folly about the Alps, God, glory, beneficence, witness of nature ...'[16*] Shelley had no difficulty in expressing emotions of awe – but not to be addressed to the orthodox God of traditional devotion. On the contrary, and to the indignation of succeeding tourists at Chamonix, he made his notorious Greek entry in the hotel register there as 'Democrat, Philanthropist, and Atheist'. The main thrust of his subsequent poem was in a contrary direction from Coleridge's, the addresses to the Deity being replaced by reference to the 'Power' which

> dwells apart in its tranquillity,
> Remote, serene, and inaccessible …

This was a radically different approach to the mystery of Being. Where Coleridge had looked up to the mountain scenery and especially its energy, taking it for granted that it was redolent of the nature of the Christian God who created it, Shelley assumed with equal certainty that it was not: if a power existed, it was that of the 'everlasting universe of things' itself and of the human mind contemplating it. Instead of Coleridge's 'thousand voices' overtly praising their divine creator, Shelley could hear in the mountain only a hidden voice, and one 'not understood | By all'. It was a voice, one must assume, much closer to those in Wordsworth's sonnet, 'Two voices are there': but if so, with an undertone of concealed reproach also, since those two voices were avowedly of 'Liberty' – that very Liberty on which Shelley thought their author to have reneged. As in Wordsworth's case, the voice he was endeavouring to transmit was not to be grasped easily: it was a kind of voice behind, or within, the voices heard in nature. Whatever it had to say was as subtle and fugitive as other features of its scenery: the harmony created by wind in the pines, the beauty of the rainbow on the waterfalls, the very caverns that echoed the sound of the rushing river. All these subtle sensations have the ability to force the observer's mind back in on itself, making it aware of similar forces and perceptions of its own. Beyond, is the spectacle of the mountain itself, displaying to the observer an image of silence and eternity and standing, above all, as a record of nature's dealings with the living world. Just as the glaciers creeping silently and slowly on their prey, or the shattered pines littering the mountain side are all that remain of their existence, or the rocky wastes that replace the overwhelmed dwellings of living things, all have a message for mankind that in its central voice has nothing to do with moral authority. On the contrary it can 'repeal | Large codes of fraud and woe'. It has also, however, a positiveness – an affirmation of the 'secret Strength of things' – which is as valuable to the contemplating imagination as it would be awful if it were to find in the scene no more than a silence and solitude merely vacant.

The same theme of an interwoven subtlety in human affairs was inherent in other writing of Shelley's at the time, notably the 'Hymn to Intellectual Beauty', where the true source of the mystery is traced to that beauty itself, and all the elements that shadow it – summer winds, moonbeams, certain human expressions –

> ... aught that for its grace may be
> Dear, and yet dearer for its mystery.

Whereas Coleridge had turned away from the attempt to find true Being in the interplayings of the 'one Life' in nature, the human mind and God, redirecting his enterprise towards a more conventional piety, Shelley was exploring a concept which would at once cultivate the love of one's fellow human beings and honour a wisdom behind all.

Although enigmetically attendant, Coleridge was evidently an important presence throughout the decade of his major writing. As long ago as his schooldays he had been at Eton with Coleridge's nephew, John Taylor Coleridge (who later wrote an extremely hostile review of Shelley's poetry for the *Quarterly*),[17]* and in 1811 had visited Keswick, hoping apparently to make direct contact, only to find, unfortunately, that Coleridge was absent. From an early stage the poems then available to him must have been an important influence; the indications are that he also read eagerly in the pages of the first version of *The Friend* – perhaps acquired through the mediation of William Calvert, who was a subscriber.[18] He continued to seize immediately on any new writing of his predecessor's: his journals record readings of various poems in 1814–16, of *Biographia Literaria* in 1817 and of the *Lay Sermons* in 1816–17.[19] Yet his sense of something also unsatisfactory in these works emerges into the open when he includes a satiric pen-portrait in 'Peter Bell the Third':

> He was a mighty poet – and
> A subtle-souled psychologist;
> All things he seemed to understand,
> Of old and new – of sea or land –
> But his own mind – which was a mist...
>
> He spoke of poetry, and how
> 'Divine it was – a light – a love –
> A spirit which like wind doth blow
> As it listeth, to and fro;
> A dew rained down from God above;
>
> 'A power which comes and goes like dream,

> And which none can ever trace –
> Heaven's light on earth – Truth's brightest beam.'
> And when he ceased there lay the gleam
> Of those words upon his face.

The skill with which Shelley turns the poetry of the gospels to assist the praise of Coleridge's poetry bespeaks an irony pointing in more than one direction at once and a respect for him, in spite of his failure to achieve clarity of stance and utterance, which looks forward to the more favourable picture to be painted only a few months later in his 'Letter to Maria Gisborne':

> You will see Coleridge – he who sits obscure
> In the exceeding lustre and the pure
> Intense irradiation of a mind,
> Which, with its own internal lightning blind,
> Flags wearily through darkness and despair –
> A cloud-encircled meteor of the air,
> A hooded eagle among blinking owls. – [20]

The brilliant image of a mind blinded by the flashing of its own internal lightning gives in fact a fine key to the nature of Shelley's own thinking – though it may miss the extent to which Coleridge's 'blindness' reflected internal contradictions produced by his attempts to appease convention while still honouring the innovative thinking of his time.

Despite important reservations, Coleridge in his turn showed strong appreciation of Shelley's gifts:

> Shelley was a man of great power as a poet, and could he only have had some notion of order, could you only have given him some plane whereon to stand, and look down upon his own mind, he would have succeeded. There are flashes of true spirit to be met with in his works …

He regretted never having had the chance to meet his fellow-poet, particularly in view of the failed encounter in Keswick, when he felt sure that he could have been more help to him than Southey, whom he did meet:

> I should have laughed at his Atheism. I could have sympathized with him and shown him that I did so, and he would have felt that

I did so. I could have shown him that I had once been in the same state myself, and I could have guided him through it. I have often bitterly regretted in my heart of hearts that I did never meet with Shelley.[21]

He had been told, he said, that shortly before his death, 'in those moments, when his spirit was left to pray inwards', Shelley had 'expressed a wish, amounting to anxiety' to commune with him, 'as the only being who could resolve or allay the doubts and anxieties that pressed upon his mind'.[22] Coleridge had a sympathetic view of such 'doubts and anxieties', no doubt, perceiving how closely they might relate to his own early anxieties and how Shelley had not had the benefit of the faith to which he himself had been able to return in some relief, giving up what he increasingly found a predicament. Whether Shelley would at any time have been convinced by the complexities of his argument is of course another matter, but he might have recognized the testimony of another man who had tried, like himself, to be a free spirit and had discovered the hazards of such a course, particularly in a post-revolutionary period now dominated by a regard for convention. Coleridge's position, however hard for a young rebel to understand, had been taken up in recognition of that fact.

Without appreciation of it Coleridge remained a puzzle, as attractive in his championing of the imagination and its power as he was reprehensible for his retreat from radical thinking and his move towards religious orthodoxy. How could the laudation of the renewing power of imagination to 'awaken the mind's attention from the lethargy of custom, and direct it to the loveliness and the wonders of the world before us; an inexhaustible treasure, but for ... the film of familiarity and selfish solicitude', in *Biographia Literaria*, resembling the 'Defence of Poetry's assertion that 'Poetry ... purges from our inward sight the film of familiarity which obscures from us the wonder of our being',[23] be reconciled to the apparent visionlessness of the Established Church? The satirical portrait in *Peter Bell the Third* retains strong signs of admiration for such insight, nevertheless. Whatever Shelley's reservations, he was bound to recognize in Coleridge the one man who had taken a path he could have sympathy with, who had acted as a pathfinder on the search for the nature of the Supreme Being – even if the identification of that Being with the God of contemporary religion was to his mind hopelessly mistaken.

If Byron, meanwhile, was also obsessed by the mystery of Being, he located that mystery rather differently. Religion was never for him the main problem; whatever the world might think, he had discovered a path of his own. As he himself put it as early as 1808:

The events of my short life have been of so singular a nature, that, though the pride, commonly called honour, has, and I trust ever will prevent me from disgracing my name by a mean or cowardly action, I have been already held up as the votary of Licentiousness, and the Disciple of Infidelity ...

... In Morality, I prefer Confucius to the ten Commandments, & Socrates to St. Paul (though the two latter agree in their opinion of marriage). In Religion I favour the Catholic Emancipation, but do not acknowledge the Pope ... I hold virtue, in general, or the virtues severally, to be only in the disposition, each a *feeling*, not a principle. I believe Truth the prime attribute of the Deity, and Death an eternal Sleep, at least of the Body. You have here a brief compendium of the Sentiments of the *wicked* George Ld. B... [24]

This adoption of an eclectic religion that contained some acceptance of orthodox Christianity, including Catholicism ('which I look upon as the best religion as it is assuredly the oldest of the various branches of Christianity'[25]) remained steady, as witnessed by his decision to let his daughter Allegra be brought up in a convent. There was a division in his mind, nevertheless, between his aristocratic urge to embrace traditional religion and his eighteenth-century scepticism, which he could never resolve. He was happy to live with such contradictions, however, observing on one occasion, 'It is has been said that the immortality of the soul is a "grand peut-être" – but still it is a *grand* one. Every body clings to it.'[26] In the same way he could declare, 'I believe doubtless in God' and express a desire to believe more, while making it clear that what he truly valued lay elsewhere – even if that too was open to questions of its own kind: 'the *moral* of Christianity is perfectly beautiful – and the very sublime of beautiful – yet even there we find some of its finer precepts in earlier axioms of the Greeks ...'[27] Although attracted for a time by Shelley's way of thinking, he was not ultimately drawn to his preoccupation with metaphysical possibilities. For him the true puzzle lay in the very nature of existence itself, in the absurd order of things that had placed the noble spirit of human beings ineluctably within the limitations of the human body. In a sense this confessed admirer of Pope (another victim of bodily existence because of physical deformity) could never pass beyond the summary of human existence found by his hero:

> Plac'd on this isthmus of a middle state,
> A being darkly wise, and rudely great...

> Sole judge of Truth, in endless Error hurl'd:
> The glory, jest, and riddle of the world![28]

Devoting *Childe Harold* to the 'glory' and *Don Juan* to the 'jest' he was left confronting the riddle of existence with fewer resources than his friend. Yet he remained devoted to both sides of the question:

> I have often been inclined to Materialism in philosophy – but could never bear it's introduction into *Christianity* – which appears to me essentially founded upon the *Soul* ...[29]

If there was an answer to the riddle, Coleridge might be thought to have found one in his cultivation of the 'one Life' as a possible key, but in that case he had then thrown it away. In the conversation poems (or as they were more accurately termed by himself the 'meditative poems'), he had developed a sensitivity to nature that ran easily with the writing of poetry such as 'Tintern Abbey' or Dorothy Wordsworth's journals. The only one of his immediate successors who could have been said to have come near to the genius of such work was Keats, the responses to him by Byron and Shelley providing another example of divisions in their beings which they were discovering in themselves and which neither could ultimately resolve.

It can be argued that the intercourse between the two earlier poets, which was touched on above, was in fact now not only being repeated in an important way, but carried to a further extreme. This is less surprising once it is recalled that in both cases there had earlier been a quarrel with society. Their predecessors had moved quite rapidly to patch up their differences, however. Wordsworth had successfully covered up the existence of his early liaison with Annette Vallon, while Coleridge did not, it seems, ever seek to consummate his love for Sara Hutchinson, remaining formally married to his wife even after separating from her.

Nevertheless Wordsworth and Coleridge too, had, like many of their time, found themselves crucially disoriented by the events of the 1790s. Brought up in the settled assumptions of the English eighteenth century, they also had found themselves questioning on a scale hitherto unknown to their contemporaries. Suppositions 'concerning God, Man and Nature' were thrown into question by arguments that introduced new radical positions in each case. Coleridge's phrase 'I found myself all afloat' was tellingly apt to describe a condition where familiar bearings had been lost. Yet the experience of disapprobation had also been enough to show them the drawbacks and pains of taking up a stance that in any way offended society. For Shelley and Byron the pains were to be greater: Shelley's loss of his children in a Chancery suit, Byron's virtual banishment into exile made them even more aware of the quiet weapons that society had at its command when it needed to manifest its disapproval.

In certain respects they were also (and to some degree unwittingly) replicating the original stances of their predecessors more than they themselves probably grasped. The work of scholars has enabled us to see increasingly the character of Wordsworth in the revolutionary period as that of a young man deeply stirred by the events of the time who then became in reaction disillusioned – adopting for a brief period a bitter, sardonic attitude to the hypocrisies of contemporary English society that was in time to be taken up with more passion by Byron. It is doubtful how far Byron himself perceived this continuity, since the early verses and the books on London in *The Prelude* where its traces are to be found were not available to him. In much the same way the young Shelley who was so attracted to radical politics and contemporary science was revivifying the Coleridge who, in the 1790s, had been an ardent advocate of political change and who after the turn of the century was still cherishing new hopes based on scientific advances for his society through his contacts with Humphry Davy. Shelley, filling his Oxford rooms with scientific apparatus in the months that he spent there before being expelled, was only a few years removed from Coleridge's short-lived plan to set up a small laboratory of his own in the Lakes. While Coleridge retreated from his enthusiasm for contemporary science, preferring later to follow the more speculative line of the German *naturphilosophen*, Shelley evidently hoped for more, further nurturing, as has been suggested, Coleridge's hope that it might be possible to produce new thinking by relating recent scientific discovery to ancient esoteric lore.

When Byron and Shelley encountered one another in the summer of 1816 and spent long hours of discussion together, an influence from Coleridge can be detected in both – though in different terms. Shelley had been interesting himself directly in his ideas (including those expressed in *The Friend*); Byron had recently been enjoying the company of the poet himself and hearing him recite poems, such as *Christabel* and *Kubla Khan*, which were not yet available in published form. The one was likely to be more impressed by his idealistic imagery and philosophy, therefore, the other by the exotic qualities of the unpublished verse.

The development that can then be traced in the relations between the two men themselves is also relevant to the issue. After the first shared intellectual excitement in Switzerland during 1816, in which the afflatus of Shelley concerning nature predominated – with the effect on Canto III of *Childe Harold* which has already been described – a second phase, beginning in 1818, was marked by a cooling of Byron's enthusiasm for discovering significance in the scenery of nature and a darker, more cynical mood: both factors coloured the contents of Canto IV.

Another issue arises at this point. As in the case of Wordsworth and Coleridge, also, the concern with matters of Being in the minds of the two poets cannot be totally separated from questions of personal identity. It need not be assumed that their personalities in everyday matters were affected radically any more than their poetry by their treatment at the hands of society. Although Byron was developing from his writings a reputation for misanthropy and sourness, this was only partly reflected in his personal behaviour. Despite the egoism of his dealings with Claire Claremont, including his refusal to allow her access to their daughter Allegra, the impression he made on Mary Shelley was unexpectedly favorable: 'How mild he is! how gentle! So different from what I expected.'[30]

Yet at the same time, and beyond the reach of social effects, it remains the case that their gestures of self-alienation from society left Byron and Shelley in those years drifting, as it were, on the ocean of Being – and more, no doubt, than they had anticipated. The effect of the conjunction of the two poets was initially heady, each recognizing the other's outlaw status. The individual nature of their respective repudiations already suggests, however, the modes in which they were inflecting the possibilities involved.

Shelley has sometimes been seen as effeminate by comparison with his manly friend. In a well-known incident, mourning the fact that he could not swim, he was persuaded to try by plunging into the water, where he then lay at the bottom without making any effort until rescued by Edward Trelawny, who believed that otherwise he would have drowned.[31] This and a few other such anecdotes have encouraged writers to locate in him an essential and pervasive passivity, which has then been transferred to his whole behaviour as offering a theme for interpretation. Myths have subsequently arisen to support an impression of general passive ineffectuality. Even the manner of his death is affected, becoming for interpreters the first of a number of fatalities in the Romantic and post-Romantic eras that were to prove ambiguous.

Trelawny was annoyed by a later biography that claimed Shelley's drowned body to have been clutching a volume of Keats's poems, since the only person to have examined the corpse was himself, and he had already described clearly how the volume had been found in a pocket, 'doubled back, as if the reader, in the act of reading, had hastily thrust it away'.[32*] The erroneous account assisted a view that Shelley had been casually reading at the time of the storm, whereas the only other report that survived at least suggested, like Trelawny's, that he had behaved actively. According to one of the Italian captains, who vainly attempted to rescue Williams and Shelley, they were urged to reduce their sails in such a heavy sea, and one of those on board was seen to make the attempt. Eventually, many years later, a confession by a sailor (mentioned by a priest but relayed also through local gossip) claimed that the boat had not in fact been lost through accident or lack of seamanship, but had been purposely run down by a local felucca bearing men who had seen money being loaded at Leghorn and were hoping to gain possession of it,[33] a story which Trelawny found consonant with his own investigations at the time. If it was true, Shelley did not even have time to be active in self-preservation. In any case, Timothy Webb rightly rebukes those who regard an attitude of passivity as having been endemic to him – particularly when it also suggests an effeminacy that is transferred to the remainder of his poetry. Many contemporary observers, by contrast, dwelt on the masculine energy he showed at times. As an antidote to the myths Webb quotes from Thornton Hunt's recollection of him, seen from the perspective of his own boyhood:

> The outline of the features and face possessed a firmness and *hardness* entirely inconsistent with a feminine character ... [His countenance] changed with every feeling. It usually looked earnest – when joyful, was singularly bright and animated, like that of a gay young girl, – when saddened, had an aspect of sorrow peculiarly touching, and sometimes it fell into a listless weariness still more mournful; but for the most part there was a look of active movement, promptitude, vigour, and decision ... [34]

It is better to assume that he enjoyed being able to shift between the active and the passive, particularly when either might be taken to an extreme; there was no habitual abdication from energy, in other words, but a characteristic alternation between modes. Those who recalled his personality were to recall how it could engage him in extraordinary feats of physical or intellectual activity. Conversely, Byron, to whom the energetic mode came more naturally, also enjoyed his times of peace when they came, as his lines in *Childe Harold*, for example, show: his psyche, it might be said, existed in the same subliminal spectrum, but habitually accented from the other end.

Their differing points of view came out well in their attitudes to Keats. Byron's dismissal of his work as 'piss-a-bed' and a kind of 'mental masturbation' are well known, though the main cause of his displeasure, he said, was impatience at Keats's attack on Pope in 'Sleep and Poetry'.[35] While the early poetry was being seen by Byron as a 'self-pollution', however, his developing works were impressing Shelley by their imaginative achievement and he urged his friend to read *Hyperion*. Byron was somewhat assuaged in his view once he became aware of such admiration; in this context his appearance as mourner in *Adonais* might be seen as a tribute by Shelley to his own powers of persuasion. On hearing of Keats's death he also withdrew some projected criticisms – only, when convinced by his friend that that had been occasioned by the review of 'Endymion' in the *Quarterly*, to produce the lines in *Don Juan* about his having been 'killed off by one critique':

> Poor fellow! his was an untoward fate;
> Tis strange the mind, that very fiery particle,
> Should let itself be snuffed out by an article.[36]

Whatever the truth, or otherwise, of Shelley's belief in his reaction (expressed most fiercely in the preface to *Adonais*) the simplicity of Byron's own physiological views, which seem here to extend no further than a conventional, if vivid, distinction between the fire of the spirit and the clay of the body, is noteworthy.

As is well known, the contemporary hostile reviews often carried a strong political content, a fact that has encouraged attention to the involvement of poets such as Shelley and Byron with contemporary liberal movements. In their earliest writings their status as rebels aligned them naturally enough with the views of young radicals who were trying to keep alive the aspirations, nourished by the French Revolution, that had had to meet with condemnation from most political thinkers in more recent years. A work such as *Laon and Cythna*, indeed, was to be important for future generations of idealistic radicals.

The strong line of realism that makes its presence felt even within the development of that poem as its characters recognize that the cult of non-violence will not necessarily be successful and that they may indeed be forced to acknowledge its impotence, suggests the line that his thought was taking however. There are signs that, without his giving up his ideals, the difficulties facing those who attempted reforms were leading him to reconsider some of his assumptions. Mary Shelley drew attention to the considerable difference to be found in the 1815 poem *Alastor* by comparison with the earlier *Queen Mab*. Speaking of his misfortunes, she remarked:

> Physical suffering had also considerable influence in causing him to turn his eyes inward; inclining him rather to brood over the thoughts and emotions of his own soul rather than to glance abroad, and to make, as in *Queen Mab*, the whole universe the object and subject of his song.

This 'turning his eyes inward' involved a redirection of his attention to the whole question of Being, which was not only to provide an apposite topic in his revision of the Mont Blanc theme, but gave him in *Alastor* another way of considering the 'spirit of solitude'. As he traces the adventures of his figure of the Poet there it becomes clear that an important element in his quest is the attempt to relate the exploration of nature to that of human inwardness, the most striking example coming at the point where he perceives the stream at his side as an emblem of his own inner Being, precise even in its variety:

> Sometimes it fell
> Among the moss with hollow harmony
> Dark and profound. Now on the polished stones
> It danced; like childhood laughing as it went:
> Then, through the plain in tranquil wanderings crept,
> Reflecting every herb and drooping bud
> That overhung its quietness. – 'O stream!
> Whose source is inaccessibly profound,
> Whither do thy mysterious waters tend?
> Thou imagest my life. Thy darksome stillness,
> Thy dazzling waves, thy loud and hollow gulfs,
> Thy searchless fountain, and invisible course
> Have each their type in me: and the wide sky,
> And measureless ocean may declare as soon
> What oozy cavern or what wandering cloud
> Contains thy waters, as the universe
> Tell where these living thoughts reside, when stretched

> Upon thy flowers my bloodless limbs shall waste
> I' the passing wind.'[37]

The central stream-image is the same as that which Wordsworth had already explored, and was to use in his Duddon sonnets a few years later, but Shelley includes more of its possible implications and the full cycle involved, leading not just to the lapse of the stream into the sea but with the eventual dissolution of some of its water into clouds, ready for its return. Although Wordsworth shows awareness of the full process elsewhere, he does not refer to it in the Duddon sonnets, preferring to accentuate the naturalistic there in a manner that will keep him closely related to humanity.[38*]

As Mary Shelley noted, political language was for Shelley giving way to that which was 'inward' – the imagery, we have argued, of 'Being'. Like Coleridge a few years before, he was turning his attention away from current political matters and towards 'what we are, and what we are capable of becoming' with the underlying assumption that it was there that true political wisdom would be found, linked to a fuller understanding of nature; he continued to explore the ideas underlying Coleridge's attempt to relate the sublimities of nature to such a Being – inquiring what, in the absence of a God, that nature might be.

While similarly trying to leave behind ordinary human aspirations, Byron was all too conscious of the curb imposed by physical limits, so that the focus of his idea of Being lay not in the investigation of super-nature but in recognizing the tension between the aspiring spirit of nobility in humans and the bounds of the clay in which it was imprisoned. At the same time, he sought to make his poetry retain complicity with its audience through his acute social sense. Such varying attitudes to bodily experience pointed the radical division within the two poets' concepts, Shelley's involving abstention and a drawing away from satisfaction of physical needs while Byron, by contrast, was drawn to the exploitation of physical experience – whether of frugality or voluptuousness – to the full, and to the recognition that a whole world of frustration existed between the spark and the clay, clogging his attempts to fathom the springs of nobility – as he acknowledged ruefully in a verse scribbled on the back of the *Don Juan* manuscript:

> I would to Heaven that I were so much clay
> As I am blood, bone, marrow, passion feeling –
> Because at least the past were passed away,
> And for the future – (but I write this reeling,

> Having got drunk exceedingly to-day,
> So that I seem to stand upon the ceiling)
> I say – the future is a serious matter –
> And so – for God's sake – hock and soda-water!

Despite the attractions of cynicism, he could not remain unmoved by the fervour of Shelley's enthusiasm, nevertheless. Even Godwin, notable for a lack of imagination rather than otherwise, found the impact of Shelley evident in the works that Byron wrote after the first meetings – notably, as already mentioned, in Canto III of *Childe Harold*, where as he describes in the Alps the stillness of nature, and the answering sensations the note is not only of Shelley but, behind him, Wordsworth:

> All Heaven and Earth are still – though not in sleep,
> But breathless, as we grow when feeling most;
> And silent, as we stand in thoughts too deep: –
> All Heaven and Earth are still: from the high host
> Of stars, to the lulled lake and mountain-coast,
> All is concentred in a life intense,
> Where not a beam, nor air, nor leaf is lost,
> But hath a part of Being, and a sense
> Of that which is of all Creator and Defence.
>
> Then stirs the feeling infinite, so felt
> In solitude, where we are least alone;
> A truth, which through our being then doth melt,
> And purifies from self: it is a tone,
> The soul and source of Music, which makes known
> Eternal harmony, and sheds a charm
> Like to the fabled Cytherea's zone,
> Binding all things with beauty; – 'twould disarm
> The spectre Death, had he substantial power to harm. (lxxxix–xc)

If the Wordsworthian quality of the lines is apparent, they fall short of that poet's faith that love of nature leads to love of man – a lack that Wordsworth himself noted in similar verses by Shelley. There is nevertheless a visible connection between the preoccupations discussed in an earlier chapter and these lines, some of the very few to use a capital for the word 'Being' and to show concern with the correspondence between the work of nature and that of the human psyche. Shortly afterwards, moreover, he turns from the peaceful calm of nature in its peaceful state to the fearful powers displayed at the opposite extreme, while dwelling on the impossibility of finding in those any adequate correlative for the energies of potentiality felt by the sympathizing observer:

> Sky – Mountains – Rivers – Winds – Lake – Lightnings! ye!
> With night, and clouds, and thunder – and a soul
> To make these felt and feeling, well may be
> Things that have made me watchful; the far roll
> Of your departing voices, is the knoll
> Of what in me is sleepless, – if I rest.
> But where of ye, O Tempests! is the goal?
> Are ye like those within the human breast?
> Or do ye find at length, like eagles, some high nest? (xcvi)

Most striking of all, however, are the terms in which he tries to figure what it would be like to experience such a moment of total immediacy in nature:

> Could I embody and unbosom now
> That which is most within me, – could I wreak
> My thoughts upon expression, and thus throw
> Soul – heart – mind – passions – feelings – strong or weak –
> All that I would have sought, and all I seek,
> Bear, know, feel – and yet breathe – into one word,
> And that one word were Lightning, I would speak;
> But as it is, I live and die unheard,
> With a most voiceless thought, sheathing it as a sword. (xcvii)

For Byron, evidently, the true focus of the sense of Being lay in a refinement of energy which could be most fully itself only if realized as lightning. This is a flashing in him of what was referred to earlier as *kairos*, going with a larger sense – that throughout his career he was always seeking for such a suitable 'occasion' that would bring all his powers into play in a single culminating act, even if the act coincided with his own death. It was an ironic subsequence that in the event his end, which he had no doubt anticipated as heroic – probably in battle in Greece – in fact came in the less glamorous mode of fatal illness, the sickness, it was said, of a 'young old man' who had 'exhausted all the nectar contained in the cup of life'.[39]

The manner in which for poets who had cast off the trammels of convention such discourses of *kairos*, aiming at a maximal engagement with the immediate, were liable to interchange with those of *aion*, reaching back from the temporal to the eternal, (many of Wordsworth's poetic meditations in *The Prelude*, for example, subsisting in either mode, or both), was discussed earlier. The dual conception makes even better sense when applied to these later Romantic poets. Shelley is overwhelmingly a poet of *aion*: indeed, once the conception is grasped it illuminates some of his most characteristic passages, particularly when describing moments of supreme insight. One could hardly imagine a better imagery for it than that in the West Wind Ode:

> Thou who didst waken from his summer dreams
> The blue Mediterranean, where he lay,
> Lulled by the coil of his crystalline streams,
>
> Beside a pumice isle in Baiae's bay,
> And saw in sleep old palaces and towers
> Quivering within the wave's intenser day,
>
> All overgrown with azure moss and flowers
> So sweet, the sense faints picturing them! ...

The West Wind is not, of course, an image of Being itself; the very first line clarifies the relation – it is 'the breath of autumn's being'. It provides an excellent subjective correlative, nevertheless, for the state it is expressing.

As far as their own beings found expression in their creative energies – those energies which essentially aspire towards *kairos* – on the other hand, Shelley and Byron found appropriate symbols for themselves in two that appear in Shelley's own *Laon and Cythna*: the Snake and Eagle. The Eagle was an obviously apposite emblem for Byron, given his exceptional soaring powers, while the Snake was one that he himself delighted in applying to Shelley – though whether he had primarily in mind its superb darting quality, or its ability to renew itself by sloughing its skin at intervals, or its emblematic power to swallow its tail and so become a circular image of eternity is not altogether clear. How far the poets were 'wreathed in fight', as one of Shelley's most potent images depicts the two creatures,[40] is harder to say, but the dual identification brings the discussion to another polarity raised by the personal geography of Being. For in accordance with that conception, artists who move beyond the boundaries of normal consciousness may find themselves, in relation to one another, either gesturing mutually and generously across the sphere of creativity or forced back upon the palisades of defensive personal identity.

While both poets entered the domains of creative Being simply by powers of language that took them beyond the denotative, their works attesting not only their facility in writing verse, but the recognition by each of the other's exceptional powers of linguistic exploration, each can also be seen at the personal level as again developing the major characteristic of his predecessor: Shelley's poetry was carrying to a greater refinement the kind of sensibility that had emerged in Coleridge; Byron's writing paid tribute to the powerful naturalism that had been championed by Wordsworth. In each case important differences existed – which were partly a matter of simple morality. Shelley paid little attention to the ordinary conventions of everyday life – particularly where marriage was concerned – that were a source of agonizing to Coleridge. Byron, it need hardly be said, sat even more lightly to conventional sexual morals: it is not at all surprising, therefore, that he should have become so firm a critic of his sententious Lakeland predecessor, often referring to him as 'Turdsworth'.[41]

The distinctiveness that was now emerging in the new wave becomes still more apparent if the development of each of the predecessors is considered in relation to the conventions with which they had set themselves in tension. Both, as has already been pointed out, made peace, at their own pace, with the Anglicanism from which they had earlier strayed. The process of doing so helped to determine the character of their writing and, in the process, its limitations; but it at least allowed that process to continue. For Shelley and Byron, the lack of respect for such conventions left the process free and unconstrained, reinforcing Shelley's devotion to current exploratory thinking – particularly in the area of esoteric philosophy and the potentialities of current science – and Byron's gift for outrageous comedy; but in each case the concluding achievements gave intimations of talents that were reaching an endgame. A dramatic change of course would have been demanded if either were to continue exercising their formidable gifts profitably.

Byron's increasing preoccupation with the dramatic and the comic masked growing reservations concerning Shelley's enterprise; although he could sometimes follow his friend into his more extreme flights, he normally managed his attitude by interspersing praise and defence with complaints concerning his 'metaphysics'. Charles Robinson has demon-strated his consistency of attitude. In March 1822 he wrote to Moore,

> As to poor Shelley, who is another bugbear to you and the world, he is, to my knowledge, the *least* selfish and the mildest of men – a man who has made more sacrifices of his fortune and feelings for others than any I ever heard of. With his speculative opinions I have nothing in common, nor desire to have.[42]

This was shrewd self-knowledge, for Byron must fully have recog-nized that the lack of selfishness which he praised in his friend was far from his own condition. In May he repeated his defence of Shelley to George Bancroft:

> 'You may have heard,' said he, 'many foolish stories of his being a man of no principle, an atheist, and all that; but he is not.' And he explained what appeared in Shelley as atheism was only a subtle metaphysical idealism.[43]

Medwin recorded another expression of his view:

> Shelley has more poetry in him than any man living, and if he were not so mystical, and would not write Utopias and set himself up as a Reformer, his right to rank as a poet, and very highly too, could not fail of being acknowledged.[44]

To James Hamilton Browne he repeated this opinion in 1823 still more elaborately:

> He maintained that Shelley, from the wonderful facility of his versification,, and aptitude at metaphor, would, but for his unfortu-nate predilection for metaphysics in poetry, have ranked in the fore-most circle amongst modern bards: asserting, that no one wrote better, when he selected a lucid theme, and allowed the reader fully to understand and appreciate his effusions.[45]

To George Finlay he repeated his exception more emphatically, tem-pering his praise with the comment that he was 'quite mad with his metaphysics'.[46] Such caveats share a kinship with Wordsworth's view of Coleridge, as recalled by R.P. Graves:

Wordsworth, as a poet, regretted that German metaphysics had so captivated the taste of Coleridge, for he was frequently not intelligible on the subject; whereas, if his energy and his originality had been more exerted in the channel of poetry, an instrument of which he had so perfect a mastery, Wordsworth thought he might have done more permanently to enrich the literature, and to influence the thought of the nation, than any man of the age.[47]

Shelley's 'metaphysics' were not identical with Coleridge's, of course, but they had qualities in common. Wordsworth's further comment that nevertheless Coleridge was 'wonderful for the originality of his mind' can be matched by Byron's extravagant praise of Shelley to Finlay as a 'most extraordinary genius'.

Just as Wordsworth was sparing of praise for Coleridge during his lifetime, Byron proved unwilling to express his admiration for Shelley's gifts very publicly. An incident concerning the matter is recorded by Trelawny, who quoted from a letter he had just received to show something of his egoism in action:

Today I had another letter warning me against the Snake. He, alone, in this age of humbug, dares stem the current, as he did today the flooded Arno in his skiff, although I could not observe he made any progress. The attempt is better than being swept along as all the rest are, with the filthy garbage scoured from its banks.

Taking advantage of this panegyric on Shelley, I observed, he might do him a great service at little cost, by a friendly word or two in his next work, such as he had bestowed on authors of less merit.

Assuming a knowing look, he continued:

'All trades have their mysteries; if we crack up a popular author, he repays us in the same coin, principal and interest. A friend may have repaid money lent, – can't say any of mine have; but who ever heard of the interest being added thereto?'

I rejoined:

'By your own showing you are indebted to Shelley; some of his best verses are to express admiration of your genius.'

'Ay,' he said, with a significant look, 'who reads them? If we puffed the Snake, it might not turn out a profitable investment. If he cast off the slough of his mystifying metaphysics, he would want no puffing.'

Seeing I was not satisfied, he added:
'If we introduced Shelley to our readers, they might draw
comparisons, and they are '*odorous*'.[48]

A story such as this is very much to the taste of critics who read literary
history in terms of power-games as between individuals, and a
reminder that writers are indeed liable to protect their *amour propre*.
Awareness of this firm persuasion at the time makes it desirable to
adopt an alternative assumption to 'human power-politics' when dealing
with writers such as Coleridge and Shelley, and to take account of their
status as people whose sensibilities were of a rare order, having been
developed in a manner that encouraged them to subordinate their
egoism to an unusual and, for their period, unprecedented degree. There
is a need, in other words, to examine the events involved through an
appropriate filter, making allowance for this bias by which their ordinary
emotions could sometimes lie unacknowledged or only half admitted as
they contrived to keep them below the level of consciousness. In the
earlier relationship Coleridge had been able to maintain an admiration
and veneration for Wordsworth that was tempered only by an occasional misgiving or surgence from his subconscious, as in the 'awakening
from a dream of ... involuntary Jealousy' recorded earlier.[49] Such a poise
was much easier in the age when traditional Christian moral beliefs
might seem supported by the philosophy of Immanuel Kant.
    Shelley's feelings concerning Byron were even more divided. Byron's
personal behaviour could repel him, as when he wrote on 17 July 1815

Lord Byron is an exceedingly interesting person, and as such is it
not to be regretted that he is a slave to the vilest and most vulgar
prejudices, and as mad as the winds.

This was early in their relationship and in some respects Shelley
warmed to his friend as it grew; but a distance always remained. His
distaste emerged strongly at Venice in 1818 when he wrote to Peacock
concerning Canto IV of *Childe Harold*, that 'the spirit in which it is
written is, if insane, the most wicked that ever was given forth. It is a
kind of obstinate and self-willed folly in which he hardens himself ...'
claiming that it was associated with his addiction to vice:

LB is familiar with the lowest sort of these women, the people his
gondolieri pick up in the streets.... He associates with wretches who
seem almost to have lost the gait and physiognomy of man, & who

do not scruple to avow practices which are not only not named but I believe seldom even conceived in England. He says he disapproves, but he endures.[50]

By the end of his career such repulsions had become part of his regular attitude, so that he could confess in March 1822:

Particular circumstances, – or rather I should say, particular disposi-tions in Lord B's character render the close & intimate exclusive intimacy with him in which I find myself, intolerable to me; thus much my best friend I will confess & confide to you.... However ... I will take care to preserve the little influence I may have over this Proteus in whom such extremes are reconciled until we meet.[51]

The sense of personal distaste continued to grow, intensified by Byron's callous attitude to his wife's half-sister Claire, happy to let her become pregnant by him, but then denying her access to her child. As Shelley put it in a further letter to Hunt:

Certain it is, that Lord Byron has made me bitterly feel the inferior-ity which the world has presumed to place between us and which subsists nowhere in reality but in our own talents, which are not our own but Nature's – or in our rank, which is not our own but Fortune's.[52]

Once again, the dialogue between the two men might be said to be reproducing, in a higher key, that between Coleridge and Wordsworth a few years earlier. In each case a free play of mind, yearning towards the freedom of infinity, was met by a sensibility more conscious of human limitations. For Shelley, the 'immortal spark' in man was essen-tially illuminating, offering a possible guarantee (if any were to be found) of his immortality; Byron, by contrast, concentrated on its fieriness, burning in ultimate impotence against the fact of its impris-onment in clay – or laughing at its plight.

A crucial document here is 'Julian and Maddalo' – the poem by Shelley in which the relationship is most explicitly projected. Maddalo, the Byron figure, rides out with Julian one evening at sunset and takes him in his gondola to a point where the sun is blotted out by a prison-like building, rearing itself as an emblem of human mortality. One of its inmates is a Maniac, whom they go to see next day, and who turns out to be a victim of love. This figure has been variously held to be a projection of Tasso, Byron or Shelley himself. One critic[53] holds him to be primarily a Byronic hero who was once a Shelleyan idealist – thus, as he says, effectively subsuming the experiences of both poets. Perhaps it is better to interpret him a shade differently, as representing Shelley's recognition of a common ground between their positions. Both men, at least, could agree that the force which stood most firmly against realization of the ideal was that of unrequited love.

The dialogue can also be pursued through *Prometheus Unbound* (seen as, among other things, a commentary on Byron's *Manfred*[54]) to a time when Shelley, impressed by the fecundity of Byron in *Don Juan*, could make a remark such as 'I despair of rivalling Lord Byron ... and there is no other with whom it is worth contending'. This suggests that he was in some sense conscious of such a contending against his friend – a supposition which throws some light on his bent at the time towards satire, as exhibited in *Peter Bell the Third*. But the two were also coming to differ more vehemently. Shelley disliked *Marino Faliero* and Byron *The Cenci*.

As the dialogue continued, Shelley refined his vision and Byron occasionally found room for apposite comments amid the sardonic flow of *Don Juan*. Shelley was bowled over by *Cain*, which he described as 'apocalyptic' and the work of 'this spirit of an angel in the mortal paradise of a decaying body'.[55] Yet he also increasingly recognized Byron's lack of altruism and his unwillingness to help his friends. On the basis of his self-confessed envy, Robinson has seen Shelley in the last period as a fallen angel, who has committed the sin of envying Byron his fame and riches and so passed into a state of Satanic despair.[56] The evidence is tenuous, however. To see Shelley as taking up the role of Milton's Satan in simple acceptance risks missing an irony. Already, a few years earlier Blake had asserted that Milton wrote so well about the devils and so colourlessly about the angels because he was a true poet and therefore of the devil's party without knowing it; whether or not he had ever come across this comment Shelley had hardly needed such prompting to write of Milton's God as 'one who in the cold security of undoubted triumph inflicts the most horrible revenge upon his enemy, not from any mistaken notion of inducing him to repent of a perseverance in enmity, but with the alleged design of exasperating him to deserve new torments'.[57]

Shelley's criticisms of Milton's God were powerful enough to make it unlikely that he accepted the rest of his theology at face value. He would surely have found the Satanic position heroic. To say further that he came to fear death because he feared that he would be pursued into the darkness by the envied sun of Byron's genius is surely to misapprehend further the nature of the relationship in its last months. In his 'Sonnet to Byron',[58] he abases himself as a worm beneath the sod before Byron's genius – but he does so on the express grounds that to do anything else might bring him into a state of envy. Unlike Milton's Satan, on the other hand, he never, it may be argued, lost faith in light; nor, by the same token, did he lose faith in Byron's genius. The tribute to *Don Juan* just quoted should be read in its full context:

> He has read to me one of the unpublished cantos [V] of Don Juan, which is astonishingly fine. – It sets him not above but far above all the poets of the day: every word has the stamp of immortality. – I despair of rivalling Lord Byron, as well I may: and there is no other with whom it is worth contending. This canto is in style, but totally, & sustained with incredible ease & power, like the end of the second canto: there is not a word which the most rigid assertor of the dignity of human nature could desire to be cancelled: it fulfills in a certain degree what I have long preached of producing something wholly new & relative to the age – and yet surpassingly beautiful. It may be vanity, but I think I see the trace of my earnest exhortations to him to create something wholly new.[59]

The contradiction which he was now facing had to do not with envy but with his awareness of the paradox contained in a Byron who combined within his person evidences of the illumination and genius he himself aimed for as unmistakable as were his lack of the virtues which, on Shelley's reading of life, ought to have accompanied genius: sympathy, open generosity, selflessness. His last poem, 'The Triumph of Life', may in fact mark his recognition that life itself seems to contain the very same ambiguity that he has had to acknowledge in his friend. 'Imagination', he had written earlier, 'is as the immortal God which should assume flesh for the redemption of mortal passion'. Yet the man whom he regarded as the greatest poetic genius of the age gave little evidence of such redemption.

The matter of personal identity and its comparative status between the participants in a relationship is again relevant. As in the case of Coleridge and Wordsworth, an outgoing personality was being pitted against a self-confirming character and finding itself correspondingly weak. Keats recognized the problems created by such a disposition straightforwardly, as has already been noticed:

It is a wretched thing to confess; but is a very fact that not one word I utter can be taken for granted as an opinion growing out of my identical nature – how can it, when I have no nature? When I am in a room with People if I ever am free from speculating on creations of my own brain, then not myself goes home to myself; but the identity of every one in the room begins [so] to press upon me that, I am in a very little time annihilated ... [60]

By his belief in the existence of 'spirit', on the other hand, Keats could conceive even of a commerce between spirits after death by their intelligence of each other.[61] In the same way, as has been noted already, Coleridge could imagine a process by which one spirit might interpenetrate another, longing for such a process between himself and Wordsworth: 'O that my Spirit, purged by Death of its Weaknesses, which are, alas! my *identity*, might flow into *thine*, & live and act in thee, & be Thou.' [62] Even as he was aspiring to an absorption of 'spirit', in other words, he was recognizing that his own 'identity' might consist in no more than a weakness. It was a recognition that he would repeat from time to time in what his friends would despairingly call his 'prostration' before his friend. The sight of a man near him who was more like a firm rock, a lighthouse even, seemed a permanent reproach to the mercurial qualities of his own personality.

The contrast both fits – and fails to fit – Byron, whose personality in many basic respects ran contrary to Wordsworth's. He had none of the self-affirming steadfastness that made the Lake Poet so impressive in his stance; on the contrary, in his equally self-affirming shifts of position he could seem as mercurial as Coleridge himself. He even claimed that a desire to get away from self was dominant in his behaviour:

To withdraw *myself* from *myself* (oh that cursed selfishness!) has ever been my sole, my entire, my sincere motive in scribbling at all; and publishing is also the continuance of the same object, by the action it affords to the mind, which else recoils upon itself.[63]

Yet this was simply to confirm the egoism of his basic attitude, the self-regarding quality that came first in his behaviour. The self-forgetting Shelley, by contrast, must necessarily seem to vanish when performing against the powerful sense of identity emitted by such self-reinforcement: in a world that would increasingly concern itself with what would work, he would be destined to suffer Matthew Arnold's dismissive adjective, 'ineffectual'.[64*]

Instead of simply seeing him as a figure taking on Byron and losing, it does more justice to the complexity of his attitude if the growing division in his mind is recognized. That its state was becoming unusual is suggested among other things by the final condition of his marital relations. Remaining closely attached to his wife, he had reserved the right to freedom of the affections for himself, as expressed in the well-known lines of 'Epipsychidion':

> I never was attached to that great sect,
> Whose doctrine is, that each one should select
> Out of the crowd a mistress or a friend,
> And all the rest, though fair and wise, commend
> To cold oblivion ...[65]

Mary presumably assented, at least at one level of her personality, to this attitude, and to the love for Emilia Viviani which was expressed in the remainder of the poem, though its position was in some respects notably confused. Richard Holmes has discussed the difficult effects produced in a poem where a paean of platonic love for Emilia mingles with autobiographical reminiscence, so that 'he was promising eternal courtly love in a poem which actually celebrated free love'.[66] In one sense, however, the situation here was simple enough, since Emilia was safely locked up in her convent, so that the invitation to liberty could remain at the level of fantasy.

The position became more complex with the advent of Edward and Jane Williams. Despite his attempts at total candour, Shelley found that there were some things that he could not say to Mary – notably the decline of her attractiveness for him. To Gisborne he wrote of his love of Italy,

> I only feel the want of those who can feel, and understand me. Whether from proximity and the continuity of domestic inter-course, Mary does not. The necessity of concealing from her thoughts that would pain her, necessitates this, perhaps. It is the curse of Tantalus, that a person possessing such excellent powers and so pure a mind as hers, should not excite the sympathy indis-pensable to their application to domestic life ...[67]

In this context, Jane was an opportune object of his affections, pre-served, just as Emily was by her convent, through the presence of her husband. But the effect of having her so near was to exacerbate still further the division in him between his everyday married life with

Mary and his yearnings for Jane. His two selves were increasingly in tension with one another.

In the last weeks of his life Shelley came to exist in an unreal state of mind that increasingly allowed subliminal elements to find expression. Shortly before his fatal voyage, he ran on one occasion into Mary's bedroom screaming. She believed him still to be under the influence of sleep, but afterwards he told her that he had seen two visions: in one he had seen Edward and Jane Williams, torn and covered with blood, staggering into his room supporting each other and crying 'Get up Shelley the sea is flooding the house & it is all coming down'; in the other, as he actually rushed into Mary's room, he had seen his own figure bending over her and strangling her. If regarded as a projection from his subliminal self, it suggests an unconscious and unwelcome wish, nursed even while he was supporting his wife. A similar projection may account for another incident, in which walking on the terrace he encountered himself, hearing from him the words 'How long do you mean to be content?'[68]

Meanwhile he sought to enlist Jane in the role of therapist, exploring another avenue that we have noticed as a ready source of subliminal awareness. Animal magnetism, which despite its decline in England had retained its fascination on the continent of Europe, naturally attracted the attention of someone who was so interested in sciences – particularly when they verged on the occult.[69] Mary tried her hand at magnetizing him, but gave up when she found that it had revived his habit of sleep-walking and feared an accident.[70] Jane, however, unvisited by such hesitations, conducted experiments with him which resulted in the poem 'The Magnetic Lady to her Patient'.[71] The first stanza of this records her success, and her reservation concerning deeper intimacy:

> Sleep, sleep on! forget thy pain;
>   My hand is on thy brow,
> My spirit on thy brain;
> My pity on thy heart, poor friend;
>   And from my fingers flow
> The powers of life, and like a sign,
>   Seal thee from thine hour of woe;
> And brood on thee, but may not blend
>   With thine.

The end of the fourth stanza, describing the healing influence of her affection on him expresses Shelley's belief in the relationship between the soul and Being:

> Its light within thy gloomy breast
> Spreads like a second youth again.
> By mine thy being is to its deep
> Possessed.

The poem ends in enigmatic fashion as the Magnetic Lady, now given her real name, asks how she might cure him when he is awake. He replies:

> 'What would cure, that would kill me, Jane:
> And as I must on earth abide
> Awhile, yet tempt me not to break
> My chain.

It is a riddling reply, its meaning uncertain;[72*] what is clear, however is a decision not to leave his life for the time being – which was not always present to him when talking to Jane. Trelawny recalled a hot day by the sea when he persuaded her forcefully how pleasant it would be if she and her babies joined him in floating offshore in his insecure boat. Having assumed that an excursion into the shallows was planned, she became alarmed when he rowed them out into deeper water and rested on his oars, 'unconscious of her fears and apparently of where he was, absorbed in a deep reverie, probably reviewing all he had gone through of suffering and wrong ...'

> Spellbound by terror, she kept her eyes on the awful boatman: sad and dejected, with his head leaning on his chest, his spirit seemed crushed; his hand had been for every man, and every man's hand against him ... At any other time or place Jane would have sympathized deeply with the lorn and despairing bard. She had made several remarks, but they met with no response. She saw death in his eyes. Suddenly he raised his head, his brow cleared, and his face brightened as with a bright thought. and he exclaimed joyfully 'Now let us together solve the great mystery.'

Jane, who was as drawn to life as he at this time to transcending it, kept calm and showed admirable presence of mind, Trelawny recalls, seeing that 'her only chance was to distract his thoughts from his dismal past life to the less dreary present – to kindle hope':

> In answer to his kind and affectionate proposal of 'solving the great mystery', suppressing her terror and assuming her usual cheerful

voice, she answered promptly 'No thank you, not now; I should like my dinner first, and so would the children.'[73]

Her prompt reaction showed Jane Williams to be living in the same common-sense world as Mary Shelley, in whose company she was destined to watch the man with whom their destinies were linked take, with Byron, their varying paths to death, each pursuing one of the polarities of Being to an utmost extreme. Both men were, in one way or the other, trying to delineate further the relation between body and spirit, Byron still relishing or tormenting the body while emphasizing its limitations, Shelley concentrating on the far reaches of sensation that might merge into the potentialities of 'soul'.

Neither was particularly interested in his own survival: various incidents bring out the degree of their indifference. Trelawny twice records exclamations on the subject by Byron: 'Who wants to live? ... Not I. The Byrons are a short-lived race on both sides ... I don't care for death a damn: it is her sting, I can't bear – pain'; and 'If Death comes in the shape of a cannon-ball and takes off my head, he is welcome. I have no wish to live, but I can't bear pain.'[74] Shelley's quiet indifference on occasion in the face of mortal danger has already been mentioned.

The basic tension between Byron and Shelley remained that of their dispositions of Being: Byron's essentially inward turning and self-consolidating, Shelley's essentially outgoing, with little self-regard. When they had both left their mortal state, no longer needing to ask the questions concerning Being that had obsessed each of them in different ways, they left behind women, Mary Shelley herself, Claire Clairmont, Jane Williams, who did not share those concerns, being more committed to living in the immediate present. For such survivors the question of Being was therefore more readily focused on a point which Wordsworth and Coleridge had passed through in their earlier period, where it had fewer metaphysical overtones and was intimately associated with the nature of Life.

At the time of her deepest involvement Mary Shelley may well have gone further, at least glimpsing the polarities involved in the relationship between Byron and her husband and grasping the possibilities of a true significance in nature, even, possibly, the desirability of probing, like them, the limits of physical experience. If so, her own mode of coping with such issues was different – not, as they did, to pursue a particular course to its extreme but to take the issues into her own psyche and dramatize them in a work of fiction where she devised a

'Being' of her own to bring out the issues involved. In the case of that constructed Being, for reasons that will by now have become clear, the questions first of Life, and then of consciousness, would be for her the most crucial – though here for the most part they would take a nightmare form.

8
Mary Shelley's Mediation

When looked at beside her companions, Mary Shelley remains an undefined, somewhat prosaic figure. Trelawny describes his first impression of her, bringing the company back from the ideal world to which her husband had tried to transport them with her requests for news of London and Paris, the new books, operas, and bonnets, marriages, murders ... In a note added later to his *Records* he asserted that she was a person as conventional as her husband had been the opposite, setting this down partly to her upbringing by her father and his wish that she should not be made to suffer as he had done for beliefs found unacceptable by her society:

> Mrs Shelley was a firm believer, and had little or no sympathy with any of her husband's theories; she could not but admire the great capacity and learning of her husband, but she had no faith in his views, and she grieved that he was so stubborn and inflexible. Fighting with the world was 'Quixotic' .... Mrs Shelley did not worry herself with things established that could not be altered, but went with the stream.[1]

Whatever the truth of this at the time when Trelawny knew her, it must be remembered that, for the most part, this was the period following a tragedy, the effect of which on her cannot be overestimated. In her editing of Shelley's works she writes that her task 'becomes inexpressibly painful as the year draws near that which sealed our earthly Fate ...'[2]; the high-flown language should not allow the reader to discount the devastating effects of the event, which no doubt left her, above all, as someone whose first thought must henceforth be to survive, along with her child. Her state of mind in 1816, when she was strongly under the spell of her husband and Byron, may well have been very different from that which Trelawny describes: it is indeed difficult to imagine Mary Wollstonecraft's daughter turning to conventional beliefs without any kind of questioning, particularly when one knows of the 'many long conversations' between Shelley and Byron that she herself describes, to which she was 'a devout but nearly silent listener', and of her own reading during the previous years. Even the names mentioned in her novel suggest a mind still simmering with such things as a reading of recent novels from England and Germany, a full knowledge of the French Revolution and of the ideas behind it, and awareness of contemporary scientific work.

For her, the facts of living and dying that contemporary scientists discussed in dispassionate terms were more immediately present, through the tragic events of her own experience. Her life, originally overshadowed by the tragedy of her mother's death at her birth, was further darkened by the effects on others of her impulsive decision to run away with Percy Bysshe Shelley, which was to induce the suicide of his wife Harriet, in time. Most recently, moreover, she had been dogged by event after event in which pregnancy, childbirth and death intermingled. In February 1815 she gave birth to a premature female child, who died twelve days later. Thirteen days after that she dreamt that her baby had come to life again, having simply been cold and that they had rubbed her back to life in front of the fire. In January 1816 she gave birth to her son William; in October, Fanny Imlay, Mary's half-sister, discovering that her father was not Godwin but Mary Wollstonecraft's American lover, committed suicide, followed on 10 December by Harriet herself, who was then pregnant by another man. The Shelleys married three weeks later and, in March 1817, were joined at Marlowe by Claire Clairmont, who had recently had a child by Byron. Child death and suicides made vivid the physical facts involved, happening in an intellectual context of inquiry where the nature of life itself was an object of debate.

Coleridge's earlier interest in the various current theories concerning this was mentioned above;[3] Marilyn Butler has drawn attention to the likely fascination for the Shelleys now of the vitalist controversy, connected particularly with the lectures of their friend William Lawrence. The fact that Lawrence was suspended by the Royal College of Surgeons and not reinstated until he withdrew his *Lectures on Physiology, Zoology and the Natural History of Man*, published in the year after *Frankenstein*, illustrates the dangers of the path trodden by any whose work might be held to support a materialist version of vitalism.[4*]

Mary's account of how, having listened silently to many such conversations, particularly on the nature of life and the probability that its principle might be discovered and communicated, she became so excited that on one occasion her thoughts rose up in visionary form has often been quoted: she saw, she said, 'the pale student of unhallowed arts' kneeling behind the thing he had put together until it began to stir with life and how then, when he went to sleep hoping that it would die again, it continued to live and to haunt him. When her companions planned that each should write a ghost story she realized that she had one already to her hand and set to work on *Frankenstein*.

For his own part her husband believed that she had created not so much a 'Monster' as what he was to term a 'Being' of her own. He found the novel enthralling: 'we are led breathless with suspense and sympathy, and the heaping up of incident on incident, and the working of passion out of passion.' Drawing on his Rousseauian presuppositions he found in the 'Being' himself a fit subject for sympathy:

> Treat a person ill, and he will become wicked. Requite affection with scorn; – let one being be selected, for whatever cause as the refuse of his kind – divide him, a social being, from society, and you impose on him the irresistible obligations – malevolence and selfishness.

He read the novel, in other words, as embodying a social deconstruction of Being as he envisaged it, and so taking on the lessons of his own ideal philosophy, according to which humans were properly created to behave as good, fully sympathizing with one another. Once take away the presence of such qualities, however, and their negatives, ill-will and selfishness, would automatically rise to take their place.

Whether Mary herself would have drawn the moral so wholeheartedly is by no means clear, but she was certainly aware of the qualities in recent literature that gave rise to it, so that in artistic terms her fiction could easily be seen to represent the positive elements that had grown up to replace such Being, the absence of which was likely to be deeply experienced in an age of conscious rationalism. The relevant elements which had appeared most often in the fiction of the time were those of sensibility and terror, in either case the appeal being to responses starved in a literature based on common-sense rationalism. The most notable examples were in English and German literature, readily available in novels of sensibility and in the popular Gothic novel.

On this dual tradition Mary Shelley drew effortlessly during her writing of *Frankenstein*. At one point the monster, living in a humble cottage in Germany, keeps watch on the family next door without their realizing it and is deeply attracted by their effortless affection towards one another. The description here is reminiscent of Goethe's *Sorrows of the Young Werther*, with its key image of a young hero forced to look on at a family happiness he knows he can never share. The monster, in his own way, is in precisely that position. Just after relating similar impressions he himself reveals how *Werther* was among three books he had stumbled across in his reading.

The Gothic tradition of sensibility and horror was a basic resource, providing access to two existing polarities within recent artistic development that complemented rationally-based performances, but Mary could not ignore new questions raised by the times in which she lived, including the ways in which they affected the criticisms of earlier works that might seem to have a firmly established position. This was most notably true of *Paradise Lost*. Her husband's view, as published a few years later, has already been mentioned; this was another work which the Monster was made to come across:

> But *Paradise Lost* excited different and far deeper emotions. I read it as I had read the other volumes which had fallen into my hands, as a true history. It moved every feeling of wonder and awe that the picture of an omnipotent God warring with his creatures was capable of exciting.

When the monster goes on to say that he found an affinity in himself to Satan, he is helping to establish the degree to which he will invite identification as a Promethean figure – more directly in some ways than Dr Frankenstein himself – being bound to the rock of a deformity which offers no hope for anything but hostility and fear from human beings. The novel's subtitle, *The Modern Prometheus*, reflects the fascination of this mythical figure for contemporary writers, including Shelley, who, of course, entitled his major poetic drama *Prometheus Unbound*. Romantic writers in general, with their concern for human liberty, developed a natural fellow-feeling for this figure as the great protagonist of humanity: instead of an obedient Son of God made to suffer by his contemporaries in accordance with their creator's decree, as promulgated in Christianity, they were drawn to the idea of a man with sufferings directly attributable to his Creator. Why, they asked, should humankind be made to feel guilty for breaking a code which was imposed in the first place by God? Why should they not be allowed simply to protest against their plight, retaining in the circumstances dignity and nobility? Prometheus on his rock provided an apt emblem for such feelings.

Something of the kind was in Mary Shelley's mind when she produced as epigraph for her novel the words of Adam's protest in *Paradise
Lost* after the Fall:

> Did I request thee, Maker, from my clay
> To mould me man? Did I solicit thee
> From darkness to promote me?

It is not surprising, therefore, that some readers have regarded the
monster as himself a Prometheus, condemned to a life not asked for,
though it is more likely that in selecting her subtitle Mary Shelley actually had in mind another part of the Prometheus myth: having stolen
the heavenly fire, Prometheus implanted it in clay and so brought
about the creation of humanity. Her Dr Frankenstein, usurping the
creator's prerogative, had brought down on himself a similar curse.

Read in its entirety, however, the novel allows for both elements of
the Promethean myth, sharing them out between creator and creation.
Dr Frankenstein is a Prometheus, stealer of fire and implanter of it in
human clay; but it is the monster he creates, forever to be tortured by
the contradictions of his being, who exhibits most fully the
Promethean predicament. If, as is sometimes claimed, Prometheus is
the greatest saint in the Romantic calendar, Mary Shelley may be cred-
ited with having seen even more fully into the possibilities of his can-
onization than her Romantic contemporaries, and in so doing to have
exposed some of the tensions inherent in Romanticism itself.

To this degree at least, then, she had managed to take on some of the
implications of her companions' interest in Being, by developing the
sense of division that they too were exploring. She also had the opportunity of glimpsing the mystery involved in its most vivid form, by
seeing in action their extraordinary powers of prolific poetic creation,
which each could make the other despair of rivalling. What power, if
not that inherent in Being itself, could explain such fountainous
overflowing? At the same time she moved the discussion to a different
level by her reverence for the nature of the life that they were treating
so negligently. The quest for dangerous knowledge which each cher-
ished in his own way was seen by her when directed to investigations
of life itself to be fraught with the perils that faced Dr Faustus: hence
her phrase 'unhallowed arts' and her insistent descriptions of
Dr Frankenstein's activities in terms of nastiness and filth.

This was one reason, no doubt, why she took the older poets of her
companions' generation more seriously than they, particularly the

authors of *Lyrical Ballads* and the work associated with their devotion to the 'one Life': as a result of her own experiences of child-bearing and death she knew on her own pulses that life was too precious to be regarded as a means to some other end. Her references to Wordsworth bear witness to the depth of her feelings. In chapter 18 of *Frankenstein* Victor pays tribute to his friend Clerval in the words: 'He was a being formed in the "very poetry of nature". His wild and enthusiastic imagination was chastened by the sensibility of his heart.' This could serve as a summary of Wordsworth's own aims in much of his poetry, where the workings of sublime feelings that separate him from the rest of mankind are constantly counterpointed by the interventions of a quiet sensibility reuniting him again with the human race: 'Love of nature leading to love of man'. Mary could not of course have known *The Prelude*, but she knew the rest of Wordsworth's poetry, and just afterwards she actually quotes a few lines taken from the 'Lines written ... above Tintern Abbey' – a poem describing his progress from a childhood of aching joys and dizzy raptures to the humane vision of the adult man – in order to describe the passionate sensibility of Clerval himself. It suggests how fully she appreciated the degree to which Wordsworth had developed the cults of sensibility and terror that had made contemporary novels popular, yet open to charges of sensationalism, into the subtle mode by which a more mature cultivation and love of nature could be induced. Precisely the kind of alternation that Wordsworth describes, between experiences of awe and fear in nature and subsequent feelings of unusual beauty and sympathy, characterizes the attitudes developed in her novel: the monster himself is shown by turns in fearsome and tender lights. There are long sequences in which he tells his own story and strikes a note of sympathy; there are others when we are aware of him only as an external and looming threat and are invited to share the nausea and terror of the other characters; the two modes can, in addition, sometimes alternate rapidly.

Mary's cultivation of the Wordsworthian ideal of persuasion through fear and tenderness follows in the same course of development as his: from a late eighteenth-century indulgence in Gothic terrors and cultivation of sensibility to a more fully realistic and human view; this, however, can help explain only some parts of her novel. The element of the supernatural there, signalled by events which are increasingly unbelievable on any basis of probability, is more reminiscent of *The Rime of the Ancient Mariner*, where a tale of the supernatural is presented more boldly, not just offering a work of delight and terror in the Gothic style, but (rather as her father

William Godwin had hoped with his novel *Things as They Are)* suggesting that it might not only effect the permanent change described in the hero, but change the reader's own perception of the world. Even the elements of firm logic in her plot remind one of the persuasively naturalistic way in which the voyage is described in Coleridge's poem.

She also showed how fully she had absorbed the impact of its author. When Coleridge had visited her father's family during the Christmas of 1799, he had been oppressed by the 'cadaverous Silence' of the children, by comparison with the boisterousness of his own.[5] Along with her reserve, however, the two-year-old Mary had later proved to have an extraordinary receptivity – activated strongly, no doubt, when she crept downstairs one evening to hear the poet himself read the *Rime* aloud.[6]

There can certainly be no doubt of the poem's presence in the novel, since it is quoted by Dr Frankenstein himself to describe his state of mind when he has just run away from the monster he has created:

> Like one that on a lonesome road
> Doth walk in fear and dread,
> And having once turned round walks on
> And turns no more his head;
> Because he knows a frightful fiend
> Doth close behind him tread.

Its presence is also there at the very beginning. In his second letter Walton writes:

> I am going to unexplored regions, to 'the land of mist and snow', but I shall kill no albatross, therefore do not be alarmed for my safety, or if I should come back to you as worn and woeful as the 'Ancient Mariner?' You will smile at my allusion; but I will disclose a secret. I have often attributed my attachment to, my passionate attachment for, the dangerous mysteries of ocean, to that production of the most imaginative of modern poets.

Fourteen years later, when Mary Shelley was looking back on the creation of the novel and particularly of the monster, her description of his appearance in her original dream, 'I saw the hideous phantasm of a man stretched out, and then, on the working of some powerful engine, show signs of life, and stir with an uneasy, half-vital motion', recalls that of the ship in Coleridge's poem:

> But in a minute she 'gan stir
> With a short uneasy motion ...

These ready quotations show how intimately the images and language of Coleridge's poem had entered her imagination, even its figure of Death having features akin to the monster's. Both the underlying preoccupation with the nature of life and the incidental imagery (the behaviour of her own figures at the end of the story being very like the phantasmagorial travellings of the Mariner from land to land) betray the continued working of the poem.

Her imagery also suggests something of Coleridge's fascination with symbolic interpretation of the world. A recent critic, Andrew Griffin, has shown how extraordinarily predominant in this novel is its imagery of fire and ice.[7] The monster seems to be encountered especially in frosty regions – but also often at times when a lightning storm is playing. Twice he expresses his despair by making a fire – the first time when he burns down the cottage vacated by the family from whom he had hoped for friendship, the second, at the end of the novel, when he plans to perish himself by fire.

Griffin further shows how Percy Bysshe Shelley's use of similar imagery – particularly in *Prometheus Unbound* – suggests a fascination with the extremes of nature displayed by these phenomena. In this sense, and given the patent improbability of the events, the novel borders on symbolic myth. Even more powerful, however, is an equally basic symbolism – that of motion. In *Frankenstein*, the Monster's movements are as unpredictable and improbable as those of the ship in *The Ancient Mariner*, while at the end there is an eerie resemblance between the last glimpse of the Mariner ('I pass like night from land to land ...') and that of the 'Daemon', 'soon borne away by the waves, and lost in darkness and distance' – in his case foreseeing his own fiery destruction, it is true, but still, in the language, an anti-type of Shelley himself at the end of *Adonais*, 'borne darkly, fearfully afar ...'.

At this symbolic level the novel retains potency in our time by very reason of the fact that the questions raised by the Shelleys remain unresolved. The monster can still be seen as a symbol of various terrors that not only haunted her consciousness but lie beneath the surface of the rational order increasingly cultivated by the civilization of her time, and our own – fears of war, oppression, violence; but it also raises, over all, the Shelleyan question that remains unanswered: whether or not it is a failure of love and affection within the human race that is ultimately responsible for the prevalence of these terrors. Because such questions are left open at the end, they can be explored by each reader in his or her own way, while another basic question, the Faustian one concerning the value to human beings of knowledge beyond a certain point, also survives, to tease further.

A good deal of the critical interest that has surrounded the novel has been based on such points, where symbolism merges into social questioning with a moralistic overtone; yet this on reflection must seem strange, since the story then tends to be treated as if a true one is being related, available to be judged from a naturalist point of view. Any judicial view of the novel must immediately take account, however, of its far-fetched nature, in which the Monster is not only endowed with life through the improbable putting together of a patchwork of organs, but the resulting body is immediately endowed with consciousness and the capacity to educate itself linguistically in a brief period. This unlikely state of affairs is then complemented by events some of which involve the Monster's apparent ability to move on occasion with impossibly high speed so as appear in a location that happens to suit the development of the plot.

While the 'Being' she created in her novel can be seen as an attempt to represent the paradoxical version of humanity that her companions recognized in themselves, then, such improbabilities mean that it must also be regarded not as realistic but as an innovatory construct, reflecting an inquiry into what might result from a successful attempt to create new life. As such the Monster cannot have the full organic validity of a normal human being but must be a contradictory creation, one that figures further tensions raised within her own mind and draws attention to matters concerning the 'life' that her companions slighted. It ignores, therefore, many of the issues that had been betraying themselves in the discussions between her two companions. In this she not only remained true to the fears that commonly surrounded Faustian aspirations, but also looked back to the reverence for life itself which she had gained from the previous generation they were looking to supersede.

She had also grasped that in the new world in which they were now living the implications of such a simple attitude, despite being known to every member of the human race and especially to those who shared her gender, were unlikely to be impressed properly on the mind of a reader simply by the presentation of an ordered narrative statement. Something other than straightforward retailing was called for. So she followed a method not unlike that to be found in *The Ancient Mariner*, where three distinct tellers may be discerned (the narrator of the ballad, the Mariner himself, and the compiler of the marginal glosses) and set up a plot where the point of view shifts between those of Walton and Victor Frankenstein, with intervening self-justifying speeches from the Monster. In doing so she was unwittingly acting as a further pioneer for works such as *Bleak House*, *Wuthering Heights* and *The Turn of the Screw* and looking forward to the varying points of view expressed in some later novels, culminating, for example, in *A Passage to India*. Such narrative complexities reflect the interplay of different strains of thought, each needing recognition, that were to be found in the new intellectual situation following the time of the French Revolution.

Frankenstein is sometimes said now to have passed – though comparatively recently – to become a part of the literary canon. If this is true, it is so in a rather special sense. Traditionally, the concept of the canon has been reserved for works which carry particular authority in terms of recognizably assessable qualities of achievement. In the case of *Frankenstein*, however, its qualities lie rather in an unseizability. Its value for the literary teacher lies not so much in the fact that it can be held up as an example to be imitated as in the many questions that it raises. It is hard to think of another work of its time that has quite this characteristic; the one instance rising indubitably to mind being again the one already discussed: *The Rime of the Ancient Mariner*. Coleridge too had Mary's capacity of absorption, albeit on a grander scale that could sometimes, however, be self-defeating when the contradictions of his mind brought his creative faculties to a standstill. *Christabel*, for instance, remained unfinished, and it can be forcibly argued that this was because its author was unable to resolve the status of Geraldine. Was she a spirit of energy and the subliminal, a mirror to the poet's own genius, or was she a cleverly subtle spirit of evil, knowing just how to undermine Christabel's innocence? The poet gives opportunities for either reading of her. *Kubla Khan* is similarly ambiguous – interpretable either as a poem about tyranny or about genius.

The difficulties raised by such ambiguities had in fact proved after a time still more insuperable for Coleridge, impelling him away from fiction and poetry at the highest level as his main concerns and causing him to press further instead his quest to reconcile the humans' sense of their Being to the nature of the Divine Being as revealed to Christians. As discussed in Chapter 6 the Coleridgean enterprise had been taken up by others, notably the Cambridge Apostles and

Tennyson, who had still hoped to give substance to the Coleridgean dream. But the attempt was always likely to be the affair of a minority, for reasons which the fate of Shelley's enterprise had already demonstrated. With the growth of the scientific attitude the 'Being' of the universe could not easily be reconciled with the God of Hebrew scripture, while human beings showed no more than temporary inclinations to fulfil the ideals promulgated by Jesus of Nazareth.

The methods of ambiguity explored in *The Ancient Mariner* remained a better guide, therefore, for Mary Shelley. Her fiction showed in fact how fully she had absorbed its impact, learning from it a means of handling nightmare in a way that could override more facile strategies by incorporating elements of the contradictory. Just as the 'crime' of the Mariner looks more like a misdemeanour, so Victor Frankenstein is punished by events that seem quite out of proportion to the act that initiated them. In both cases the reader is invited to question further. And since the contradictions in her novel take the reader to the very core of the problems besetting humanity in a post-Enlightenment world her novel would remain, like Coleridge's poem, endlessly re-interpretable – a better guide to the post-Romantic world, it would turn out, than a conscious 'philosophy' and a truer image, for many readers, of what they could hope to discover concerning the enigmas and pleasures that are caught up in questioning the relative natures of consciousness and Being.

Appendix: Wordsworth's Later Sense of Being

The play of words and imagery around the concept of Being reached its greatest intensity for Wordsworth around the first decade of the new century, when he was engaged on work such as the Immortality Ode and some of the more intense passages of *The Prelude*. The intricacy of the writing then is well illustrated by some of the revisions: Jared Curtis's edition of the *Poems in Two Volumes* reproduces, for instance, a loose manuscript leaf,[1] where Wordsworth can be seen working his way towards the long section about the insight of the child. He begins

> (I speak not in delusion – tis a feeling
> Of my past self, and insight, a revealing
> And trusting to the same
> Child as Thou art I give thee highest name)
> Thou best Philosopher who yet dost keep.

He then plays with some further possible lines, including one or two, which are finally formed into the couplet

> Though little child yet glorious in might
> Of heavens effulgence from thy beings Light.[2]

The reason why the lines did not find their way into the poem in this form is fairly clear. Once started on this track Wordsworth felt the urge to extend his idea further; on the one hand, he cut out the reference to his own experience as authority for what he was saying, while on the other, he transformed the image of the child transmitting the light of its Being – an image which he perhaps distrusted in its simple form – into a more extended and complex one whereby the child becomes likened to the moon that had revealed itself over Snowdon:

> Thou best Philosopher who yet dost keep
> Thy heritage, thou Eye among the blind,
> That, deaf and silent, read'st the eternal deep,
> Haunted for ever by the eternal mind –

That idea of an eye haunted by the power which gives it its vision, as the moon can be said to be haunted by the unseen sun that gives it its light, is far more complex than the straightforward one of effulgence from one's own Being – which Coleridge might readily have retained – and closer to the developing idea that Being is something that may be glimpsed in the creation but can never reveal itself directly. As descriptive of a child's vision the lines are unexpected to the reader who comes on them unawares, and, as is well known, Coleridge himself found their sentiment impossible to accept,[3] but Wordsworth evidently kept them because they expressed with precision his own idea of the way that Being was to be viewed. Once they were there, of course, the original lines he had written became redundant, and in the later manuscripts of the poem that have survived they find no place. It was not until the actual printing, in fact, that Wordsworth found a way of introducing them. Feeling perhaps that the lines about the child finding the grave 'A place of thought where we in waiting lie' were in themselves so passive as to make the child begin to seem unreal, and that the sense of light needed to be complemented by that of energy, he rescued his draft lines and turned them into a more vigorous version:

> Thou little Child, yet glorious in the might
> Of untam'd pleasures, on thy Being's height.

'Though' has turned into 'Thou', 'Light' into 'height' – a good example, it seems, of the serendipitous way in which a poet may (consciously or unconsciously) misread his own writing creatively. The new version gives the child the benefit of its full energies, so that having been pictured as a Snowdon moon, reading the deep beneath, it now becomes a vigorous young animal cavorting on the mountain-top of its own Being. So in the 1807 edition at least; but then Wordsworth seems to have felt that image to be a little too anarchical, and returned to a concept which was there at the beginning of his thinking about Being, the concept of freedom. Not only is the child the true visionary; the child alone knows what it is to be truly free. So Wordsworth now sanctifies its energies: from 1815 onwards the lines read:

> Thou little Child, yet glorious in the might
> Of heaven-born freedom, on thy Being's height ...

The word 'Being' continues to invite attention throughout Wordsworth's verses of this period, particularly when it appears with the capital letter that for him usually signals a certain stress. Within the 80 lines, for example, of 'The Old Cumberland Beggar', a poem composed in 1797 and published in 1800, it is first asserted to be Nature's law that no living things should exist

> Divorced from good – a spirit and pulse of good,
> A life and soul, to every mode of being
> Inseparably linked.[4]

Then the Beggar is described as 'this solitary Being', while Wordsworth's own neighbour, with her gifts of charity, is referred to as 'one kind Being'.[5] This is all in a low key, yet the effect of the iterations is to suggest a providential chain of Being, capable of working for good, in which Beggar and neighbour are each essential links. In 'Hart-Leap Well', published in the same collection as 'The Old Cumberland Beggar', the Shepherd comments on the tragedy,

> 'The Being that is in the clouds and air,
> That is in the green leaves among the groves,
> Maintains a deep and reverential care
> For the unoffending creatures whom he loves.'[6]

In 'She was a Phantom ...', Mary Wordsworth is characterized as 'A Being breathing thoughtful breath'.[7] Throughout this period the word sounds an impersonal note, as if the act of describing someone as a 'Being' focuses attention on his or her place in the total scheme of things – drawing from its central powers and contributing to its sustaining – rather than on individual characteristics.

In time, the moral emphasis in the concept was fortified for both poets. In *The Friend* Coleridge's discussions lead to an emphasis on the play of active and passive elements. 'Under the term Sense, I comprize whatever is passive in our being ...' This leaves him free to associate that which was truly active with the Reason, and to set up a further link with the moral. 'A Barbarian,' he writes, 'so instructed in the Power and Intelligence of the Infinite Being as to be left wholly ignorant of his moral attributes, would have acquired none but erroneous notions even of the former ... (For the Idea of an irresistible invisible Being naturally produces terror in the mind of uninstructed and unprotected man ...)' So the conscience becomes 'an Element of our Being'. Coleridge relies upon an idea of permanent Being, to which belong 'all the Truths and all the Principles of Truth' that do not lie within the sphere of the senses.

As the impulse to probe the nature of Being by investigating the phenomena of consciousness waned moral issues were increasingly raised, with the correlative that the moral nature of Being would constantly involve the active element rather than the passive. Wordsworth's *Excursion* follows a similar pattern: one comes to see that it has two main creative centres. The first is to be found in the first book, where the great early narrative 'The Ruined Cottage' becomes the starting-point for a more complex meditation, taking in the original pathos and extending it to the human condition at large. The other is to be found in the fourth book, which contains some of the earliest writing apart from 'The Ruined Cottage' and sets out some of Wordsworth's thinking on subjects such as superstition. In this book the word 'Being' has particular force. First the Wanderer affirms his faith

> That the procession of our fate, howe'er
> Sad or disturb'd, is order'd by a Being
> Of infinite benevolence and power ...[8]

This Being is then addressed as

> Thou, dread source,
> Prime, self-existing cause and end of all
> That in the scale of being hold their place ... [9]

The paradox of a self-existing Being who is yet the source of the whole scale of being, thus including all other Beings, is taken for granted, as is the equal paradox that Being is still subject to laws:

> those transcendent truths
> Of the pure intellect, that stand as laws
> (Submission constituting strength and power)
> Even to thy Being's infinite majesty![10]

Later in the book comes a long dissertation on the state of human beings in earlier times, which seems to have been one of the first pieces accomplished when Wordsworth began work on *The Excursion* in real earnest. Here he speculates on the custom of casting some locks of one's hair on a running stream and its likely effect:

> And, doubtless, sometimes, when the hair was shed
> Upon the flowing stream, a thought arose

> Of Life continuous, Being unimpaired;
> That hath been, is, and where it was and is
> There shall endure ...[11]

After a reference to ascent in 'dignity of being', the Wanderer speaks of the displeasure of the Divine at the work of philosophers who

>   prize
> This soul, and the transcendent universe,
> No more than as a mirror that reflects
> To proud Self-love her own intelligence;
> That one, poor, finite object, in the abyss
> Of infinite Being, twinkling restlessly![12*]

Later still in this book the Wanderer inquires:

> Has not the Soul, the Being of your Life
> Received a shock of awful consciousness,
> In some calm season ...?[13]

– going on to describe the experience of a sublime sunset. Describing further the experience of communing with the forms of nature, he comments,

> – So build we up the Being that we are;
> Thus deeply drinking in the Soul of Things,
> We shall be wise perforce ... [14*]

The final book of *The Excursion* develops similarly. It has its origin in a passage in a manuscript belonging to the Alfoxden period which begins:

> There is an active principle alive
> In all things, in all natures, in the flowers
> And in the trees[15]

and which later continues,

> All beings have their properties which spread
> Beyond themselves, a power by which they make
> Some other being conscious of their life, ...
> Spirit that knows no insulated spot,
> No chasm, no solitude; from link to link
> It circulates, the Soul of all the worlds.[16]

These lines, veering towards pantheism and to the idea of the 'active universe' proposed by some French philosophers,[17] are scaled down in the opening of the last book of *The Excursion*:

> 'To every Form of being is assigned,'
> Thus calmly spake the venerable Sage,
> 'An *active* Principle: – howe'er removed
> From sense and observation, it subsists
> In all things, in all natures ...[18]

By acknowledging that the principle is removed from sense and observation, Wordsworth locates it firmly in the mind, and so facilitates the link with an active moral principle. Later in the book this becomes overt, with the assertion that

> ... when we stand upon our native soil,
> Unelbowed by such objects as oppress
> Our active powers, those powers themselves become
> Subversive of our noxious qualities,
> And by the substitution of delight,
> And by new influxes of strength suppress
> All evil, then the Being spreads abroad
> His branches to the wind, and all who see
> Bless him rejoicing in his neighbourhood.[19*]

The same striking metaphor is used in the manuscript, though in the final version Wordsworth seems to have become uneasy with the image, substituting the lines 'whence the Being moves | In beauty through the world ...'

Such developments suggest that while Wordsworth had no clear figuration of Being in his later poetry to compare with the oceanic imagery of earlier years the word always retained something of its earlier charge. For him, the effects on his poetic achievement of having known Coleridge was always to remain something of a mystery; what he could not relinquish, however, was the effect of enhancement. Through the creative work of the two minds his sense of what it was to be human had received a gift of grandeur. As he put it in his 'Afterthought' to the Duddon Sonnets,[20]

> Enough, if something from our hands have power
> To live, and act, and serve the future hour;
> And if, as toward the silent tomb we go,
> Through love, through hope, and faith's transcendent dower,
> We feel that we are greater than we know.

He was always a man whose words were weighed; but never more portentously weighted than in that last line.

Notes

Chapter 1

1. Antonio R. Damasio, *Descartes' Error* (1996) p. 150.
2. Ibid., 129.
3. Ibid., 248.
4. Roger Penrose, *The Emperor's New Mind* (1990) p. 7.
5. Ibid., 548–9.
6. Ibid., 13.
7. *Mill on Bentham and Coleridge*, with an introduction by F.R. Leavis (1950) pp. 99–100.
8. 1926. See for example his third chapter, entitled 'The Deep Well'.
9. *Europe*, pl. 14: *BE* 64; *BK* 244.
10. 'Eternity', ll. 1–2: *BE* 461; *BK* (var) 179.
11. Saint Augustine, *Confessions* (tr. Rex Warner, 1963) XI, 14.
12. Acts 17: 28. The Greek word means simply 'are', but its position in the sentence suggests the more emphatic reading which the Authorized Version licenses.
13. See Colossians 3: 3 and cf. Ephesians 3:9. Wordsworth's feeling about idiots carries some suggestion of the kind: quoting the Colossians phrase in this connection, he goes on to describe the worship of them in some cultures and to comment that the conduct of parents in the lower classes towards them displays 'the strength, disinterestedness and grandeur of love': *WL* (1787–1805) 357.
14. An account of this aspect of Coleridge's achievement can be found in my *Coleridge the Visionary* (1959). The story was later amplified, so far as the poetry of the 1790s was concerned, in Ian Wylie's *Young Coleridge and the Philosophers of Nature* (Oxford 1989). For my own investigation of Blake's myth-making, see particularly *Blake's Visionary Universe* (1969). Kathleen Raine's *Blake and Tradition* (1969) was directed particularly to traditions such as the Platonic, which she regarded as being more surely based metaphysically.
15. *KL* II, 102.
16. *SP* 202.
17. *Prel* (1805) xii, 254–5.
18. See his *Treatise of Human Nature* (1739) IV, vii (ed. Selby-Bigge, 1896) pp. 270–1.
19. Both in this volume and the companion one, *Post-Romantic Consciousnesses: Dickens to Plath*.

Chapter 2

1. For various accounts of the saying, see *Blake Records*, ed. G.E. Bentley Jr (Oxford 1969) p. 291 and n.

2. See especially Job 4. 14 and 21. 6 – texts which he did not, however, quote directly in his *Illustrations* to the book.
3. *BE* 680; *BK* 799.
4. Sources of this story are given in *Blake Records*, 32.
5. Ibid., 34–7.
6. Annotations to Lavater's *Aphorisms on Man*: *BE* 584; *BK* 80.
7. 'There is no Natural Religion' ii: *BE* 2; *BK* 97.
8. *BE* 462–3; *BK* 171.
9. *BE* 490 and 779; *BK* 185.
10. *BE* 555; *BK* 617.
11. For the evidence of his father's having been a worshipper in the relevant years, see *Blake Records*, 8 and n.
12. 'Divine Wrath and Mercy': Isaac Watts, *Hymn and Spiritual Songs* (1755) p. 37.
13. 'Divine judgments': Isaac Watts, *Horae Lyricae* (1779) p. 5.
14. *BE* 56; *BK* 203.
15. 'God's Eternity': *Hymns and Sacred Songs*, 166.
16. 'The Faithfulness of God in the Promises': Watts, *Hymns and Sacred Songs*, 220.
17. *The First Book of Urizen*, *BE* 71; *BK* 224. The accompanying illustration is from the title-page to that volume.
18. 'Auguries of Innocence', *BE* 482; *BK* 432.
19. *Milton* 2: 5Z6: *BE* 95; *BK* 481.
20. *The Four Zoas*, Night 9: *BE* 389; *BK* 376–7.
21. *Visions of the Daughters of Albion*, 7.15: *BE* 49; *BK* 194.
22. *The Four Zoas* Night 2.21: *BE* 309; *BK* 280.
23. *The Four Zoas* Night 2. 422; 3. 211: *BE* 391, 324; *BK* 291, 297.
24. *Jerusalem* 32[36].22: *BE* 176; *BK* 663.
25. *The Book of Los* 36–7: *BE* 90; *BK* 256.
26. *Jerusalem* 98.33–4: *BE* 255; *BK* 746.
27. *The Book of Ahania* 1.10–11: *BE* 83; *BK* 249.
28. 'All Religions are One': *BE* 2; *BK* 98.
29. This example appears on the opening page of *The First Book of Urizen* (1794).
30. Various portraits by John Linnell in the Fitzwilliam Museum, Cambridge bring out these traits. The allied alternative aspects, human and visionary, are well illustrated in the double portrait by Frederick Tatham which is reproduced as the frontispiece for my *Blake's Humanism* (1968).
31. Francis Oliver Finch, quoted in A. Gilchrist, *Life of William Blake* (London and Cambridge 1863).
32. pp. 298–9.
33. 'Auguries of Innocence', 109–10: *BE* 483; *BK* 433.
34. See the fate of Uzzah, II Samuel vi, 6–8, I Chron. xiii, 9–10, alluded to in his *Annotations to Lavater*, *BE* 585; *BK* 82.
35. *BE* 475–7; *BK* 424–7.

Chapter 3

1. Letter to Southey, 29 July 1802; *CL* II, 830; cf. ibid., 812.
2. There, where it was still more influential, the fashion was associated with the ferment that surrounded the revolutionary events. See Robert Darnton,

Mesmerism and the End of the Enlightenment in France (Cambridge, Mass., 1968).

3. See my *Coleridge the Visionary* (1959), chapter 2, and *Coleridge's Poetic Intelligence* (1977) p. 73. As mentioned in the first, the contemporary relevance of 'that, which comes out of thine eye' (addressed to the Mariner) in the first version was first noticed long ago, notably in Lane Cooper's article 'The Power of the Eye in Coleridge' (in *Studies presented to J.M. Hart* (New York 1901), pp. 78–121; reptd in his *Late Harvest* (Ithaca, NY 1952)). Rather surprisingly, however, Cooper did not perceive any further significance in Coleridge's use of the phenomenon, concluding, 'It is disappointing to find his "poet's eye" so continually "fixed" by so trivial a "fact of mind"' (1952 edn., 95).
4. See my studies *Wordsworth and the Human Heart* (1978) and *Wordsworth in Time* (1979).
5. This theory with its ramifications is discussed more extensively in my *Coleridge's Poetic Intelligence* (1977); see especially pp. 81–8, 247–8, 256–7.
6. *Coleridge on Imagination* (1934) p. 58.
7. Letter to Southey, 21 October 1794, *CL* I, 115.
8. *C Lects* (1795) 49.
9. *W Prel* (1805) ii, 220–6.
10. *CL* I, 397.
11. Milton, *Church Government.*
12. *W Prel* (1805) x, 896–900.
13. *CBL* ch. 10 (*CC*) I, 200–1. Coleridge had very little to say about Descartes' most famous formulation, though he was probably responsible for the underlining of it in the copy he used of the *Works*. In statements that have survived, his concern was far more with his doctrine of ideas and his consequent relationship to Locke. But he did contend, with emphasis, that when Descartes used the term 'cogito' he meant 'I am conscious'.
14. *CL* I, 294–5.
15. A notable exception is Edward Kessler's *Coleridge's Metaphors of Being* (Princeton, NJ 1979).
16. *CL* I, 173.
17. Ibid., 491.
18. Ibid., 453.
19. *CN* II, 2712.
20. L.105: *CPW* (EHC) I, 247.
21. *CL* II, 649.
22. Ibid., I , 470.
23. Ll. 17–20: *CPW* (EHC) I, 179.
24. *CN* III, 4073.
25. *CN* III, 4073 f. 146ᵛ.
26. *CPW* (EHC) I, 106–8.
27. L. 47, ibid., 77.
28. Ll. 1809–10, *WPW* I, 200.
29. *Paradise Lost* ii, 147.
30. Ll. 1818–19. *WPW* I, 200.
31. V, 54–6, *CPW* (EHC) II, 584.
32. L. 12: ibid., I, 328 (cf. II, 1130).
33. *CN* I, 582 (cf. I, 1589); I, 1779.

34. See 'This Lime-Tree Bower' ll. 58–9 (*CPW* (Beer) 168); *CAR* 389–90; my *Coleridge's Poetic Intelligence* (1977) p. 240; the 'Letter to Sara Hutchinson', ll. 90–1 (*CPW* (Beer) 394); and (for Sylvia Plath) *Post-Romantic Consciousness*, p. 171.
35. Wordsworth himself claimed that he left the poem unpublished in order that his heirs would have something to live on, but it is very hard to believe that he would have withheld so massive a work had he felt confident of a sympathetic reception. What dedicated poet would behave so?
36. *W Prel* (1799) I, 412.
37. *W Prel* (1805) iii, 171–7.
38. *W Prel* (1805) iii, 182–94.
39. *W Prel* (1805) iii, 246–9.
40. *WPW* v, 343–4.
41. Ibid., I, 119–22 (from MS JJ).
42. *W Prel* (1799) I, 69–73.
43. Ibid., ll. 389–90.
44. Ibid., II, 26–31.
45. Ibid., ll. 267–9 (corrected from ms).
46. Ibid., 295–6.
47. See Hugh Sykes Davies, *Wordsworth and the Worth of Words* (Cambridge 1986) pp. 272–6.
48. See H.W. Piper, *The Active Universe* (1962) *passim*.
49. *W Prel* (1799) ii, 446–51.
50. *W Prel* (1805) iii, 539–41.
51. Ibid., vi, 488–90.
52. Ibid., vii, 710–13.
53. Ibid., xiii, 69–73.
54. In the 1805 Book Eleven, for instance, Wordsworth tells how he

> In Nature's presence stood, as now I stand,
> A sensitive, and a creative soul. (xi, 255–6)

By 1850 this has become:

> A sensitive being, a creative soul. (xii, 206–7)

The word appears here in its weaker form, not easily to be distinguished from a sense such as 'person'. The stronger sense can equally be enlisted in the revisions, however. 'Those mysteries of passion' that have made one brotherhood of all the human race (xi, 84) become, in 1850, 'Those mysteries of being'(xii, 85); while in the last book of the poem the 1805 lines

> The feeling of life endless, the one thought
> By which we live, infinity and God. (xiii, 183–4) become

> Faith in life endless, the sustaining thought
> Of human Being, Eternity and God.(xiv, 204–5)

55. *W Prel* (1805) vi, 525–9.
56. Ibid., vi, 592–6.
57. *W Prel* (1805) xiii, 62–5.
58. Ibid., xiii, 72–3.

59. See Appendix, pp. 179–83.
60. *WPW* III, 17.
61. Ll.154–6: *WPW* iv, 284.
62. Having written first 'fructifying', then this, Wordsworth corrected both fair copies finally to 'renovating'. See *The Prelude 1799, 1805, 1850*, ed. Jonathan Wordsworth, M.H. Abrams and Stephen Gill (New York 1979) 428n.
63. Henry Taylor, *Autobiography* (2 vols., 1885) I, 188.
64. *CL* I, 491.
65. *CN* I, 1379 and n.
66. Ibid., 524.
67. Ibid., 1554.
68. *CL* I, 481.
69. Ibid., 479.
70. Ibid., ii, 1032.
71. 'Dejection: An Ode', ll. 87–93. *CPW* (EHC) I, 367.
72. 'To W. Wordsworth' ll. 12–15. My quotations are from the 1807 version: *CPW* (Beer) 436–42. The two lines in square brackets here are from the 1817 version, ll. 19–20: *CPW* (Beer) 437.
73. Ll. 33–6.
74. Ll. 67–70. The 1817 version reads in the second line 'The pulses of my Being beat anew'.
75. Ll. 115–16.
76. See above at note 65.
77. CN I, 1606. In her note, Kathleen Coburn tentatively but persuasively identifies the 'A' and 'B' of the anecdote as Coleridge and Wordsworth.
78. Ibid., II, 3148 (September 1807).
79. A notorious case is the film 'Pandaemonium', where Wordsworth is cast as the villain of the piece.
80. See, e.g., the examples of his bemusement given in Jennifer Ford's *Coleridge on Dreaming* (Cambridge 1998) pp. 142–6 and the surrounding discussions of his attempts to account for them.
81. *CBL* I, 241 and n; repeated, II, 60.
82. The distinction is discussed learnedly and eloquently by Thomas MacFarland in *Coleridge and the Pantheist Tradition* (Oxford 1969).
83. According to Sara Coleridge in her 1847 edition (I, 297), her father 'stroked out' the last clause, beginning 'and as a repetition', in one copy.
84. 'A Shakspere, a Milton, a Bruno, exist in the mind as *pure Action*, defecated of all that is material & passive.' (The nature of genius related the active and the passive.) The term 'actus purissimus' is used in a letter to Clarkson of October 1806 (*CL* II, 1195) and frequently in later notebook entries and mss (for an extended list see *CAR* 555). In a marginal annotation on Jeremy Taylor (*CM* v, 594) he characterized 'actions' as, like the Will, existing out of time altogether and to be distinguished, therefore, from 'deeds'.
85. *CN* III, 3593.
86. See especially *CAR* 313 and n for further references.
87. Letter to Matilda Betham, 14 March 1811: *CL* III, 310.
88. This was a first impression, of course, preceding by a quarter of a century the more caustic portrait in his *Life of John Sterling*.

89. Marginal annotation on Southey, *Life of Wesley* (2 vols., 1820) I, 301–5 (*CM* V, 141–2).
90. *WL* (1787–1805) 366. Interestingly, after the prominence given to 'was' in the manuscript version, 'By which an old man was', the word disappeared from the line in the published 'Resolution and Independence'; this may reflect a despair at ever being able to convey the depth of his feeling. (Other things were omitted from the original, including a description of the old man's skin being so dry that the leeches would no longer stick to them – which so amused Fanny Allen as to send her into convulsions of laughter, much to Coleridge's displeasure. See *Coleridge the Talker*, ed. R.W. Armour and R.F. Howes (Ithaca, NY 1940) pp. 104–5.)
91. C *Friend* I, 514.
92. *CLS* 72.
93. Ibid., 78–9.
94. Letter to Coleridge of 29 March 1804: *WL* (1787–1805) 464; 'A Complaint', *WPW* II, 34; Graves, reported in *Prose Works* (Grosart) III, 469.
95. See his Table Talk for 31 March 1830 (*CC* I, 96–7 and nn), with the comment and amendment by John Sterling (ibid., II, 308).
96. *CN* II, 2070.

Chapter 4

1. *KL* II, 279. In *The Recluse* I, 793f (*WPW* v, 338) Wordsworth locates the 'haunt and the main region' of his song in 'the Mind of Man'.
2. Ibid., 203.
3. From Severn's report of Haydon's party: see Sidney Colvin, *John Keats* (1918) p. 248.
4. Ibid., 250–2.
5. *KL* II, 88–9.
6. Ibid., I, 193–4.
7. Quoted in C *Lects* (1808–19) I, 233.
8. *DQW* II, 56.
9. In the summer of 1820 according to Allsop (and possibly during a similar walk) he praised the sweetness of the birdsong in Ken Wood, the wood that he and Keats were passing in Millfield Lane during their conversation. He commented: 'Would to God I could give out my being amidst flowers, and the sight of meadowy fields, and the chaunt of birds. Death without pain at such a time, in such a place as this, would be a reward for life' (*CTT* II, 355). This, especially the desire for death without pain, links interestingly with Keats's Nightingale Ode. Hazlitt tells how during his 1798 visit to Alfoxden he got into a metaphysical argument with Wordsworth, 'while Coleridge was explaining the different notes of the nightingale to his sister, in which we neither of us succeeded in making ourselves perfectly clear and intelligible': 'My First Acquaintance with Poets' (*HW* XVII, 119). If this should mean that Coleridge was already so possessed by his idea of primary consciousness that he was applying it to the nightingale's song, the reference to nightingales and poetic sensation in the course of the Millfield Lane conversation was not produced extempore but had a much longer provenance. If one then makes a link to Coleridge's poem 'The Nightingale', composed in April

1798, a month before Hazlitt's visit, the implication would seem to be that for him at this time the 'primary' was to be identified with the joyous.

10. For the survival of related speculations in his mind during the subsequent period, nevertheless, see my *Coleridge's Poetic Intelligence*, especially chapters 8 and 9. The long note on 'The Soul and Its Organs of Sense', which he contributed to Robert Southey's *Omniana* in 1812 (see his *Shorter Works and Fragments (cc)*, 332–6), shows how much he reflected on similar mental phenomena during these years.

11. See, for example, Jack Stillinger, 'Keats and Coleridge', in *Coleridge, Keats, and the Imagination: Romanticism and Adam's Dream*, ed. J.R. Barth and J.L. Mahoney (1990) 11.

12. In the article cited in the previous note, Stillinger mentions discussions by H.W. Garrod, Mary Rebecca Thayer and myself, but maintains that they 'ignore the facts of Keats' chronology': 'Keats had been writing about dreams, poetry, the supernatural, fairy creatures, knights, caves, nightingales and the rest – and in his letters, even about Coleridge's poetry and philosophy – for two years or more before the meeting.' So far as the theories to be presented here are concerned, however, my contention is not that he took new *topics* from the conversation, but that he found his existing ideas being transformed into a new pattern – which then affected the form of his own poetry. As Stillinger points out, Keats had already written a first draft of 'The Eve of St Agnes', with its presentation of the contrast between the cold forms of death and the life of warm sensuousness, before the Highgate meeting. I have never proposed a direct influence on that poem, however, which, as he says, the known chronology precludes (though Keats did, of course, know 'Christabel', where the sense of entering a 'world of death' is enhanced by the chilliness of the night). What I am suggesting, rather, is a reorientation of ideas already strong in his mind – which may have extended further, given the length of their encounter: if, for instance, Coleridge's discussion of 'first and second consciousness' extended to his relating of the warmth sense to 'primary consciousness' and cold to the 'secondary' (see *Coleridge's Poetic Intelligence*, 81–9), this could have reinforced Keats's strong sense of the difference by giving him a fresh way of organizing his ideas about that particular sensuous distinction.

13. (Oxford 1991).

14. (Cambridge 2001). See especially Chapter 5.

15. Letter of 9 June 1819: *KL* II, 115.

16. *KL* II, 90–1.

17. See e.g. *Lear* III. iv. 55, *Measure for Measure* I. ii. 133; also *II Hen IV* I. xi. 48; *I Hen VI* V. iv. 29.

18. *KL* II, 181.

19. For a fuller list, see *KP* 500–1.

20. Number 413.

21. See F.S. Ellis's reminiscence, recorded by Sidney Colvin in his *John Keats* (1918) p. 470.

22. When in Book iv the Wanderer maintained, for instance, that the superstitions of mankind kept alive a source of truth which had, in its most direct form, been lost, he was voicing an idea which Coleridge had explored previously in 'The Destiny of Nations' (ll. 80–7: *CPW* (EHC) I, 134). It might

indeed be said that the whole conception, that of certain minds being privileged with knowledge beyond the rest of mankind, however derived, was one that would hardly have been voiced so potently by Wordsworth without Coleridge's earlier advocacy.

23. See below, p. 182.
24. II, 97.
25. 'Psyche', l. 67, 'Ode to Indolence' v. 8.
26. Letter to Woodhouse, 27 October 1818. *KL* I, 386–7.
27. For example, *KL* I, 369, 387, 392, II, 5, 77.
28. *KL* II, 103. See also above, pp. 8–9.
29. *The Tempest* III. ii. 152.
30. These, by their differing punctuations, leave it doubtful whether the second statement is to be linked with the first, placed within inverted commas, or to be taken separately. Nor is it clear (as discussed below) whether the 'ye' of the last line is addressed by the urn to mankind, by the poet to his readers, by the poet to the urn, or by the poet to the figures on the urn.
31. Letter of 22 November 1817: *KL* I, 184.
32. See above, p. 32.
33. *Paradise Lost* I, 730–2.
34. 'Comus' 476. These lines were quoted by Keats in his long journal-letter of March 1819: *KL* II, 81.
35. 'Lamia' 2, 93–7.
36. To Hazlitt: see his essay, 'My First Acquaintance with Poets': *HW* XVII, 112.
37. See Wordsworth's 'Elegiac Stanzas suggested by a Picture of Peele Castle', ll. 53–4: *WPW* IV, 260.
38. *KL* II, 142.
39. *KP* 700.
40. See above, p. 22.
41. H.W. Garrod, *Keats* (1926) pp. 132–3.
42. *KP* 686–7.
43. L. 93: *KP* 73.
44. Letter of 19 February 1819, *KL* II, 67.
45. Letter of December 1817, *KL* I, 213–14.
46. Letter of 24 September 1819, *KL* II, 213.
47. Letter of 1804, *CL* II, 1116.
48. Se Colvin, *Life of Keats*, 523–4 (Houghton *Life of Keats*, II, 91).
49. See Christopher Ricks, *Keats and Embarrassment* (1974) especially pp. 218–19.
50. *CPW* (Beer) 214–17.

Chapter 5

1. *DDQ*, 188.
2. *DQD*, 192.
3. *DQD*, 163.
4. Thomas Carlyle, *The Life of John Sterling* (1851) p. 71. Cf. De Quincey's comments on Coleridge's conversational eloquence (*DQW* II, 152).
5. See *Posthumous Works*, ed. Japp (1891) II, 7–59.
6. Ibid., II, 57.

7. See J. Hillis Miller, *The Disappearance of God: Five Nineteenth-Century Writers* (1963) pp. 17–23, 79–80; A.S. Plumtree, 'Freedom and the Labyrinth: An Existential Study of Thomas De Quincey' (PhD diss., University of Nottingham, 1977). I am indebted to Plumtree's thesis, both for its general stimulus as a study of De Quincey and for a number of individual references.

8. H.A. Page (A.W. Japp) *Thomas De Quincey: his Life and Writings* (1877) 1, 10.

9. Ibid., 1, 9.

10. *DQCS*, 71.

11. *DQW* I, 43.

12. *DQW* II, 139.

13. Shadworth H. Hodgson, 'The Genius of De Quincey', in *Outcast Essays and Verse Translations* (1881) pp. 10–11.

14. See above, p. 22.

15. *DQW* XI, 56.

16. *DQW* II, 443.

17. *DQW* II, 444.

18. *DQW* II, 445.

19. *DQW* III, 283.

20. 'To William Wordsworth', (1817 version) l. 40, *CPW* (Beer) 439.

21. *The Borderers*, ll. 1543–4. *WPW* I, 188.

22. Letter to Cottle, 8 June 1797: *CL* I, 325.

23. *CBL* I, 80.

24. 'The Old Cumberland Beggar', l. 153: *WPW* IV, 239.

25. *DQW* II, 205.

26. Letter of 12 April 1810 to Catherine Clarkson, *WL* (1806–11) 399.

27. *DQW* III, 410.

28. *DQW* X, 447.

29. See his comments on Lear: *CShC* I, 65, quoting from *Literary Remains* (1836) II, 198–9 (but not to be found in *CM* IV at this point); and on Don Quixote, *C Lects* 1808–19 II, 162.

30. See Alethea Hayter, *Opium and the Romantic Imagination* (1968) pp. 119–20.

31. *CN* I, 1176, 1250, 1649; II, 2055; III, 3404.

32. *DQW* I, 101–8.

33. *DQW* I, 100–1.

34. *DQW* VI, 149–51; X, 365.

35. *DQCS* 149.

36. Letters of 19 December 1813 to Thomas Roberts and Mrs J.J. Morgan, *CL* III, 463–4.

37. *DQW* III, 362.

38. *DQW* II, 204–5.

39. *DQW* XII, 173–4.

40. See my 'Coleridge and Wordsworth: The Vital and the Organic', in *Reading Coleridge: Approaches and Applications*, ed. Walter B. Crawford (1979) pp. 160–90. For further applications to De Quincey, see my 'The Englishness of De Quincey's Ideas', in *English and German Romanticism: Cross-Currents and Controversies*, ed. James Pipkin (Heidelberg 1985) pp. 323–47.

41. *DQW* XII, 208–9. See e.g. lines 117–19 of the Immortality Ode and p. 179 below.

42. *DQW* II. 443.

43. *DQW* II, 239.
44. *DQW* II, 304.
45. *DQW* I, 35.
46. *DQW* I, 103.
47. *DQW* XIII, 347–8.
48. *DQW* III, 435.
49. *DQW* III, 198.
50. For a full and detailed discussion of the estrangement and reconciliation see John E. Jordan, *De Quincey to Wordsworth: A Biography of a Relationship* (Berkeley and Los Angeles 1962) pp. 203–36, 278–302. Jordan suggests that the Wordsworths' disapproval was aroused primarily by the initial illicitness of the relationship.
51. *DQW* III, 394.
52. *De Quincey to Wordsworth*, 358. One might also note how, when the opium-eater in his best state 'feels that the diviner part of his nature is paramount – that is, the moral affections are in a state of cloudless serenity, and high over all the great light of the majestic intellect' (*DQW* III, 384), De Quincey's imagery merges that of the Immortality Ode and that of the Snowdon vision in *The Prelude*. That Wordsworth actually describes the moon as the 'type of a majestic intellect' in the version of 1850 is particularly interesting. De Quincey might have seen a version later than that of 1805, where the moon is the 'image of a perfect Mind'; it is even possible that Wordsworth picked up the phrase in the *Confessions* and conveyed it back into his own poem.
53. *DQW* VIII, 291.
54. Ann Radcliffe, *The Italian*, ed. Garber (1968) p. 35.
55. Leigh Hunt, *The Autobiography of Leigh Hunt*, ed. Ingpen (2 vols., 1903) II, 21.
56. See my discussion in *Coleridge the Visionary* (1959) pp. 213–18.
57. *DQD* 192.
58. See, for example, *DQW* I, 29, 12, 228.
59. Thomas De Quincey, *Reminiscences of the English Lake Poets*, ed. John E. Jordan (1961) pp. 122–3. This edition contains the entirety of De Quincey's 'Reminiscences' as they originally appeared in *Tait's Edinburgh Magazine*.
60. Letter of 10 December 1798 to Wordsworth, *CL* I, 452–3.
61. H.A. Page (A.W. Japp) *Thomas De Quincey: his Life and Writings*, (1877) I, 326–7.
62. See William Wordsworth, *The Prelude: 1799, 1805, 1850*, ed. Jonathan Wordsworth, M.H. Abrams and Stephen Gill (New York 1979) iv, 400–504, xiii, 1–119 (1805). See also my discussions in *Wordsworth in Time*, 121–5, 186–90.
63. See Miller, *Disappearance of God*, 17–18.
64. *DQW* XII, 158.
65. *DQW* VII, 203.
66. *DQW* III, 232.
67. *DQW* III, 224.
68. The essay appears in *De Quincey and his Friends* ... , ed. James Hogg (1895) pp. 295–313, and is picked out for discussion by Miller, *Disappearance of God*, 74–5.
69. *DQW* I, 41–2.
70. *DQW* I, 41n.

71. *DQW* VIII, 17.
72. See above, p. 42 and my discussion in *Wordsworth in Time*, 30–42.
73. 'Elegiac Stanzas suggested by a Picture of Peele Castle', l. 54. *WPW* IV, 260.
74. *DQW* III, 295–7, 346–7.
75. I am indebted here to Alethea Hayter, *Opium and the Romantic Imagination* (1968) pp. 247–50.
76. *DQW* VII, 203–4.
77. *DQW* I, 129.
78. *DQW* I, 8–9.
79. See 'Home at Grasmere', ll. 205–29. *WPW* V, 321.
80. *DQCS* 210.
81. *DQW* II, 401–2.
82. *DQW* II, 402.
83. *WPrW* I, 339.
84. *DQW* XI, 56.
85. *DQW* I, 50.
86. *DQW* XIII, 325.
87. *DQW* XIII, 326–7.
88. *DQW* XIII, 348.
89. *DQW* II, 305.

Chapter 6

1. 'Yes! in the sea of life enisled...': *APW* 130.
2. 'The Sea of Faith / Was once too at the full...': 'Dover Beach', ll. 21–2: *APW* 254–6.
3. *CBL*, chapter 10, I, 200.
4. Hallam Tennyson, *Alfred Lord Tennyson, A Memoir* (1897) I, 50.
5. Allingham, *Diary*, quoted *Tennyson: Interviews and Recollections*, ed. Norman Page (1983) p. 150.
6. Hallam Tennyson, *Memoir*, I, 50.
7. Peter Allen, *The Cambridge Apostles: The Early Years* (Cambridge 1978); Paul Levy, *Moore: G. E. Moore and the Cambridge Apostles* (Oxford 1979); Joyce Green, 'The Development of the Poetic Imagination in Tennyson, with Particular Reference to the Juvenilia and to the Influence of Arthur Hallam' (unpublished PhD thesis 1954, in Cambridge University Library); W.C. Lubenow, *The Cambridge Apostles, 1820–1914* (Cambridge 1998). Richard Deacon's *The Cambridge Apostles* (1985), although a more coarse-grained account, contains some useful information not otherwise available, including a glossary of Apostolic terminology. Frances Brookfield, *The Cambridge Apostles* (1906) may also be consulted.
8. Levy, *Moore*, quoting *Letters of Roger Fry*, ed. D. Sutton (1972) I, 108.
9. Marginal note by Kemble in a copy of Connop Thirlwall, *Letter to the Rev. Thomas Turton* (1834) now in the London Library, quoted Allen, *Cambridge Apostles* 8.
10. Allen, *Cambridge Apostles* 8, quoting Arthur Helps, *Realmah* (1868) Ch. 12.
11. Allen, *Cambridge Apostles*, 6, quoting A. and E.M. Sidgwick, *Henry Sidgwick: A Memoir* (1906) pp. 34–5.

12. In *Monckton Milnes: The Years of Promise, 1809–1851* (1949) p. 17, James Pope-Hennessy quotes such expressions of romantic affection as 'Sir Jacob and I are inseparable, he is one of the dearest creatures I have ever seen. You would I am sure approve of our friendship, it is so unlike the routine of Cambridge arm-in-arms'; 'Garden and Monteith have not cooled at all' and 'Cavendish's brother is a charming creature and so well fitted for Fitzroy'. On Fitzroy's departure from Trinity in 1831, several of his friends were so affected that they burst into tears. See Robert Bernard Martin, *The Unquiet Heart* (1980) p. 95, for further instances.
13. See *The Writings of Arthur Henry Hallam*, ed. T.H. Vail Motter (New York 1943) preface, pp. v–vii and Appendix 7, pp. 317–21.
14. See Christopher Ricks's headnote to *In Memoriam*, TP II, 313–14, and references.
15. Allen, *Cambridge Apostles*, 1, 38, 143, and cf. Brookfield *Cambridge Apostles*, 10. The 'Ark' refers, of course, to the biblical Ark of the Covenant in which the tables of the law and other sacred relics were kept. (See Exodus 16, etc. and Hebrews 9: 4.)
16. Deacon, *Cambridge Apostles*, 6; cf. Brookfield, *Cambridge Apostles*, 6.
17. Ibid. Deacon states that 'illumers' appears to have gone out of circulation after the 1840s. It is no doubt cognate with the favourite word '*illuminati*' of the period. After the visit to Oxford the Apostles reported the Oxonians to be 'a very wise gentlemanly set, about a hundred years behind the illuminati' (Wyndham Farr, letter to Gladstone, 1 January 1830, quoted Joyce Green, *Cambridge Apostles*, 217).
18. Ibid.; Allen, *Cambridge Apostles*, pp. 3, 8. McTaggart, a later nineteenth-century member, reported on one occasion that a fellow Apostle had 'taken unto himself a phenomenal wife'. See Deacon, *Cambridge Apostles*, 6.
19. Allen, *Cambridge Apostles*, 81.
20. CL vi, 797, 849.
21. Sir John Frederick Maurice, *Life of F D. Maurice* (1884), I, 165; He was also, incidentally, to become Hallam Tennyson's godfather and to receive, in that capacity, one of Tennyson's finest epistolary poems: 'To the Rev. F. D. Maurice', TP II, 497–500.
22. Carlyle, *Life of John Sterling* (1851) Ch. viii, p. 72.
23. John Sterling, Preface to *Essays and Tales* (1848) I, xxv. Sterling goes on to declare Coleridge's conversation superior to Johnson's.
24. *The London Magazine*, as cited in *Athenaeum*, 3 September 1828, pp. 716–17
25. R.C. Trench, *Letters and Memorials* (1888), I, 10, cited Green, *Cambridge Apostles*, 182.
26. *Athenaeum*, 30 April 1828, p. 423. Coleridge's name was spelt out when this was reprinted in Sterling's *Essays and Tales*, II, 9.
27. Letter to W.E. Gladstone, 26 August 1828: *Letters*, ed. J. Kolb (Columbus, Ohio, 1981) p. 233.
28. Green, *Cambridge Apostles*, 134.
29. Letter to J. Frere, 23 December 1828, ibid., pp. 260–1.
30. A brief account may be found in Hallam, *Letters*, 346–7. Tennant married and went as English Chaplain to Florence, where he died of consumption in 1842.

31. Letter to Gladstone, 8 November 1828, Hallam *Letters,* 244.
32. Allen, *Cambridge Apostles,* 152, citing letter from J.W. Blakesley to W.H. Thompson, 16 April 1833, Blakesley MSS, Trinity College, Cambridge.
33. Letter to Jack Kemble, 18 October 1832, Hallam, *Letters,* 667.
34. T.W. Reid, *The Life, Letters and Friendships of Richard Monckton Milnes* (1890) II, 432.
35. Hallam, *Writings,* 42–3. Milton's tenth sonnet refers to Isocrates, who died on hearing of the Athenian defeat at Chaeronea, as 'that old man eloquent'.
36. Ll. 160–71, ibid.
37. See his half-ironic self-description as 'Heraclitus redivivus' in a letter of September 1817, *CL* IV, 775, and flattering references elsewhere.
38. Allen, *Cambridge Apostles,* 49, citing a letter to his father (post-marked 19 February 1829) in the Houghton MSS at Trinity College, Cambridge.
39. F. D. Maurice, *The Kingdom of Christ* (2nd edn., 1842) Dedication, p. xxiv.
40. In 1827 Coleridge took communion for the first time since his first year in Cambridge: see CN,V, S704 (36 ff. 32v–33), quoted in J.R. Barth, *Coleridge and Christian Doctrine* (Cambridge, Mass. 1969) pp. 178–9nn.
41. *Life of Sterling,* Ch. 8, 69.
42. See his letters to Milnes of 21 July and 1 September 1829, Hallam, *Letters,* 301, 312.
43. *CCS* 182; Hallam, *Writings,* 204.
44. *CAR* 333–4. (The spelling of the Greek is as printed.)
45. Hallam, *Writings,* 210–11.
46. See, e.g., William Beveridge, *Exposition of the XXXIX Articles of the Church of England* (1710) p. 2.
47. Ll. 221–4; *TP* I, 453.
48. Hallam, *Writings,* 199.
49. Hallam Tennyson, *Memoir,* 213–79 *passim*; see also, for instance, P.J. Toynbee, *Dante in English Literature* (1909) II, 416–24.
50. Hallam, *Writings,* 203.
51. Hallam, *Letters,* 360.
52. *CAR* 358.
53. 'How is't for every glance of thine ...?' Hallam, *Writings,* 83.
54. Ibid., 154.
55. 'Maud', l. 144: *TP* II, 531.
56. *TP* II, 370–4; lv–lvi.
57. The line was not in the first edition of 1859, however. but added later, appearing, e.g., as stanza xlvii of the fourth (1879) – just before lines viewing life as 'A Moment's Halt – a momentary taste | Of BEING from the Well within the Waste...': see Edward Fitzgerald's *Works* (NewYork and London 1887) I, 44–5.
58. *Excursion,* iv, 10–17; Hallam, *Letters,* 317–18.
59. He had been fined at the Eton Society on 19 May 1827 for annotating the line from 'Ruth', 'The breezes their own languor lent' with the words 'By Jove they did! at three percent!!!' See H.N. Coleridge in *The Etonian* I, 103, cited Hallam, *Letters,* 301.
60. See 'Wordsworth at Glenarbach', ll.73–9; Hallam, *Writings,* 72; and letter to Milnes, 21 July 1829, *Letters,* 301.
61. See below, p. 134.

62. Letter to Blakesley, 25 November 1829, Blakesley MSS,, cited Allen, *Cambridge Apostles*, 90–1.
63. For accounts of the enterprise and its failure, see Carlyle, *Life of Sterling*, Chs. 9–13, and Allen, Cambridge Apostles, Ch. 7.
64. Hallam, *Letters*, 387–91.
65. See, e.g., letter to W.B. Donne, 29 January 1832, Hallam, *Letters*, 512, and 'The influence of Italian upon English Literature' (1831–2): Hallam, *Writings*, 233.
66. Hallam, *Letters*, 438.
67. *Tennyson: The Critical Heritage*, ed. J.D. Jump (1967) p. 42.
68. Hallam, *Letters*, 453, 570.
69. See his letters to Derwent Coleridge and to Edward Coleridge of 11 January and 27 July 1826, *CL* VI, 537, 600. The latter was worked up as an appendix to *CCS* (1829) and so directly available to contemporary readers.
70. See above, note 13.
71. *TP* II, 315 and note.
72. St John, 1. 18. Tennyson's immediate turning to the will ('Our wills are ours, we know not how, | Our wills are ours, to make them thine'), which is later echoed in the opening to the last-but-one section, 'O living will that shall endure...', squares interestingly with a similar movement of mind in Coleridge (see, for example, *CAR* 74–8, 135–41); given the centrality of the will in Christian doctrine, however, this may well be coincidence.
73. Letter to B.P. Blood, 7 May 1874, Houghton Library, quoted Martin, *Unquiet Heart*, 28–9.
74. Martin, *Unquiet Heart*, 84, quoting a record of Tennyson's conversation from an unpublished notebook of Aubrey Tennyson's in the Tennyson Research Centre.
75. See my *Wordsworth and the Human Heart* (1978) especially pp. 71–8.
76. iv, ll. 28–34; *TP I*, 85.
77. Ll. 37–40; *TP II*, 91.
78. *BE* 1; *BK* 97.
79. 'Locksley Hall', ll. 182, 184; *TP* II, 130 *TP* II, 121, 130.
80. Milnes, letter to his father, post-marked 19 February 1829, Houghton MSS, cited Allen, *Cambridge Apostles* 47–8. He also states that Blakesley 'gave a most eloquent commentary' on the poem.
81. *TP* I, 239–40.
82. See Green, *Cambridge Apostles*, 160, citing Milnes, letter to his father 13 March 1830: Reid, *Milnes* I, 92; R.C. Trench, letter to Blakesley, 24 January 1830: *Letters and Memorials* (1888), I, 50.
83. *TP* I, 240 ll. 25–30.
84. *TP* I, 187.
85. This anecdote is given, without source, both in Charles Tennyson, *Alfred Tennyson* (1968) p. 70, and Martin, *Unquiet Heart*, 116.
86. *TP* I, 281.
87. Ll. 36–40; *TP* I, 253.
88. *TP* I, 247, 249.
89. *TP* I, 216.
90. *TP* II, 403–4; *In Memoriam*, lxxxvii, 21–40. Ricks (*TP* II, 404n) draws attention to a striking parallel in the 'bar, ridge-like, above the eyebrows' of the

truly wise in Coleridge's 'Allegoric Vision', printed in his 1817 *Lay Sermon* (CC) 135, and included in his *Poetical Works* from 1829 onwards.
91. Edward Young, *Conjectures on Original Composition* (1759) pp. 30–1. In Young's formulation, 'Genius' was judiciously balanced against 'Conscience', but the exuberance of his imagery for genius was likely to point readers further in that direction. The book was immediately translated in Germany and widely influential there.
92. *CL* I, 470. See above, p. 29.
93. *TP* II, 366–7; l, 1–4. Ricks notes a parallel to the mood of a 'Meditative Fragment' of Hallam's, Hallam, *Works*, 73–4, and Shelleyan uses of 'prick and tingle' (with 'sickness') and of 'wheels of being': cf. *The Cenci*, IV I, 163–5, and *Queen Mab*, ix, 151–2 (noted by J.D. Jump). Tennyson is, however, transferring to a torpid mood what in Shelley is hectic.
94. See, for instance, his *Poems* (1867) p. 109: 'Heaven's aeonian day'.
95. *TP* II, 412–3; xcv, 21–44 (1850–70 text here cited). Tennyson's other use of the word in *In Memoriam* is in sect. xxxv, 10–11: 'The sound of streams that swift or slow I Draw down Æonian hills ...', where any sense of 'Æonian music' comes rather from the 'moanings of the homeless sea' and the sound of the streams than from the erosion of the hills themselves.
96. *TP* II, 413n
97. *TP* II, 399; lxxxv, 42–4. The term 'Footsteps', at one time apostolic slang for those who had made their way in the world, (Deacon, *Cambridge Apostles*, 7) may have left a distant echo here in the wake of 'being'.
98. *TP* II, 457; Conclusion, ll. 123–4.
99. *TP* III, 67, 138, 235.
100. See Ricks's headnotes to each poem and Hallam Tennyson, *Memoir*, II, 372.
101. *TP* III, 69 ll. 42–7.
102. A. and E.M. Sidgwick, *Sidgwick Memoir*, cited Allen, *Cambridge Apostles*, 9.
103. See my discussion in *The Achievement of E.M. Forster* (1962) pp. 77–83, written when I had not yet fully seen its relationship to apostolic thinking.
104. See *Post-Romantic Consciousness*, pp. 109–20.
105. Allen, *Cambridge Apostles*, 218, quoting the text enclosed in a missive from Donald MacAlister to William Everett, 24 June 1908: William Everett MSS, Massachusetts Historical Society, Boston.
106. *TP* III, 490: ll. 901–15.

Chapter 7

1. See Charles Tennyson, *Alfred Tennyson* (1968) pp. 33–4.
2. See above, p. 121.
3. See his MS note to 'Churchill's Grave': *BPW* IV 46n–47n.
4. Note to stanza xcix.
5. *BL J* V, 105.
6. See the early chapters of my *Coleridge the Visionary* (1959) and *Coleridge's Poetic Intelligence* (1977), especially chapters 2 and 3.
7. *C Friend* II, 514. Cf. above, p. 50.
8. *CL* II, 842.

9. Ibid., 864–5.
10. For a considered account of the questions, see *CPW* (*CC*) I, 717–23, and for one more hostile to Coleridge's achievement, Norman Fruman, *Coleridge, the Damaged Archangel* (1972) pp. 26–9.
11. *CL* II, 830.
12. His perplexity continued. Even after Coleridge's death, when his friendship ceased, he was at a loss how to answer satisfactorily charges which should have been easy to refute, given Coleridge's indisputable gifts, and regretted he had not been more punctilious in recording his debts when they were incurred: 'I used to beg he would take the trouble of recording his obligations, but half his time was passed in dreams, so that such hints were thrown away.' *WL* (1840–53) VII, 49–50.
13. *WPrW* (Grosart) III, 442.
14. *CL* IV, 974.
15. *Correspondence*, ed. Toynbee and Whibley (Oxford 1935) I, 125, quoted Timothy Webb, *Shelley: A Voice not Understood* (1977) p. 141.
16. Quoted by Gavin de Beer, *On Shelley* (Oxford 1938) p. 45, from Swinburne's 1875 *Essays and Studies*; in pp. 35–54 of his volume, De Beer gives a full account of nineteenth-century discussions of the incident. According to Timothy Webb (*Voice not Understood*, p. 140) a previous comment ran 'Such scenes as these, then inspire most forcibly the love of God'.
17. Being the son of James Coleridge his views may have been coloured by the family's sceptical view of his uncle. Fortunately for his relations with Coleridge himself, however, Shelley always believed the review to have been written by Southey.
18. *The Friend* II, 419. See also Richard Holmes, *Shelley: the Pursuit* (1974) p. 100n.
19. 'The Ancient Mariner', 15 September and 5 October 1814, 22 February 1821; 'France: An Ode' and 'Ode to Tranquillity', 6 January 1815; *Christabel*, 26 August 1816. See *SL* II, 471–2.
20. Ll. 202–8, *SPW* 368.
21. Report from 1830 by J. H. Frere: *TT* I, 574.
22. Comment recorded by Allsop: *TT* II, 379.
23. See *CBL* chapter 14, II, 7 and n; *SW* VII, 137.
24. Letters to R.C. Dallas of 20 and 21 January 1808, *BLJ* I, 148.
25. Ibid., VIII, 98.
26. Ibid., VIII, 35
27. Ibid., III, 120.
28. *Essay on Man*, ii, 3–4, 17–18.
29. *BLJ* IX, 46.
30. Quoted ibid. V, 296.
31. *SBT* 7, 41–2. It should also be borne in mind that if the story is to be regarded as literally true, the natural activity of the water would have required considerable muscular energy from him to *retain* his position. It is far more likely that his passiveness left the very practical Trelawny with a vivid impression for a moment before taking the prompt action called for – which then (in the manner of such a happening experienced at a crucial moment) left an enduring impression of lastingness.
32. Ibid., chapter 11, 81. Interestingly, Trelawny recorded the book that was in his other pocket as a 'volume of Sophocles' but by his 1878 version the

name had been transposed into 'Aeschylus'. Most subsequent biographers have mentioned the volume only as one of Sophocles, without noting the curious discrepancy; which Timothy Webb mentions in passing.

33. E.J. Trelawny, *Records of Shelley Byron and the Author* [1878] (New Universal Library, n.d.) pp. 112–17.
34. Quoted (without reference) by Webb, *Voice not Understood*, 16–17.
35. *BLJ* VIII, 104 and n.
36. Canto XI, lx, 6–8.
37. Ll. 496–514; *SPW* 25–6.
38. This was in line with his general attitude to Shelley's poetry, of which in 1819, he had expressed a low opinion (*SBT* 3–4). Later, he took a more favourable view, praising his artistry and setting him above Byron (*Henry Crabb Robinson on Book and their Writers* (ed. E.J. Morley, 1938) I, 351); yet he also maintained that he had suffered through trying to reach beyond the human: 'For the most part he considered that Shelley's works were too remote from the humanities ...' Aubrey de Vere, *Essays, chiefly on Poetry* (1887) I, 201. Though the poem on the skylark was full of imagination it did not, he thought, show the same observation of nature as did his own poem on the same bird: see F. Maurice, *The Life of Frederick Denison Maurice* (New York 1884) I, 199.
39. Quoted by Phyllis Grosskurth, *Byron: The Flawed Angel* (1997) p. 468 (without reference).
40. I, viii, 4. Charles Robinson took this line for the title of *SBR*, the most comprehensive study so far of the relationship.
41. *BLJ* VII, 158, 167,168,253; VIII, 66, 68.
42. *BLJ* IX, 119.
43. George Bancroft, 'A Day with Lord Byron', *History of the Battle of Lake Erie, and Miscellaneous Papers* (New York 1891) p. 200. Cited *SBR* 232.
44. *Medwin's Conversations*, p. 235
45. James Hamilton Browne, 'Narrative of a Visit, in 1823, to the Seat of War in Greece', *Blackwood's Edinburgh Magazine*, IIIVI (1834) p. 395. Cited *SBR* 232.
46. Quoted in Leicester Stanhope's *Greece, in 1823 and 1824 ...* (1825) p. 513. Cited *SBR* 232–3.
47. *WPrW* (Grosart) III, 469.
48. *SBT* 5, 31–2.
49. See above, p. 46.
50. *SL* II, 58.
51. Ibid., II, 393–4.
52. Ibid., II 405.
53. *SBR* 94.
54. See, e.g., ibid., 91–101 and 113–37.
55. *SL* II 388, 376.
56. *SBR* 205–11.
57. Shelley's comments were not written until 1821, but are fully consonant with his lifelong attitudes.
58. *SPW* 658.
59. *SL* II, 323.
60. *KL* I, 387. See above, p. 66 (but see also pp. 8–9).

61. Ibid., II, 5.
62. *CN* II, 2712: see above, p. 28.
63. Journal for 27 November, *BLJ* III, 225.
64. Arnold's well-known phrase 'a beautiful and ineffectual angel, beating in the void his luminous wings in vain' appears in his Essay on Shelley: *APrW* XII, 327. He was evidently proud of it, since he was quoting it from his essay on Byron (ibid., IX, 137).
65. Ll. 149–53.
66. Holmes, *Pursuit*, 633.
67. *SL* II, 435.
68. *ML* I, 180.
69. Nigel Leask has explored Shelley's obsession with the phenomenon at length in his article, 'Shelley's 'Magnetic Ladies': Romantic Mesmerism and the Politics of the Body' for the collection *Beyond Romanticism*, ed. Stephen Copley and John Whale (1992) pp. 53–78.
70. Holmes *Pursuit*, 627.
71. *SPW* 667.
72. Medwin took the reply to refer to Shelley's fear of having to undergo lithotomy as a cure for his gallstones, since he had used precisely the same phrase when referring to it, but in this context it strikes one as a curious and uncharacteristically literal-minded reading; it is not necessary to assume that when employing the paradox he always used it of the same thing.
73. Trelawny, *Records*, 91.
74. *SBT* ch. 5, 36; Trelawny, *Records*, 172.

Chapter 8

1. E.J. Trelawny, *Records of Shelley Byron and the Author* [1878] (New Universal Library, n.d.) p. 256.
2. *SPW* 662.
3. See p. 27.
4. See her World's Classics edition (Oxford and New York, 1994). She believes that this official hostility may help to explain why, in the 1831 version, Mary introduced changes likely to tilt the reader's balance of sympathies further in favour of Dr Frankenstein by reinforcing his religious and moral attitudes.
5. Letter to Southey, 24 December 1799: *CL* I, 553.
6. See William St Clair, *The Godwins and the Shelleys* (1989) p. 295.
7. See Andrew Griffin, 'Fire and Ice in *Frankenstein*' in *The Endurance of Frankenstein*, ed. Levine and Knoepfelmacher (Berkeley, Calif. 1979) pp. 49–73.

Appendix

1. *Poems in Two Volumes, 1800–1807*, Cornell Edition (Ithaca, NY 1983), p. 397.
2. Here I differ slightly from Curtis's transcription of a notably difficult manuscript text.

3. See *Biographia Literaria*, chapter 2; CBL II, 138–9.
4. Ll. 77–9; *WPW* IV, 236.
5. Ll. 110, 154.
6. Ll. 165–8; *WPW* II, 254.
7. L. 23; ibid., 214.
8. *The Excursion* iv, 13–15
9. Ibid., 79–81.
10. Ibid., 96–9.
11. Ibid., 752–7.
12. Ibid., 989–94. In the earlier manuscript this reads: 'prize the frame | Of nature, this transcendent universe' and 'in the abyss | Of Mind and Being'– which is even stronger.
13. Ibid., 1156–8.
14. Ibid., iv, 1264–6. The first line of this dates back to an early stage, when Wordsworth had just concluded 'The Ruined Cottage'.
15. From MS 18A; see ibid., ix, 1–7, app. crit.: *WPW* V, 286.
16. Ibid., 10–12, app. crit. and 13–15; ibid.
17. See Piper's study, mentioned at n. 48 in chapter 3 above.
18. *Excursion* ix, 1–5.
19. Ibid., 128, app. crit.: *WPW* V, 290. (The final text reads '... the Being moves | In beauty through the world ...') There is a curious resemblance between the last lines here and Blake's passage in *Milton* describing 'every space that a Man around his dwelling-place':

> And if he move his dwelling-place, his heavens also move
> Where'er he goes & all his neighbourhood bewail his loss. (*BE* 126, *BK* 516, pl. 29: 12–13)

The convergence of imagery, and even the common word 'neighbourhood', are no doubt to be regarded as coincidence, since Blake could hardly have seen Wordsworth's text, but they show a remarkable meeting of minds from different starting points. Wordsworth's 'neighbourhood' rejoices in the stability of the man's rooted Being, whereas Blake's enjoys the work of his energetic Genius as a 'son of Los', to be mourned if lost.
20. *WPW* III, 261.

Index

Printed in the United States
26101LVS00001B/91